# Mobilizing at the Urban Margins

In October 2019, unprecedented mobilizations in Chile took the world by surprise. An outburst of protests plunged a stable democracy into the deepest social and political crisis since its dictatorship in the 1980s. Although the protests involved a myriad of organizations, the organizational capabilities provided by underprivileged urban dwellers proved essential in sustaining collective action in an increasingly repressive environment. Based on a comparative ethnography and over six years of fieldwork, *Mobilizing at the Urban Margins* uses the case of Chile to study how social mobilization endures in marginalized urban contexts, allowing activists to engage in large-scale democratizing processes. The book investigates why and how some urban communities succumb to exclusion, while others react by resurrecting collective action to challenge unequal regimes of citizenship. Rich and insightful, the book develops the novel analytical framework of 'mobilizational citizenship' to explain this self-produced form of political incorporation in the urban margins.

**Simón Escoffier** is an assistant professor at the School of Social Work at Pontificia Universidad Católica de Chile. His research focuses on social movements, citizenship, conservative countermovements, political exclusion, human rights, public policy, urban democracy, and Latin America.

# Mobilizing at the Urban Margins

## Citizenship and Patronage Politics in Post-Dictatorial Chile

SIMÓN ESCOFFIER

*Pontificia Universidad Católica de Chile*

# CAMBRIDGE
## UNIVERSITY PRESS

Shaftesbury Road, Cambridge CB2 8EA, United Kingdom

One Liberty Plaza, 20th Floor, New York, NY 10006, USA

477 Williamstown Road, Port Melbourne, VIC 3207, Australia

314–321, 3rd Floor, Plot 3, Splendor Forum, Jasola District Centre, New Delhi – 110025, India

103 Penang Road, #05–06/07, Visioncrest Commercial, Singapore 238467

Cambridge University Press is part of Cambridge University Press & Assessment, a department of the University of Cambridge.

We share the University's mission to contribute to society through the pursuit of education, learning and research at the highest international levels of excellence.

www.cambridge.org
Information on this title: www.cambridge.org/9781009306928

DOI: 10.1017/9781009306904

First published 2023
First paperback edition 2024

*A catalogue record for this publication is available from the British Library*

*Library of Congress Cataloging-in-Publication data*
NAMES: Escoffier Martínez, Simón, 1983- author.
TITLE: Mobilizing at the urban margins : citizenship and patronage politics in post-dictatorial Chile / Simón Escoffier.
DESCRIPTION: Cambridge, United Kingdom ; New York, NY : Cambridge University Press, [2023] | Includes bibliographical references and index.
IDENTIFIERS: LCCN 2022047892 (print) | LCCN 2022047893 (ebook) | ISBN 9781009306942 (hardback) | ISBN 9781009306928 (paperback) | ISBN 9781009306904 (epub)
SUBJECTS: LCSH: Political participation–Chile–Santiago. | Community organization–Chile–Santiago. | Social movements–Chile–Santiago. | Sociology, Urban–Chile–Santiago. | Marginality, Social–Chile–Santiago. | Santiago (Chile)–Politics and government. | Santiago (Chile)–Social conditions.
CLASSIFICATION: LCC JL2681 .E84 2023 (print) | LCC JL2681 (ebook) | DDC 323/.0420983315–DC23/eng/20230118
LC record available at https://lccn.loc.gov/2022047892
LC ebook record available at https://lccn.loc.gov/2022047893

ISBN  978-1-009-30694-2  Hardback
ISBN  978-1-009-30692-8  Paperback

# Contents

# Figures and Tables

## Figures

## Tables

# Acknowledgments

Books like this are written by and assigned to a single author. Yet, they are collective endeavors. I want to begin by thanking all those urban residents, activists, and leaders who placed their trust in me and spent time telling me about their lives. Their tireless commitment to improving their communities inspired this book and made me stay connected to their work throughout the years. I particularly appreciate the help and support I received from the organizers of La Casita Periférica and Mrs. Uberlinda, in Nuevo Amanecer. In Lo Hermida, the Morales and Ceballos families welcomed me into their homes and taught me about their neighborhood when I knew very little about it.

This book began as my doctoral project when I was a DPhil student in the Sociology department at the University of Oxford. Although I earned a master's degree in Sociology from LSE, my core training was in clinical psychology (and I treated patients for a while in public and private institutions in Santiago). My doctorate, therefore, required me to broaden my understanding of sociology and politics and reformulate much of my existing academic knowledge. Along the way, I had amazing help from the most incredible people. I exchanged many of my plans for this project with Hugo Rojas and Julia Zulver – excellent friends who inspired me and helped think through the challenges I was experiencing with my doctoral project. Heather Hamill, Federico Varese, and Michael Keith also read my dissertation at different stages and gave me very insightful comments that helped me perfect my methodology. Alan Angell was also extremely generous to me; he read my work several times and gave me detailed feedback. I would also like to thank Javier Auyero for traveling to Oxford all the way from Austin, Texas, to act as one of my final doctoral examiners. He was one of the first people to encourage me to publish my dissertation as a book.

I will be forever grateful to my doctoral advisor and mentor, Leigh Payne. She has read and commented upon countless versions of this book's manuscript. Her feedback was always impressively detailed and thoughtful. If this book encapsulates the rigor and freedom of thought that I believe it does, it is largely because her advice always pushed me to develop my unique academic approach. As we kept in touch and eventually collaborated in other projects, she became my mentor, colleague, and friend. Her generosity and commitment to social justice have deeply inspired my academic career.

The Pontificia Universidad Católica de Chile's Institute for Urban and Territorial Studies (IEUT) awarded me two non-stipendiary research visit fellowships when I did my doctoral fieldwork. It was very helpful to get feedback and support from a welcoming academic community outside my time in the urban margins. I would like to thank Roberto Moris and Arturo Orellana for their support. I am also grateful for the help I obtained at IEUT from Felipe Irarrázabal, a geographer and activist who taught me a great deal about urban Chile. I also want to thank Mario Garcés and Lautaro Guanca, who introduced me to activists in Chile's urban margins in the early days of my doctoral fieldwork.

In early 2015, while I worked on the final draft of my doctoral dissertation, I traveled to California and spent almost six months as a visiting research student at UC Berkeley's Sociology department. I learned a great deal from the people I met there. I was lucky enough to attend Löic Wacquant's course on the sociology of Pierre Bourdieu and had very stimulating conversations about Chilean politics and US academia with Michael Burawoy. Both encouraged me to broaden my conceptual tools and strengthen my comparative analysis. I am also grateful to Bonnie Prestridge, Julien Debonneville, Jonathan Smucker, and Christian Ulbricht, with whom I discussed my project at Berkeley.

Upon returning to Santiago in 2016, I became involved in an increasingly vibrant academic community. Like me, many other early career scholars had leveraged Becas Chile grants to pursue doctoral studies in elite universities abroad and were settling back down in Chile to infuse the country's universities, state institutions, and civil society organizations with new ideas. I joined the Chilean Institute for Municipal Studies (ICHEM) at the Universidad Autónoma de Chile, where I worked as an assistant professor. During my time there, I collaborated with other academics advancing inclusive and democratic policies at the local level.

I was lucky to benefit from the support of colleagues like José Hernández and Camilo Vial, who believed in my work and encouraged me to pursue this book project. Alongside Stéphanie Alenda, at the Universidad Andrés Bello, I co-organized a large international conference that sought to redefine political sociology as a tool of critical analysis and social change. I also taught courses on social movements and political sociology at the Pontificia Universidad Católica de Chile (PUC). I would like to thank Juan Pablo Luna, Julieta Suarez-Cao, and my other colleagues at PUC's Political Science Institute, all of whom gave me insightful comments when I presented an academic article that grew out of this book in their departmental seminar. I would also like to thank several other friends in Chile and beyond who gave me their time and helped make this book possible: Esteban Ceballos, Félix Bezares, Carolina Besoain, Gustavo Valenzuela, Daniel González, Claudio Hernández, Cathy Schneider, Macarena Bonhomme, Javier Sáez, Richard Wilkinson, and Juan Pablo Miranda.

I returned to Oxford for a postdoctoral fellowship in 2018 and 2019. In those two years, the University of Oxford's Latin American Centre (LAC) became my academic home. Together with Carlos Solar, a friend and postdoctoral fellow there, we decorated and shared the LAC's Annexe, a small house that was adapted into a large and comfortable office next to the Centre's main building. I exchanged many ideas for this book in countless conversations over lunch at St. Antony's College with my dear friends Francesca Lessa and Markus Hochmüller. I also appreciate the detailed comments I got from Ezequiel Gonzalez-Ocantos, Cristina Flesher Fominaya, and Juan Pablo Rodríguez in a workshop about this book that I organized at St. Antony's College and LAC in 2019. Other friends and colleagues I would like to thank for their support at the LAC are Diego Sánchez-Ancochea, Eduardo Posada, Annette Idler, Finn Lowery, Andreza De Souza Santos, Juan Luis Ossa, and Carlos Pérez. Additionally, Marti Rovira and Aino Järvelin are two amazing people I could never thank enough. They were close friends of mine at Oxford who read my work, gave me feedback, and provided me with the emotional support I needed to continue improving this book.

This research would not have been possible without the financial support, in the form of several grants, provided by the Chilean government through its National Agency for Research and Development (ANID), which I used at various stages of this book's development. Through its Programa de Capital Humano Avanzado, ANID contributed to this book by providing me with the Becas Chile fellowships for my doctorate and postdoctorate. I am also grateful to ANID's Fondo Nacional de Desarrollo Científico y Tecnológico (FONDECYT) for giving me a grant that I used to cover the expenses for this book's follow-up fieldwork (Fondecyt de Iniciación Proyecto Código 11190870). I also would like to thank Alejandra Pérez for her help creating the maps and gathering some of the data from the Chilean census in the book's appendix and to Gonzalo Miranda, at Ausencia de Color, for allowing me to use one of their photographs in the cover.

Finally, I would like to thank my close family members. Without their love, I would not have finished this book. My mother, Patricia, always understood how important finishing this book project was for me and gave me her unconditional support. Rodrigo gave me his continued love and was always available when I needed his advice. Armando, my father, was there for me every time I needed a motivational boost. I am also grateful to Gonzalo, Catalina, and Pascale, my siblings, who have accompanied and helped me in their own way throughout this journey.

# Abbreviations and Acronyms

AD          Democratic Alliance (Alianza Democrática)
AFP         Pension Funds Administrator (Administradora de
            Fondos de Pensiones)
CCB         Grassroots Christian Communities (Comunidades
            Cristianas de Base)
CMSP        Peñalolén Council of Social Movements (Coordinadora
            de Movimientos Sociales de Peñalolén)
CORVI       Housing Corporation (Corporación de la Vivienda)
COTLH       Lo Hermida's Territorial Coalition (Coordinadora
            Territorial de Lo Hermida)
DC          Christian Democratic Party (Partido Demócrata
            Cristiano)
FENAPO      Underprivileged Urban Dwellers' National Federation
            (Federación Nacional de Pobladores)
FPMR        Manuel Rodriguez Patriotic Front (Frente Patriótico
            Manuel Rodríguez)
GRUJUDEMA   Mary's Youth Group (Grupo Juvenil de María)
IC          Christian Left Party (Izquierda Crisitiana)
LOCE        Organic Constitutional Law of Education (Ley
            Orgánica Constitucional de Educación)
MAPU        Popular Unitary Action Movement (Movimiento de
            Acción Popular Unitaria)
MDP         Popular Democratic Movement (Movimiento
            Democrático Popular)
MIR         Revolutionary Leftist Movement (Movimiento de
            Izquierda Revolucionaria)

| MJL | Lautaro Youth Movement (Movimiento Juvenil Lautaro) |
| MPL | Movement of Urban Dwellers in Struggle (Movimiento de Pobladores en Lucha) |
| MR | Manuel Rodriguez Militias (Milicias Rodriguistas) |
| NRP | Neighborhood Recovery Program (Programa de Recuperación de Barrios or Quiero Mi Barrio) |
| PC | Communist Party (Partido Comunista de Chile) |
| PEM | Minimum Employment Program (Programa de Empleo Mínimo) |
| PI | Equality Party (Partido Igualdad) |
| PNDU | Urban Development National Policy (Política Nacional de Desarrollo Urbano) |
| POJH | Occupational Program for Heads of Household (Programa de Ocupación para Jefes de Hogar) |
| PRPM | Politics of Mass Popular Rebellion (Política de Rebelión Popular de Masas) |
| PS | Socialist Party (Partido Socialista) |
| PUC | Pontifical Catholic University of Chile (Pontificia Universidad Católica de Chile) |
| R | Resistance Committees (Comités de Resistencia) |
| RAP | Autonomous Neighborhood Rap (Rap Autónomo Poblacional) |
| RHA | Hip-Hop Activist Network (Red de Hip-Hop Activista) |
| SMC | Social Movement Community |
| TAC | Cultural Action Workshop (Taller de Acción Cultural) |
| UCH | University of Chile (Universidad de Chile) |
| UP | Popular Unity (Unidad Popular) |
| UV | Neighborhood Unit (Unidad Vecinal) |

# Terms

This book includes multiple words in Spanish whose meaning is highly contextual. The list below provides translations and brief explanations for those terms.

| | |
|---|---|
| *Alianza por Chile* | Coalition of right-wing parties (1989–2015). |
| *Allegados* | People or families with no home of their own and living in overcrowded conditions in other people's homes (often relatives). |
| *Apitutados* | People who receive undeserved benefits from privileged contacts. |
| *Arpilleras* | Groups of urban residents (most often, women) who create burlap in the shape of colored patchwork pictures representing their daily experience. |
| *Autogestión* | Self-management methods used to create autonomous collective action. |
| *Autogestionado* | Person, event, or action that uses self-management methods. |
| *Auto-formación* | Self-training. |
| *Bolsas de trabajo* | Employment cooperatives. |
| *Cabildo* | Town hall or meeting of stakeholders and neighborhood residents concerned with issues affecting the local community. |
| *Callampas* | Mushrooms. Urban informal settlements that emerged and grew in an improvised manner. |

| | |
|---|---|
| *Campamento* | Camp. Highly organized and mobilized urban informal settlement created through a land takeover (also *campamentos* [plural]). |
| *Casas nuevas* | New houses. Settlement built in the neighborhood Nuevo Amanecer between 1973 and 1976. |
| *Centros de madres* | Mothers' centers that function as neighborhood organizations dealing with women's affairs. |
| *Centros juveniles* | Youth centers that function as neighborhood organizations dealing with young people's affairs. |
| Chile Vamos | Coalition of right-wing parties (2015–present). |
| *Chora* | Person whose confrontational behavior replaces institutionally validated systems of redress or justice (also *choro* [masculine] and *choros* [masculine, plural]). |
| *Clubes deportivos* | Neighborhood soccer clubs including teams of different ages in which some local dwellers play and/or act as coaches. |
| *Colonias urbanas* | Children camps that involve games, competitions, workshops, and even summer trips for children in the neighborhood. |
| *Color político* | Political color. It refers to the political allegiance attributed to places of the neighborhood, such as buildings or squares. |
| *Comandos* | Defense groups composed of urban dwellers that participated in clashes with the police during the 1980s. |
| *Comité de mejora* | Infrastructure development committee. A local organization used by urban dwellers to channel state subsidies for residential and neighborhood improvements. |
| *Comprando juntos* | Cooperative supply acquisition groups. |
| Concertación | Coalition of center-left-wing parties (1988–2013, also Concertación de Partidos por el No or Concertación de Partidos por la Democracia). |
| *Cordones* | Territorial coalitions encompassing several neighborhood assemblies, each composed of several local organizations. |

| | |
|---|---|
| *Cuico* | Derogatory term referring to snob, upper-class people (also *cuicos* [masculine, plural]). |
| *Favelados* | Social movement of residents in Brazil's impoverished urban areas. |
| *Frente* | Informal term referring to the Manuel Rodriguez Patriotic Front, or FPMR. |
| *Funas* | Organized informal public denunciations against perpetrators of socially condemned violence. |
| *Jota* | Communist Youth. |
| *Juegue* | Play. As a command in Chilean Spanish, it may be informally used to encourage someone to carry out the necessary actions leading to any given result. |
| *Juntas de vecinos* | Neighborhood councils. |
| *La calle* | The street. Informal knowledge obtained by experiencing events and interactions on the streets and other public spaces of Chile's urban margins (also *calle* and *tener calle*). |
| *Lautaro* | Informal term referring to the Lautaro Youth Movement, or MJL. |
| *Leyes de amarre* | Binding laws. A group of laws limiting Chile's democracy after 1990. |
| *Lo popular* | Cohesive collective identity that emerged in Chile's urban margins in the 1980s. |
| *Lonco* | Mapuche tribe chief. |
| *Lucha* | Struggle. Collective endeavor with politically motivated means. |
| *Machi* | Mapuche tribe doctor. |
| *Mapudugún* | Mapuche language. |
| *Maquineras* | People skillful at imposing their will and influencing others at the grassroots level, often with electoral political means. |
| *Masacre* | Indiscriminate killing of people, massacre. |
| *Milicos* | Derogatory term referring to military people. |
| *Movimiento villero* | Social movement of residents in Argentina's impoverished urban areas (also *movimiento villero peronista*). |
| *Movimiento de pobladores* | Social movement of residents in Chile's impoverished urban areas. |

| | |
|---|---|
| Nueva Mayoría | Coalition of center-left-wing parties (2013–2018). |
| *Ollas comunes* | Community kitchens that feed the poor and hungry in Chile's urban margins. |
| *Operación Sitio* | Site Operation. Government policy that provided lots with very basic social houses to impoverished families between 1965 and 1970. |
| *Pasar máquina* | Actions by which someone disregards democratic, inclusive procedures to impose their will in collective decision-making processes, which benefits that person's political network. |
| *Pascuas populares* | Popular Christmas. Events in which neighbors organize Christmas celebrations with the homeless and destitute. |
| *Pastoral Juvenil* | Youth Ministry functioning within a chapel to promote the evangelization of young people in a community. |
| *Peña* | Community party that functions as a crowdfunding event in the neighborhood (also *peñas* [plural]). |
| *Población* | Chilean underprivileged neighborhood (also *pobla* [more informal] or *poblaciones* [plural]). |
| *Poblaciones hermanas* | Sister neighborhoods. Similar urban communities in their urban location, and their social and political configuration. |
| *Pobladora* | A resident of Chile's impoverished urban areas (also *poblador* [masculine], *pobladoras* [feminine, plural], *pobladores* [masculine, plural]). |
| *Poder popular* | Popular power. A type of power that emerges from the grassroots and creates structural social change. |
| *Popular* | Referring to the underprivileged masses or the excluded grassroots. |
| *Primera línea* | First line. Well-coordinated group of people that regularly clashed with the police in Chile's 2019 outbreak of protests. |
| *Red de Iniciativa Ciudadana* | Network for Active Citizenship. |
| *Recuperación* | Reappropriation tactics. Set of actions implemented by underprivileged communities to |

repossess resources from the wealthy or for-
profit institutions (also *recuperaciones* [plural]).

| | |
|---|---|
| *Recuperación de terreno* | Land reappropriation, which usually occurs in an underprivileged neighborhood. |
| *Represión* | Repression carried out by institutional actors and with political goals. |
| *Revuelta* | Outbreak of protests beginning in October 2019 (also *revuelta social* or *estallido*). |
| *Ruka* | House. A building of Mapuche spiritual and medical significance. |
| *Sapa* | Snitch (also *sapo* [masculine]). |
| *Sede* | Local community building, which is managed by the neighborhood council. |
| *Toma* | Land takeover. The word has two meanings, depending on the context. As a verb, it means the collective action carried out by people to informally invade urban land and erect dwellings to occupy it. As a noun, it refers to the settlement resulting from that urban land occupation (also *tomas* [plural]). |
| *Villa* | Settlement comprising an area within a larger neighborhood (also *villas* [plural]). |

# Introduction

It was late in the evening and Giorgio's mother met him in the lobby of Santiago's Northern Prosecutor Office. He had spent the day being processed by the police after being detained at a protest in a metro station that morning, and his sister was there to help him and pick him up. As they walked out of the building, she emphatically told him: "There is a revolution out there!" Unprecedented events had unfolded throughout the day, she explained. She described riots that were severely disrupting the city with roadblocks, bonfires, lootings, and clashes with the police. Protestors were setting public transportation buses and metro stations on fire. They had also attacked one of Enel's buildings, a company providing the electric supply for the city. The whole of Santiago's transportation system had been shut down at rush hour, when workers across the city were commuting back home, which added to the chaos.

Mobilizations had erupted a few days before, when high-school students went to a few metro stations in Santiago's city center to evade the transportation fare. In large groups, they entered metro stations suddenly and opened the ticket barriers to allow the public to dodge the metro fare for a few hours. They were protesting a recent increase in the price of public transport. Over the next few days, more and more students joined these demonstrations. The mobilizations also expanded across the city, attracting non-student demonstrators, and clashes between protestors and the police led to a spiral of violence.

In the early morning of October 18, and after coordinating actions with a few student leaders, Giorgio and other young *población* (underprivileged neighborhood) dwellers had participated in one of these demonstrations at a metro station near his neighborhood. On that day, dozens of similar demonstrations took place in the city, which overwhelmed the security forces trying to control the protests. The resulting escalation of violence led to severe damage in over 70 metro stations, 7 of which were completely burned down. Looters also attacked 450 supermarkets (Gonzalez and Le Foulon 2020). This explosive upsurge of social unrest became known as *estallido* or *revuelta social* (social outburst). Over the next few days, President Piñera declared a State of Emergency and imposed a curfew in Santiago, which handed over much of public security to the military. As shocking scenes of police and military brutality in handling these demonstrations spread across social media, the protests gained increasing public legitimacy and expanded across the country. People's cries for dignity and democracy encapsulated long-standing demands over education, healthcare, pensions, human rights, and the environment, among many others.

Giorgio's *población* reacted swiftly to the situation and spearheaded the mobilizations. In less than 24 hours after the unrest exploded, a coalition of neighborhood organizations united to support the protests and demand the protection of human rights. Soon after, this group of organizations became part of an alliance that coordinated large-scale protests with several other neighborhoods in the area. They organized marches, mural paintings, and urban art installations. The coalition coordinated large disruptive urban demonstrations with burning barricades and roadblocks, and participated in clashes with the police and the military. It also publicly denounced human rights violations and created health brigades that attended to the wounded protestors.

In the following weeks, civil society at large, as well as a huge number of citizens, engaged in the mobilizations. Many more neighborhood organizations in the urban margins joined the marches and roadblocks. For months, peaceful and violent daily demonstrations continued to overwhelm authorities and defy security measures. The sheer intensity and massive scale of the social unrest was able to shake Chile's political institutions to the core and opened opportunities for a broad democratizing process. As I write these lines, a democratically elected Constitutional Convention – that includes gender parity and reserved seats for indigenous peoples – is drafting a new political constitution. This constitutional process is the result of an agreement reached on November 15, 2019, across most political parties in the country that sought to channel Chileans' grievances through institutional means.

Key to this process was the quick and committed action of urban communities like Giorgio's. Protests were more prevalent and intense in those *poblaciones*, and their activists had leading roles in the functioning of broader mobilizing coalitions. This is because the neighborhoods in Chile's urban margins were prepared to support large-scale mobilizations. They hold highly politicized local organizations that have created mobilizing capabilities through decades of sustained community organizing and collective action. Consequently, their activists have the resources, networks, and knowledge to engage in intense and enduring disruptive challenges to the authorities. As others have shown (Staggenborg 1998; Staggenborg and Lecomte 2009; Van Dyke and Amos 2017), people's prior experience of sustained community-building and collective action makes them more likely to engage in protest coalitions and achieve structural impact.

This is not the case of all *poblaciones*, however. In fact, organizers and citizens in most neighborhoods of the urban margins engaged in Chile's *estallido* only once organizational structures allowed larger coordination and made protesting relatively safer. In contrast with Giorgio's neighborhood, these urban communities are regularly depoliticized and demobilized. The repressive policies implemented by Pinochet's dictatorship (1973–1990), together with different systems of exclusion in Chile's democratic transition and post-transition, managed to erode those neighborhoods' mobilizing potential.

The question therefore arises: Why and how has mobilization survived since the dictatorship in some communities of the urban margins but not in others? How have collectives in some *poblaciones* overcome political marginalization since the 1980s? Or, more broadly, how do the urban poor sustain collective action in shifting contexts of authoritarian rule and democratization? This book answers these questions through a comparative analysis of Chilean *poblaciones*. In doing so, it produces the concept of mobilizational citizenship, which analytically explains how activism can endure over time in the areas most affected by violence, institutional neglect, and urban marginalization.

This notion goes beyond traditional, liberal conceptions of citizenship, which rely on the nation-state as people's core political community. According to that liberal framework, becoming a citizen depends exclusively on a state's (often preexisting) policies of citizen incorporation and exclusion. The effectiveness of protests should therefore be measured by their impact on state policy. The concept of mobilizational citizenship takes issue with this liberal tradition. It understands citizenship as a relational construction of political community that emerges in collective endeavors. While it does not deny the role of formal institutions and people's preexisting citizenship status, it stresses the identities by which collectives build alternative political incorporations. This prism allows the study of the multiple ways in which community and the state are constructed, and it sides with those academic strands examining culturally embedded alternative forms of politicization (Holston and Appadurai 1996; Isin 2002; Purcell 2003; Lazar 2008; Sassen 2008; Coll 2010; McNevin 2011). Later in this book, for example, I show how using the notion of "*poblador*" (underprivileged city dwellers) is a key identity statement because it directly contributes to *población* activists' creation of mobilizational citizenship. In Chile's urban margins a *poblador* refers to an urban dweller who participates in a century-old grassroots struggle within Chilean cities to defend the poor. Self-defining themselves as *pobladores* is, therefore, a way of imagining community, as Anderson (1991) conceived it. Performatively, those activists are becoming members of a revolutionary and long-standing political community with its own values, ideals, identity symbols, and methods of action.

In later chapters of this book, I outline a theory to explain how and why some communities in the urban margins develop mobilizational citizenship while others do not. I provide a framework that analytically differentiates four components of mobilizational citizenship: agentic memory, mobilizing belonging, mobilizing boundaries, and decentralized protagonism. Agentic memory looks at the non-linear processes by which neighborhood activists re-signify historical developments and build a continuity with the past that activates agency in the present. Mobilizing belonging refers to activists' use of collective action frames to promote group identity, social cohesion, and contentious collective behavior. Through mobilizing boundaries, activists create distance and antagonism toward other social actors. Finally, decentralizing protagonism involves activists' tactics to spread a collective identity that promotes people's engagement in contentious politics. This process is implemented through routine practices of political socialization that use collective identity as political capital. The result is activists' individual and collective sense of protagonism and their local validation as community-builders. Decentralizing protagonism also promotes the renovation of leaders in the urban margins, which sustains contentious grassroots activism over time. While Chapter 3 in this book looks at a neighborhood in Chile's urban margins in which local dwellers failed to produce mobilizational citizenship, Chapters 4, 5, and 6 deliver an empirical analysis of an urban community in which these components successfully developed. In this latter case, a *población* called Lo Hermida, mobilization has endured over time and allowed local activists like Giorgio to actively support the *estallido*'s expansive democratizing process.

## 1.1 THE CASE, THE CASES, AND THE COMPARISON

The decades of the mid-twentieth century saw the consolidation of the urban poor as a collective political agent in several Latin American societies. After the industrial boom of the 1930s, Latin American cities attracted millions of impoverished rural migrants. Cities swelled with new arrivals living in highly precarious conditions. They lived in impoverished, insanitary, and overcrowded housing, in which landlords had the power to evict them as they pleased. The urban poor, often in coordination with political parties, organized land takeovers and demanded social housing from the state. While some were more politicized than others, these movements consolidated over time and began to shape Latin American cities. The *favelados* in Brazil (Lima 1989; Cortés 2013) and the *movimiento villero peronista* in Argentina (Dávolos, Jabbaz, and Molina 1987) are two prominent examples. The Chilean *movimiento de pobladores*, or underprivileged urban dwellers' movement, is another particularly politicized example that impacted policy-making during the 1960s and 1970s (Garcés 2002). *Población* mobilization developed in close collaboration with political institutions, such as political parties, radical political groups, labor unions, student organizations, the Catholic Church, and state agencies. From the margins of society, the urban poor were able to reclaim their dignity and become rights bearers (Angelcos and Pérez 2017).

In the 1960s and early 1970s Chile was one of the most politically vibrant societies in the region. Social and political movements multiplied and permeated all realms of society. The Socialist Salvador Allende took power in 1970 and implemented an intense program of reform that included nationalizing large companies, intensifying land reform, raising the minimum wage, and implementing inclusive social programs. Political polarization progressively increased and led to a military coup d'état that toppled President Allende in 1973 and imposed an authoritarian regime. Between 1973 and 1990, General Pinochet's military dictatorship conducted a repressive campaign to defeat the Chilean left. The dictatorship considered *pobladores*' mobilization to be a subversive threat to the state; it persecuted, tortured, and killed many of their leaders. Dictatorial repression made political party membership illegal, and initially managed to dismantle and prevent further popular mobilization. However, collective action in *poblaciones* eventually recommenced in the years following the coup (Oxhorn 1995). Later, between 1983 and 1986, *población* activism reconnected with political parties working underground in a large wave of national protests that resisted dictatorial rule (Schneider 1995). These were large-scale, country-wide mobilizations demanding democratization. These protests managed to build international awareness and give local political leaders the leverage they needed to activate a national referendum that in 1988 decided that electoral democracy should return. For a decade, the dictatorship had prohibited elections and repressed collective action. These mobilizations therefore produced new networks and political identities, and gave people a renewed sense of public engagement. However, the years under the dictatorship had eroded the politicization of the poor living in the urban margins. Indeed, after this wave of anti-dictatorship protests, most *poblaciones* demobilized. The new democracy did not manage to reactivate the high levels of social and political engagement that *poblaciones* had experienced before the coup d'état.

What the dictatorship and the democratization process had managed to deactivate in most cases was an engagement with contentious politics – that is, people's collective action that challenged cultural, social, and political institutions. In other words, the majority of *poblaciones* still have local organizations, but their collective initiatives supplement the state's service provision at the local level, rather than claiming rights and advancing social change.

My argument in this book, however, is that politicization and mobilization survived in some areas of the urban margins where urban dwellers use memory and community-making to recover their identity legacies of past activism. The result is a new type of citizenship, a mobilizational citizenship that empowers *pobladores* and avoids corporatist forms of collective action. Rights-claiming, dignity, and mobilization grow from urban dwellers' rejection of institutional authoritarian legacies. They have consequently abandoned their historical collaboration with political parties and other political institutions to promote informal, horizontal leadership structures.

I develop a comparison between two *poblaciones* – Lo Hermida and Nuevo Amanecer – both located in eastern Santiago. These neighborhoods caught my attention because, while they share many things in common, their trajectories of contentious social mobilization have been starkly divergent since the democratic transition (see Appendix 1). To investigate this puzzling contrast between two otherwise similar communities, I carried out a paired comparison, in line with Skocpol and Somers's (1980) Causal Analysis method. This comparison provides us an opportunity to understand why politicization and collective action survive only in particular *poblaciones*. I also explored the causal mechanisms involved in answering this question through a process-tracing (King, Keohane, and Verba 1994). Implementing this inferential methodological tool involved gathering data from different sources to build the evidence linking the events underlying those broader causal mechanisms.

The *poblaciones* I picked as case studies include a substantial proportion of self-built housing. Their urban location and access to services is similar (see Figure 2.1). They both feature criminality and drug trafficking: Some areas in the two neighborhoods are known to be unsafe among residents and authorities. The socioeconomic situation of residents is also similar, as is the degree of inequality and poverty, and the political configuration of the districts that contain them. Moreover, the two *poblaciones* have strikingly similar histories. They were both created in the late 1970s through urban land seizures coordinated by leftist political parties and the Leftist Revolutionary Movement (MIR), a revolutionary guerrilla group that was prominent at the time. At that stage, the two neighborhoods were informal settlements located in the urban outskirts and were known to be prominent strongholds of the famous *movimiento de pobladores*. In coordination with many other shantytowns, movements, and parties, their residents mobilized to demand social housing. With the arrival of the dictatorship, however, came military raids, violence, and the persecution of neighborhood leaders. In the mid-1970s, and with the assistance of the Catholic Church, both *poblaciones* organized initiatives to defend human rights. During the wave of anti-regime national protests between 1983 and 1986, the two shantytowns again became bastions of resistance against the dictatorship.

What is remarkable, though, is that while Nuevo Amanecer followed most other *poblaciones* and demobilized during the democratic transition in the early 1990s, Lo Hermida is one of the examples of *poblaciones* where politicization and activism have remained strong. In the decade that followed the transition to democracy, Lo Hermida continued to play a central role in resisting the segregating effects of market-oriented urban policies. Indeed, in collaboration with other leaders in their district, Lo Hermida's activists organized the largest and most contentious land takeovers of the new democratic regime in the 1990s and early 2000s, the settlements Esperanza Andina and Toma de Peñalolén. Later, in 2011, Lo Hermida organizations protested and campaigned to successfully resist the implementation of a new municipal urban masterplan. Although the plan promised to attract new investments to the area, it was viewed by *población* leaders as a Trojan horse for further gentrification. Thus, they pushed authorities to conduct a binding district referendum and, in the end, forced the municipality to withdraw the masterplan. Furthermore, mobilized urban communities like Lo Hermida were instrumental in leading and expanding the reach of the 2019 Chilean protests. In these communities, protests erupted earlier, were better coordinated, and became more prevalent than in other areas of the urban margins. Comparatively, their tactics were also more violent and defiant toward authorities (see Table A.1.1).

## 1.2 METHODOLOGY

The development of collective action within marginalized urban communities is often invisible to the media, policymakers, politicians, and even surveys in Latin America. Like in the United States and Europe, Latin American states tend to portray such agency as a deviation from normative, neoliberal conceptions of bourgeois behavior. As a result, the contentious politics of the urban underprivileged are often stigmatized and criminalized (Wacquant 2009). In this book, I react to these forms of marginalization and discrimination through an ethnographic approach to grassroots politics. Thus, while I use analytical distinctions to advance the book's arguments, these are based in the nuanced knowledge that only an on-the-ground experience can provide.

I began my fieldwork for this book in 2012 and 2014, when I spent over 14 months living in Santiago's *poblaciones* and participating in local neighborhood activism as part of research for my doctoral thesis. In this period, I built reliable relationships through direct engagement with local initiatives. I got to know *población* dwellers closely and obtained first-hand insights into their daily lives. To understand why and how people organize contentiously to build social change in their neighborhoods, I carried out participant observations, archival research, and 110 interviews with residents, activists, and authorities in Lo Hermida and Nuevo Amanecer, which provides the core material for this book. This work included engaging in local organizations myself. As a result, I often became part of political and mobilizing social dynamics: I helped organize neighborhood anniversaries; I joined a group of activists putting up posters and banners that advertised an upcoming march; I participated in meetings between politicians and *población* leaders; and I accompanied those leaders in their meetings with local residents. During the first couple of months, I was labelled a "*cuico*,"[1] and was excluded from many meetings. Nevertheless, I gradually earned the trust of activists and was progressively included in their regular activities. In my various roles, I gained insider access to different dimensions of *población* micro-mobilization. At the same time, my academic orientation allowed me to situate my experiences in broader conceptual, historical, and regional contexts.

In the years after this first fieldwork experience, I remained closely connected to the work of several *poblaciones*, which included regularly checking in with grassroots activists, participating in meetings, and attending local events. For several months, in 2016 and 2017, I attended the regular meetings of a group of young underprivileged residents in Lo Hermida who mobilized against police discrimination and to tackle their fellow neighbors' lack of life opportunities. Additionally, since early 2020, I have been attending meetings and collaborating with another *población* organization devoted to promoting cultural and social awareness in under-privileged neighborhoods. The networks I have nourished in *poblaciones* for the past seven years have allowed me to also include in this book six interviews that I conducted in 2017 with people involved in social policy implementation and with *población* members who were political militants in the 1980s, as well as ten interviews that I carried out in 2020 and 2021 with activists and local dwellers in the urban margins who participated in the protests of October 2019.

## 1.3 PLAN OF THE BOOK

This book's arguments unfold in six chapters. In Chapter 1, "The Mobilizational Citizenship Framework," I develop an innovative analytical framework to explain how mobilizational citizenship works. This concept is this book's fundamental contribution as it synthesizes how and why mobilization endures over time in highly inhospitable conditions at the urban margins. Theories of the political process and collective identity have already analyzed collective action in *poblaciones* in the past, but they have been unable to address how people's cultural development in Chile's urban margins translates into contentious tactics. They consequently ignore the political dynamics underlying some urban communities' differential mobilizing potential. The chapter conceptualizes citizenship beyond traditional, liberal approaches. It develops a more

---

[1] This is a Chilean derogatory term that refers to snobbish, upper class people.

flexible and informal notion of political incorporation, one that depends on how collectives create identity and rescale community-building beyond the framework of the nation-state. It therefore describes how groups produce alternative types of politicization, mobilizational citizenship being one of them. The functioning of the framework's components as well as their interactions are addressed in detail. Activists produce mobilizational citizenship when they instrumentalize a mobilizing collective identity as political capital, which they seek to diffuse among activists and potential challengers within the community. The resulting decentralization of protagonism among activists makes them legitimate community-builders, both individually and collectively. When available and implemented, the tactics described allow communities in the urban margins to overcome barriers to their mobilization. Mobilizational citizenship allows communities in the urban margins to build the mobilizing capabilities needed to support large-scale protests and broader democratizing processes that extend beyond their immediate community, district, or city. The framework outlines the barriers to mobilization in the urban margins. It explains how political institutions regularly withdraw and control political capital within urban communities with the goal of demobilizing them. When mobilizational citizenship fails to develop, local dwellers engage in political capital hoarding dynamics within their neighborhoods, which further deactivates collective action.

In Chapter 2, "The History of Mobilization in Chile's Urban Settings," I describe the past events serving as context for the development of mobilizational citizenship in *poblaciones*, starting in the 1960s. Differentiated sections provide a parallel account of historical developments in Chile's urban margins in general as well as in the case studies that the book focuses on, the *poblaciones* Lo Hermida and Nuevo Amanecer. While descriptive in its nature, the chapter makes several key arguments. Firstly, it addresses what I synthesize as prior mobilization, which refers to the events of collective action occurring in *poblaciones* before the coup d'état in 1973. Participating in these mobilizations installed a socialist project of society within communities in the urban margins, which strongly marked people's political experience at the time. This socialist project acted as a discursive framework for people's engagement in collective action and built the political and livelihood expectations that organized community-building for many *población* dwellers. Secondly, the chapter describes the powerful disrupting impact of the dictatorship in communities of the urban margins after September 1973. This was the beginning of diverging paths in civil society development between the two case studies. Thirdly, I pay special attention to the wave of anti-dictatorship protests in the 1980s. I show how these mobilizations consolidated distinct developments of citizenship between Lo Hermida and Nuevo Amanecer, as well as in other communities of Chile's urban margins. Groups and parties on the far left created a subversive leadership structure that transmitted a mobilizing identity to grassroots activists in some *poblaciones*. Simultaneously, more moderate political parties on the left and the center produced managerial leaderships that sought to coordinate and control protests in the urban margins. Fourthly, and finally, the chapter describes the dynamics of mobilization and civil society in *poblaciones* after the democratic transition in 1990. I address the several factors of demobilization in most of the urban margins during this time. I claim that while most urban communities have maintained functioning local organizations, their ability to conduct autonomous contentious politics has been strongly diminished. Nuevo Amanecer is an example of this trend. In contrast, some communities like Lo Hermida have remained active and continued mobilizing for the past three decades. Since the early 2000s an increasing number of social groups are demonstrating over social rights in Chile, and in late 2019 large-scale, highly disruptive protests erupted. The chapter shows how active communities in the urban margins reacted promptly and provided the needed organizational structure for protest diffusion; others joined the protests only later, when demonstrating seemed safer and more socially validated.

In Chapter 3, "Political Exclusion and Acquiescent Collective Action," I begin my comparative ethnographic enquiry. While research has provided a set of explanations for the post-dictatorial deactivation of the Latin American underprivileged, we know little of the trajectories by which mobilization survives in some neighborhoods. In this chapter, I focus on the case of Nuevo Amanecer to examine the specific mechanisms that led to the demise of collective action in transitional and post-transitional *poblaciones*. I begin by describing the specific ways in which party activists in Alianza Democrática (AD) developed a managerial style of leadership in many *poblaciones* when coordinating anti-dictatorial protests in the 1980s. This tactic did not include politically training neighborhood dwellers, which was in large part responsible for maintaining people's sense of historical discontinuity produced by the dictatorship. As symbols of community-building from the neighborhood's period of prior mobilization were unavailable, creating agentic memory – the first step of mobilizational citizenship – was also precluded. The relationships fostered by these moderate political activists with neighborhood dwellers during the 1980s often evolved to become networks of political loyalty after the democratic transition. These networks are current and ongoing. I draw on my ethnography to explain how local leaders engage in these networks in two ways: clientelism and false protagonism. Clientelist relationships forge strong bonds between community leaders and politicians, which allows political machines to socialize those leaders. Simultaneously, by gaining access to political authorities, those local leaders acquire a sense of impact in the policies that shape their community. This impression is actively promoted by these leaders' political networks. Yet, as I show, this experience of protagonism is deceiving because decision-making processes regularly develop from top to bottom. To feed their political loyalty networks, community leaders learn to insistently monopolize political capital at the grassroots level. This dynamic has further prevented mobilizational citizenship from developing. It also fragments *población* spaces, deactivates local initiatives of governance, and depoliticizes the youth.

In Chapters 4, 5, and 6, I shift the focus of my analysis to draw on my ethnographic experience in Lo Hermida and other *poblaciones* that have sustained mobilization in Santiago. Chapter 4, "Memory of Subversion," explains how memory-building creates the conditions for the emergence of mobilizational citizenship. I begin by providing a historical account of how radical movements socialized young *población* dwellers in some neighborhoods during the anti-dictatorial protests in the 1980s, which is key to understanding the development of mobilizational citizenship in some *poblaciones*. By providing political training to neighborhood dwellers, radical groups and parties on the left managed to update the socialist project of society that had been so popular in many areas of the urban margins before the coup. They therefore activated a historical continuity between the present construction of identity and the past, pre-coup insurgent project of *población* mobilization among local activists. Then, I explore how activists develop agency in the present through memory-building. They do this by using memories of successful collective action to performatively subvert oppressive past events. I show how activists carry out this subversion in their interactions, in idealizations of past radical groups, and in their repertoires of contention.

In Chapter 5, "We, the Informal Urban Dwellers," I look at how activists' cohesiveness and their differentiation from other social actors produce a mobilizing identity that advances contentious politics. I draw on my participant observations and interviews in Lo Hermida to outline the contents and dynamics of political consciousness production. The languages of informality and marginality combine in activists' inter-actions to boost a sense of pride about their neighborhood that resists hegemonic narratives of stigmatization. Notions such as *pobladores*, *población*, *lucha* (struggle), and *represión* (repression) are fundamental to understanding collective identity in Chile's urban margins. I further explain how thick boundaries promoting mobilization are symbolically anchored in the dictatorship and depend on the dynamic division that activists build between two realms of their collective experience, the formal and the informal. The informal represents the protected space of confidence and close connections within *población* organizations. Activism works as a way of keeping the informal alive. Simultaneously, the formal is the world of institutions and norms, a world that has historically excluded *población* dwellers. For *población* activists, I argue, the formal insistently seeks to formalize the informal. It is there-fore a threatening force working as a powerful call to action to oppose it. Finally, I show how a sense of self-determination results from activists' reactive and defensive mobilization.

In Chapter 6, "Protagonism and Community-Building," I explain how activists in the urban margins decentralize protagonism. I focus on my ethnographic fieldwork in Lo Hermida to explore dynamics of micro-mobilization in *poblaciones*. Specifically, in line with Gamson's typology of micromobilizing acts, I analyze their face-to-face interactions within three types of encounters: organizing, divesting, and reframing acts. My interviews and observations show how activists transmit their collective identity of mobilization as political capital. In other words, they teach each other the identity symbols and values that both promote and validate collective action locally. Informal leaders are key to this dynamic, although organizational structures tend to be horizontal, and activists regularly reject hierarchies. The tendency to diffuse political capital within the local social movement community usually flows from informal leaders to younger, less experienced activists and potential challengers. This dynamic progressively certifies young local activists as *población* community-builders, both individually and collectively. It makes it more likely for individual leaders to be replaced by others once they decide to quit their role. It also maintains strong informal networks and motivates emerging groups to autonomously lead new initiatives. In turn, this decentralization of protagonism feeds mobilizational citizenship, thus furthering citizenship-building and enduring mobilization.

# 1

# The Mobilizational Citizenship Framework

## 1.1 INTRODUCTION

"What does citizenship mean to you?" I asked an active leader in one of the neighborhood organizations I studied. "Citizenship is for the *cuicos*, it's not for us," she said, enthusiastically clarifying: "we are not citizens, we are *pobladores* (underprivileged urban dwellers)!"

While at the time of this interview I had already spent enough time in *poblaciones* to understand what this woman was trying to tell me, her answer stuck with me for several days. Her words synthesized several discussions, meetings, and experiences I had when engaging in local *población* activism. Far from expressing her distance from matters of citizenship, this leader was describing how powerfully cohesive the notion of *pobladores* is in Chile's urban margins. She was also unveiling that becoming a citizen for her and her fellow activists is a matter of collective self-production, which is at odds with formal institutionally recognized frameworks of political incorporation.

This chapter outlines the theoretical grounds for the exploration of what I call "mobilizational citizenship." This concept analytically examines how underprivileged urban mobilization is fueled by an alternative sense of political incorporation that survives beyond contingent political opportunities and cycles of protest. Mobilizational citizenship, therefore, conceptually addresses how local politicization and organizing survives contexts of comparatively stronger political exclusion, in which inequality, neoliberalism, and the cultural and institutional legacies of authoritarian regimes discourage activists' access to political support.

The skepticism and ambivalence of *población* activism toward political institutions resembles the position of so many other movements using alternative strategies of politicization. This combination of durable mobilization and alternative citizenship construction developed in *poblaciones* speaks to all the highly contingent movements that, across the world, appear to have highly diffuse leadership structures and appeal to people as opportunities to have an impact in sustainably shaping their communities; we see this in factions of the Argentinean Piquetero Movement, Black Lives Matter, the Alt-Right Movement, Extinction Rebellion, the Yellow Vests, Occupy Wall Street, and many others.

This chapter unfolds in four steps. It begins by explaining the book's theoretical contribution, both to citizenship theory and to the social movement literature. Two subsequent sections define and develop the components of mobilizational citizenship, explaining their role in advancing broader processes of social change and democratization. A final part addresses the exclusionary barriers that often preclude collective action in the urban margins and prevent the development of mobilizational citizenship.

## 1.2 CONTRIBUTION

The dominant academic approach to citizenship draws on a liberal conception of the term and is heavily influenced by Marshall's theorization in the 1950s (Marshall 1950). According to this view, citizenship refers to our membership in the nation-state. It is formal by essence, since it results from rights enacted into laws. Becoming a citizen means to acquire access to those legally granted rights in a specific country. These rights are conceived as universalistic, which means that they refer to public goods and reach all citizens.

Initially, only a few people could enjoy the status of citizen (e.g., elites in Athens or England). However, modern nation-states have evolved to grant citizenship to the large majority of their population (Turner 1986). Marshall's (1950) influential work outlined three types of rights. Civil rights provide people with freedom and basic equalities, and include, for example, freedom of speech, freedom of reunion, freedom of religion, and equal access to justice, among others. The rights to vote, join political parties, run for positions of representation, and protest are political rights, and they ensure people's full participation in their community's civil and political life. Social rights are those that provide us with the conditions to perform our life and citizenship adequately. They include housing, education, healthcare, and employment. While the equality of citizenship works in conceptual and legal terms, in substantive terms nations rarely provide equal access to rights to all citizens. Economic inequality and discrimination often keep some groups marginalized from accessing the goods and services needed to fully exercise their rights.

Often described as liberal, this notion of citizenship has its supporters and detractors. Despite citizenship and rights' universalistic quality, liberals understand citizens exercising their rights as an individual endeavor. Citizenship is viewed as fundamentally individual, even if at times it is analyzed as the status that individuals may enjoy in a group. The liberal citizen is an autonomous, self-governing subject who regularly pursues their interests through rational analysis (Schuck 2002). Each person may hence access citizenship rights, have duties, and decide to participate in their community's public affairs depending on their rational assessment and citizenship status. Using this framework, many researchers of citizenship have analyzed how those living in excluded conditions are granted access to rights, thus making societies more equal and prosperous (Marshall 1950; Young 1990; DuBois 1998; Hill 2006; Thompson and Tapscott 2010).

Stressing the nation-state as the entity that organizes our incorporation in a political community is fundamental to this view (Isin and Turner 2002). The state sets the norms that include and exclude natives, denizens, and subjects from participating in a territorially bound nation. This participation provides the nation-state with the cohesiveness and sovereignty that it needs to exist within the modern global order. Modern states regularly combine two broad criteria to determine a person's status as a citizen. A state may grant citizenship to those who were born in their territory (*jus soli*) and based on their family origin (*jus sanguinis*) (Davidson 1997).

Despite its wide acceptance, this mainstream, liberal approach to citizenship has well-established critics. They argue that liberal citizenship places too much emphasis on individuals, hence missing subjects' embeddedness in cultural, collective processes. Nuanced, historical and cultural analyses are consequently lost. Furthermore, novel analyses of citizenship in the past couple of decades have rescaled the notion of political community beyond the nation-state (Holston 1999; Caldeira 2000; Isin 2002). In other words, they use citizenship to explain how people produce alternative forms of political incorporation at scales like cities, regions, historically oppressed identities and communities, and even at the global level. As a result, the dominance of the state in the analysis of citizenship is eroded, which contradicts the liberal framework I outlined above. An equally fundamental concern posited by students of citizenship is liberals' passive conception of the citizen. The liberal citizen recognizes the value of protest as it allows the historical progress of citizenship in modern Western societies. Yet, while in this framework the citizen may influence citizenship, citizenship is a status that conceptually precedes (in the shape of formal procedures and laws) the citizen. The liberal citizen, therefore, acquires and possesses rights and duties; it does not actively produce them. In truth, our commitment to different dynamics of interaction in our culture, family, religion, and ethnicity is required for us to engage in society as citizens. In other words, our ideational and behavioral adherence to shared cultural symbols may be considered more important than formal norms and procedures to assess our full incorporation into a political community. This is why the establishment of free elections is not sufficient for people to experience voting as a fulfilling act of political engagement. Since Chile's return to democracy in 1990, its youth has, in fact, demonstrated that withdrawing from institutional mechanisms of political impact while also increasing informal means of public involvement is a plausible option to strengthen their citizenship (Venegas 2016).

When feminists claim that "the personal is political" they are outlining a realm of politics and citizenship that exceeds the liberal notion. They are suggesting that what are often understood as private matters can be made issues of political contention. Citizenship emerges in this process of politicization. The citizen, in this context, is collectively "made, not born" (Tulchin and Ruthenburg 2007, 281). In other words, we become citizens as we join others in building our political realm, as we participate in creating and recreating the codes by which we shape our community (Isin and Wood 1999; Lazar 2013; Zerilli 2016; Alldred and Fox 2019).

In this book, I side with these critical definitions of citizenship. I define citizenship as a set of culturally symbolic practices that bring people together in the act of collective organizing, shape their social positioning, and make them valid agents of community-building. As Anderson (1991) puts it, by participating in collective endeavors people are able to "imagine community." In other words, citizens emerge as individuals who join and identify with a community that extends beyond their direct experience. Through this act of imagination people become part of an abstract representation of community, one that extends in time – from past to future – and overcomes the idea of national boundaries (Staeheli 2003). While community-making also involves representing the state, it does not need to have the nation-state as its primary political community. In fact, by generating novel forms of incorporation, identities reposition people's community membership and territorially rescale their political incorporation (Purcell 2003; Sassen 2005; Stahl 2020).

Concerned with giving empirical substance to this critical approach, researchers have focused on highlighting the emergence of citizenship in the context of collective action. They show how mobilization allows groups to build new urban subjectivities, which in turn enables them to create alternative political incorporations. To do so, scholars highlight the way in which movements establish particular claims, take specific political positions, and implement certain tactics that allow their access to new political subjectivities. Because they are often in need of developing alternative incorporation tactics within societies with varying policies of inclusion and exclusion, migrants have been a primary target for this research. In her work on the Sans-Papiers, an irregular migrants' movement in France, McNevin (2011), for instance, describes how its members explicitly rejected being portrayed through notions of illegality. They staged protests to challenge their institutionally ascribed status as an illegal group that operates informally underground and assert their legitimate ability to claim rights.

The idea of urban citizenship has drawn special attention among scholars of citizenship and mobilization in the past couple of decades (Holston 1999; Isin 2002). They argue that cities concentrate exceptionally large flows of capital and make the contrasts of inequality particularly apparent to their dwellers. Simultaneously, urban spaces offer people a persistent proximity to others, thus giving the powerless an opportunity to rearticulate social relations in their interaction with each other as well as with authorities (Sassen 2008). Consequently, researchers of urban citizenship suggest, cities have become platforms that enable new political subjectivities among those who have been excluded. In other words, urban interactions provide privileged opportunities to mobilize and challenge unjust distributions of power in entrenched unequal regimes of citizenship (Isin 2000; Sassen 2008). The urban margins work as a magnifying glass to show how local residents build alternative identities in their collective endeavors to claim rights. Underprivileged local organizations in El Alto, Bolivia, have created what Lazar (2008) calls a "collective self," which allows them to produce territorial cohesion, politicize their neighborhoods, shape interactions with the state, and stand up to injustice. In a similar analysis but focused on the Brazilian urban margins, Holston (1991, 2008, 2011) highlights urban dwellers' *autoconstrução* (auto-construction), to refer to underprivileged people who built their own houses. His work explains how the Brazilian urban poor became competent rights-claimants and creators of an "insurgent citizenship" by producing a collective sense of protagonism in the act of self-building the urban peripheries. According to Holston, poor urban dwellers transformed themselves into empowered, valid agents of community-building by establishing their right to urban infrastructure and property claims to build their houses, learning to use the law to their advantage, and becoming modern consumers.

This literature does an excellent job in describing the multiple collective subjectivities that underlie contemporary processes of politicization. However, these authors have been less concerned with theorizing mobilization in the events and groups they study, which is a critical task if we want to understand how novel political subjects lead processes of social change. The concept of mobilizational citizenship that I put forward in this book provides an analytical answer to this issue. It builds on social movement and citizenship theories to develop a framework that explains how collective action can endure and build mobilizing capabilities in the urban margins in contexts of intense political exclusion. As I show, mobilizational citizenship allows urban communities to support large-scale processes of democratization and social change.

To produce this concept, I draw on the sustained development of collective action and citizenship in Chile's urban margins. This is not uncharted territory; several academics of social mobilization have addressed this issue since the country's return to democracy in 1990. They can be grouped into two dominant approaches, and both predicted the demobilization of *poblaciones*.

First, political process theorists are concerned with activists' perceptions of opportunities in the institutional political structure. Mobilization grows when new political coalitions, cleavages, and elite allies open additional windows of opportunity for movements. When facing threats, like police repression or counter-mobilization, collective action tends to be discouraged (Tarrow 2011). For the urban poor, opportunities also take the shape of supporting resources provided by elite allies (Piven and Cloward 1977). In the context of authoritarian rule, mobilization may flourish despite the relatively high levels of repression when civil society's organizational traits, resources, and ideology allow it. This happened under several of Latin America's dictatorships in the 1980s, including Chile's. Simultaneously, the institutionalization of social movements in Latin American societies after the dictatorships led to the deactivation of social mobilization (Kurtz 2004; Bellinger and Arce 2011).[1] Students of

---

[1] Oberschall (2000) makes a similar point for the democratization processes experienced in eastern Europe in the 1980s.

the political process diagnosed that, segregated and deprived of resources, civil society in the urban margins of countries with enclosed political systems, such as Uruguay and Chile, suffered this deactivation more acutely (O'Donnell and Schmitter 1986; Canel 1992; Foweraker 1995; Hipsher 1996, 1998; Garretón 2003).

Second, new social movement scholars studied the same outcome from the perspective of collective identity. Oxhorn (1995) called *lo popular* (the popular) a cohesive collective identity that emerged in *poblaciones* in the 1980s. This identity transcended material interests and motivated *población* dwellers to mobilize even when military repression increased. Yet, once the referendum in 1988 consolidated the new democracy and political elites withdrew their support for activism, *población* grassroots organizations experienced frustration and fragmentation. As predicted by Dubet and other social movement scholars (2016) in 1989, this identity of *lo popular* seemed to fade away with the democratic transition, as under-privileged dwellers showed "no systematic efforts ... to create any kind of popular social movement" (Oxhorn 1995, 273).

These findings are consistent with studies on culture and citizenship in *poblaciones*, which report that market-driven public policies, poverty, and urban segregation produced highly individualistic identities in the urban margins (Greaves 2005; Sugranyes and Rodríguez 2005; Jara Ibarra 2016; Angelcos and Pérez 2017). Underprivileged urban dwellers became docile citizens, disinterested with public affairs, even in cases of abusive treatment by the state or private corporations (Han 2012; Rodríguez, Saborido, and Segovia 2012).

Although useful to understand the context of generalized social deactivation in post-dictatorial underprivileged urban Chile, these approaches do not deliver insights for the study of cases that do not fit their predictions, such as those analyzed in this book. The reality is that collective action survived in some exceptional areas after the dictatorship (see Garcés and Valdés 1999; Figueroa 2003; Escoffier 2018; Pérez 2022). Activists in *poblaciones* reacted to their increased marginalization in the early 1990s by rejecting elite support and avoiding participatory funds offered by local governments. Instead, many neighborhood organizations sustained collective action by adopting strategies of *autogestión* (self-management) as their core source of funding. From then on, activists have organized community parties, neighborhood soccer tournaments, children's workshops, and other events whose revenues are used to fund larger mobilization initiatives. The additional effort that *población* activists go through to obtain resources while also avoiding engaging in collaborative interactions with political institutions could be understood as a very poor benefit maximization strategy. Presumably, the additional time, work, and effort they invest in obtaining resources for mobilization contradicts the rational assumption governing political process theory by which people seek political opportunities (e.g., state funding) to lower the costs and increase the benefits of collective action. But *población* activists see organizing additional events as beneficial because they are especially concerned with strengthening a sense of community. For decades, the local community they nurture has pushed political institutions away and promoted mobilization. Yet, why these urban dwellers sustain a sense of collective identity and community – and its resulting mobilization – over time has so far remained unanswered.

The mobilizational citizenship framework that I outline in the following sections draws on critical conceptions of citizenship to build on social movement theory. It allows to analytically understand the endurance of mobilization from the perspective of political incorporation and belonging. Furthermore, the evidence that substantiates this framework attests to the work that activists in the urban margins have developed as part of Chile's struggles over citizenship in the past three decades.

## 1.3 MOBILIZATIONAL CITIZENSHIP

Mobilizational citizenship involves claiming rights, which is not the same as framing a collective demand with the word "right." People claim rights when they join others in producing and self-defining political community. This act creates a hitherto nonexistent relational sense of empowerment and public engagement. Rights-claiming means adopting a collective political position according to which one intrinsically deserves access to public goods.

As I showed earlier in this chapter and will show in the rest of this book, the activists I study in the urban margins tend to reject the notion of citizen to describe their political struggles. They are also unlikely to use other categories of formally recognized citizenship development, including "citizenship" and "rights." Instead, they reclaim the idea of *"poblador"* as a way of legitimating the legacy of a movement that has suffered from and struggled against exclusion for almost a century. Throughout most of the twentieth century, the mobilized Chilean urban poor sought to build different versions of power from the left, all of them seeking to access the state or larger forms of national social organization. After the dictatorship, from 1990, *población* activists who continued to mobilize over time began to pursue a different political incorporation. They decided to resist neoliberalism by promoting an alternative form of community-building, one based on communitarian socialization and insurgent cultural values. In this case, citizenship and rights-claiming occurs through a set of discursive strategies that escape traditional, Euro-centric norms of institutional engagement and framing. Activists perceive the category of *poblador* as granting them dignity and empowerment, as it provides them with the opportunity to avoid the neo-corporatist forms of collective action that political parties and labor unions once offered to claim rights.

Following Zivi (2012, 24), I here understand rights-claiming as a performative collective practice that "shapes and changes our sense of self, our relationships to others, and the communities in which we live." In other words, by claiming rights, people change themselves and the sociopolitical context in which they are making that claim. Rights-claiming may appear to reify identity. Indeed, movements reify their identity when they crystallize their self-definition through fixed categories, traits, and demands. Yet, as a form of historicizing rights-claiming, memory-building contributes to "signify rather than simply reify identity" (Zivi 2012, 89). In recognizing the institutional and social historical dynamics of community oppression, rights-claiming enables the construction and reconstruction of collective identity.

Collectives claim citizenship rights as they use their identity to locate themselves as proper authors or protagonists of community development. Shotter's (1993) work is especially useful in this case. He explains how people build citizenship when their demands, narratives, and actions express their position as unconditional community-builders. This unconditional position dispenses with those credentials often employed to undermine the voice of marginalized people (Shotter 1993). In other words, groups claim rights when they understand that no proof of qualification is conditional to their ability to publicly establish their demands and identity; when they conceive themselves as valid political agents who shape their community and act accordingly (Shotter 1993). This act of joining others in producing and self-defining political community is what this book calls *protagonism*. In fact, in the case of excluded populations or undocumented migrants, the performative act of claiming spaces and making political demands creates a hitherto nonexistent relational sense of empowerment and public engagement. It is this right of producing political community in circumstances of exclusion and beyond institutionally recognized formal norms of political incorporation that Arendt (1973) calls "the right to have rights."

Mobilizational citizenship is the process by which mobilization becomes a source of political incorporation. It happens when, in the face of strong political exclusion, activists in the urban margins learn that mobilization allows them to become valid community-builders. The framework I provide here includes tactics to spread this protagonism among activists, thus making mobilization sustainable.

Studying *pobladores'* development of mobilizational citizenship means examining what Buechler (1990) calls "social movement communities" (SMCs). An SMC is a set of organizations and individuals that advance the goals of a social movement. Including both informal and state-recognized organizations, these SMCs keep relatively malleable boundaries and promote flexible leadership structures. In the study of the urban margins, SMCs may connect organizations and activists across neighborhoods; however, often their primary sources of mobilizing networks, resources, and collective meanings are based at the neighborhood level.

Mobilizational citizenship is the dynamic interaction of four components: agentic memory, mobilizing belonging, mobilizing boundaries, and decentralized protagonism. The first three components analytically outline the engagement in a collective identity that promotes contentious politics, a mobilizing identity. Collective identity is the process of building meaning and belonging inspired by shared cultural attributes. Cohesion occurs as collectives stress specific cultural attributes over other sources of meaning (Castells 2010, 10). The mobilizing identity advanced by the three first components in the framework involves sharing identity symbols that not only foster social cohesion, but that also promote actions that defy the cultural, social, or political institutions sustaining systems of inequality and exclusion. By identity symbols I refer to sources of meaning construction – words, narratives, or actions – whose sense can vary depending on the cultural context and on their relationship with other symbols (Cohen 1989). Groups with particular identities use distinctive shared symbols to classify and signify the experience of themselves and of other social actors (Goffman 1986; Zerubavel 1999). While symbols' meanings are not fixed, they function as the cultural web that allows community members to signify social reality within a set of semantic boundaries. In other words, symbols promote identification and bring people together, not by clearly setting a set of meanings that everyone will agree upon, but by defining the boundaries within which communities interpret their social world and position themselves in relation to other actors (Cohen 1989).

While interconnected, these dimensions of mobilizing identity complement each other by playing different roles. Together they set the standards of legitimacy within an SMC. *Agentic memory* can be understood as a first step and a condition of possibility in the mobilizational citizenship framework. It occurs when activists politicize community by creating a sense of continuity in time. It involves people's sense of communion with past events and social actors. Activists use this communion to draw lessons from the past to inform present experience, thus reproducing an imagined community that extends in time. Furthermore, agentic memory develops when activists use the past to create a sense of agency in the present. As activists create and recreate symbols that define them, bring them together through similar traits, and encourage their mobilization, they produce *mobilizing belonging*. This mechanism of identity fosters distinctiveness, cohesion, and pride among actors. Simultaneously, activists produce *mobilizing boundaries* when they create symbols that differentiate them from institutions, values, or other groups, and motivate collective action.

To develop *decentralized protagonism*, activists understand their mobilizing identity symbols as potentially transmitted, acquired, and even lost (when people stop adhering to particular systems of interpretation and recognition). Mobilizing identity becomes a tool for creating legitimacy (or discredit) within an SMC. As transmission tactics disseminate mobilizing identity, every SMC member becomes a locus of leadership and an agent of community-building. This promotion of leadership across members and generations allows for this alternative form of citizenship and mobilization to be sustained over time. Mobilizational citizenship is this recursive process. I here explain the mechanisms underlying each of these factors in more detail.

### 1.3.1 Agentic Memory

Narratives of the past often differ from actual historical events. Historians and students of memory are used to hearing stories of the past that do not match the evidence in archives or official records. This is because individuals and collectives use their narratives of the past to construct their self in the present. For example, people who have faced traumatic situations develop their personalities and strengthen their confidence in the present by continually interpreting and reinterpreting past events in a way that provides them with coherent, positive explanations of their present position (Harris 2006; McAdams, Josselson, and Lieblich 2006; McLean, Pasupathi, and Pals 2007). In doing so, they tend to fill gaps, include or exclude elements, or even reorganize the order of events. In his research, Eyerman (2004, 159), for example, describes how a former concentration camp inmate in Poland

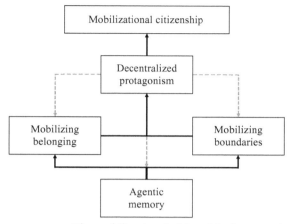

FIGURE 1.1 The mobilizational citizenship framework.

during World War II many years later remembered interacting with a particularly evil guard. Historical records, however, placed that guard elsewhere at the time the prisoner describes. When confronted with this incongruence, the victim was shaken and insisted on the veracity of his memory. This difference between narrated memory and documented history should not be seen as a mistake or a lie, but rather as a strategy of identity-building. As Polletta (1998, 141) suggests, "in telling the story of our becoming – as an individual, a nation, a people – we establish who we are." Through memory-building, collectives obtain lessons to produce and reproduce the identity symbols functioning as building blocks of belonging and boundaries. To be sure, memory is fundamental to collective identity-building, but studying agentic memory's ability to mobilize and claim rights requires a specific account of its underpinnings.

In cities in a state of permanent renovation and change, identity and memory are undermined. Private property, reinvestment, urban expansion, zoning, and building are at the core of urban development in the present day. The resulting increasing size, fluidity, and high fragmentation of cities occur at the expense of memory (Dagger 1981). However, aware of how important memory-building is for people's production of identity and citizenship, some groups have resisted these urban trends. They build community by avoiding the individuation and atomization imposed by capitalist societies at the local urban level. Agentic memory is a first step in this process of resistance. It feeds mobilizational citizenship by using symbols of the past to build a position of agency in the present. This position results from activists' performative interplay, which include the stories that they tell each other and to potential participants in face-to-face interactions. Activists in *poblaciones* would, for example, share anecdotes about the actions of leftist insurgents during the dictatorship after their organization's meetings, while sitting in a square in the neighborhood or smoking a cigarette. Often told by older leaders within local organizations, these stories regularly glorify radical militants and highlight the fundamental role of the community in resisting dictatorial rule. More recent events about injustice, police abuse, and successful collective action were also part of these stories. These acts of remembering usually depict *pobladores* as empowered agents of community-building.

Agentic memory develops when collectives create a sense of continuity with the past. In this process, the past provides symbols and standards of legitimacy in current actions. I demonstrate this dynamic in Lo Hermida's SMC, as well as in other *poblaciones* with enduring mobilization. Conversely, in other urban communities where mobilizational citizenship failed to develop, like in Nuevo Amanecer, the past is simply a lost project of community, unable to promote cohesion and dignity in people's lives.

In building agentic memory, communities produce what Sommers (1994) calls "relational settings." Relational settings are shared structures of interaction that express the community's position toward other social and political actors when performing identity. Narratives of the past construct and teach about interactions with other social agents to produce relational settings. We can speak of agentic memory when the act of remembering teaches empowering relational settings to community members. In other words, through the act of remembering, people become relationally situated as active, successful agents of community-building and social change. Memories of past mobilization generally activate present quests for dignity and empowerment in marginalized communities (Castells 1982; Gutman 2017). People use the lessons on past interactions to create new symbols in the present. In this way, collective memory's relational settings impact communities' processes of belonging and boundary-building. Agentic memory is, therefore, the initial source of communities' attributions toward other social and political actors, which translate into relationships of solidarity, differentiation, and antagonism.

Agentic memory-building is also a starting point for the politicization of place. Place-making is a collective experience that fixes time and space. It connects a mosaic of metaphors, scenes, characters, and experiences of the past to a physical environment that is relatively stable in time. Surviving in places, these experiences and characters become inevitably present to people, despite their current absence. In fact, in her ethnographic exploration of memory and place-making in Berlin, Till (2005) refers to the experience of being "haunted" by the past. "Being haunted involves the desire and repetitive practice of returning to a past time and self that never was," she explains (Till 2005, 13). By using place to bring a partially fictional past to the present, people metaphorically perform their relational settings. Manifestations of this include memorials, photographs, museums, songs, and murals; all of which connect past and present. As relational settings acquired through memory-building take issue with power imbalances, they make place-making a political matter. Neighborhood activists, therefore, use place to refer to historically oppressive relationships with authorities, express their identification with past community leaders, and honor successful events of resistance.

Communities may advance rights-claiming as they validate alternative form of remembering. Often, excluded communities authentically own narratives of the past by opposing mainstream historical narratives or hegemonic memory accounts (Gonzalez-Vaillant and Savio 2017; Badilla 2019). Feminist and indigenous movements' memory tactics brilliantly attest to this dynamic. Their narratives of the past have successfully unveiled explanations of oppression that question colonial, male, and heteronormative-dominated hegemonic notions of history. SMCs will politicize identity as their notions of the past construct a sense of authorship and self-determination in their relational settings (Shotter 1993). By politicizing identity, rights-claiming not only recognizes the history, institutions, and power dynamics that have oppressed a community in the past, but also enables the production and reproduction of mobilizing identity in the present (see Zivi 2012). The result is, therefore, not a fixed past for a fixed identity, but the opportunity of participating in creating and re-creating community.

### 1.3.2 Mobilizing Belonging

Sociologists and social psychologists who research collective identity pay attention to the symbols that address people's commonalities (Jenkins 1996). Identification requires symbolic mechanisms promoting social cohesion, a sense of sameness, an idea of "us," or as I call it here: *belonging*. In the case of urban communities, belonging is often territorially based. In other words, people's neighborhood (its name, history, location, etc.) is usually one of the local community's strongest sources of identification (Cuba and Hummon 1993; Lewicka 2010). Moreover, the personal becomes political through belonging. Individuals produce belonging by personally adopting identity symbols that sustain their connection with other community members. As a result, as academics often show, the boundaries between the personal and the collective become blurred among people sharing cohesive identities (Jenkins 1996; Craib 1998; Flesher 2010). Taylor and Whittier's (1992) work on feminist identity construction in the early 1990s in the United States, for example, explains how activists embraced collective, public ideals in their private lives. As a result of their engagement in cohesive identities of social mobilization, women rejected patriarchy in their personal relationships and promoted solidarity with other women in their daily behavior.

Belonging becomes a source of mobilization and rights-claiming under more specific conditions. As the positionality of identity also places collectives in a system of political actors struggling for recognition and power, it is key to the analysis of why and how people mobilize. Melucci, for example, thinks of identity-based political conflicts as a prime source of collective action. In his words, "a collective action implies the existence of struggle between two actors for the appropriation and orientation of social values and resources, each of the actors characterized by a specific solidarity" (Melucci 1980, 202). Melucci (1996, 23) refers to mobilizing belonging more broadly when he makes reference to the notion of "solidarity" among activists: "the ability of actors to recognize others and to be recognized, as belonging to the same social unit." More specifically, however, mobilizing belonging refers to communities' ability to activate identity symbols that promote both social cohesion and contentious politics. On the grounds of agentic memory-building, SMCs in marginal urban settings will generally use their neighborhoods as their primary inspiration for mobilizing belonging construction. The neighborhood is, after all, urban dwellers' most direct source of cohesion. Two mechanisms are activated in this process: political consciousness and positive assertion.

The first, political consciousness, is activated when people build cohesion through a shared sense of opposition toward a broader unjust system. In other words, this consciousness emerges when communities attribute their grievances to a system (either structural, cultural, social, or economic) rather than to a personal or individual failure. Crucially, this mechanism is at the core of mobilizational citizenship's ability to challenge dominant ways of understanding social, cultural, or material realities. In fact, as Taylor and Whittier (1992, 114) suggest, "[political] consciousness not only provides socially and politically marginalized groups with an understanding of their structural position, but establishes new expectations regarding treatment appropriate to their category." In other words, it results from a collective identity that promotes a strong sense of self-worth as well as people's disposition to defend their dignity. For instance, in describing themselves as *pobladores*, activists in Chile's urban margins reject self-accusation. Rather, they performatively portray themselves as politically aware actors who are ready to stand up to historically anchored systems of oppression and exclusion. They also use the notion of *lucha* (struggle) to locally validate their tactics. This struggle refers to both past and present events of collective action, and, by engaging in it, local dwellers symbolically reject entrenched systems of inequality and injustice. They might label a fundraising event or a soccer match as *lucha*, just as they would with a protest. This allows them to highlight how initiatives that may seem docile or submissive can become part of a broader challenge to institutions when they seek to advance community-building in marginalized neighborhoods.

The second, positive assertion refers to people's ability to use symbols that positively portray their community. This mechanism often involves idealizing the neighborhood or local environment. Social movement theorists have called this phenomenon "frame amplification" (Benford and Snow 2000). By praising their neighborhood, urban activists make themselves and other people more inclined to engage in processes of identification with their local community. Furthermore, positive assertion locally validates the behaviors, spaces, aesthetics, vocabulary, or artistic expressions in the particular community. While this promotes cohesion among community members, its empowering and mobilizing potential lies in its rejection of stigmatizing community conceptions, both inside and outside the neighborhood. In other words, underlying positive assertion is the community's ability to cognitively resist external criminalization and discrimination. A sense of community that strengthens self-esteem and pride is highly empowering. Collective initiatives are understood as part of a local, unique culture that boosts people's self-esteem. Positive assertion thus feeds mobilizational citizenship by legitimizing and exalting collective action among community members.

### 1.3.3 Mobilizing Boundaries

Identification also involves difference. A sense of "we" is also relationally shaped in contrast to other external actors. Collective identity, hence, involves the processes advancing collective cohesion through symbolic strategies of differentiation. Scholars of collective identity call these processes *boundary construction* (Lamont and Molnar 2002). Identity boundaries can be more or less porous depending on how congruent and rigid identity symbols are and on how externally threatened people perceive their identity to be. Identification results from the conflicts and negotiations that collectives carry out in their ongoing processes of differentiating the internal and the external. In other words, although strongly interconnected with processes of belonging, the symbols articulating boundary construction are those with the strongest power to determine what actions, meanings, values, and actors should be excluded or included in the identity or community. For example, symbols of class strongly determine racial identity boundaries in Brazilian culture. Some studies show that, in fact, as people are able to demonstrate symbols of upward class mobility (e.g., wealth or educational attainment), they begin to change their perceptions about their racial identity; that is, as they become richer or more educated, they are considered "whiter" (Degler 1971; Schwartzman 2007).

Mobilizing boundaries relationally feed mobilizational citizenship by protecting the SMC's local systems of legitimacy and by fostering autonomy. Abstract and vague approaches to injustice tend to dilute resentment among activists, making it look absurd to other community members. Instead of mobilizing, people tend to rationally discredit collective action when unfair social forces appear impersonal and vague to them. Yet, as community members use boundary-building to make more concrete attributions of antagonism and interpretations of injustice, this sense of protection sparks strong feelings among community members and mobilization becomes urgent. As Gamson (1995) argues, the emotional activation of indignation is the crucial, mobilizing component in the boundary-making equation (see also Flam 2014). For example, *población* activists often employ the symbol *"represión"* when referring to institutional interventions in the neighborhood. Regularly used to describe human rights violations – either during Pinochet's dictatorship or in the widespread protests that erupted in 2019 – the idea of repression has a powerful emotional impact on the Chilean left. It sparks strong feelings of frustration and anger. By using this notion, neighborhood activists elicit a sense of urgency among other residents that reinforces the need for mobilization.

Three mechanisms activate mobilizing boundaries: differentiation, defining antagonists, and self-determination. A first step in the boundary-making process involves symbolic strategies of differentiation. Identity symbols of differentiation build distance from other social entities, such as other groups, organizations, or institutions. Through these symbols, SMCs highlight how their history, values, methods, and language, among other things, differ from these other entities. Differentiation also allows a movement community to symbolically construct a relatively unique and protected realm from which it can oppose dominant cultural narratives.

As community members construct political consciousness and make interpretations of injustice, they may identify concrete adversaries. In other words, they may attribute their grievances to the acts of identifiable people, groups, or institutions. I call this act of attribution defining antagonists. Emotions of anger and frustration emerge as a result, and people feel compelled to mobilize. Urban movements often use this attributional work as a way of protecting their community from other actors threatening their symbolic or material existence. This is the case of movements fighting against eviction or gentrification. By gaining a sense of control over their own actions, community members experience self-determination. The processes of differentiation and identifying adversaries set a variably porous system of inclusion and exclusion that discourages some externally validated values and behaviors. Highly valued by activists, this sense of self-determination may also strengthen their inclination for defensive forms of mobilization. Antagonists, in this context, can be seen as an obstacle to differentiation and autonomy, and hence a threat to identity. Empowerment and mobilization may then incorporate strategies to exclude antagonists.

Activists in *poblaciones* use these boundary-building tactics. They define antagonists and create self-determination. As I explain more thoroughly later, in Chapter 5, local dwellers use locally validated notions to create a realm of security and confidence that I label "the informal." This realm outlines a system of legitimacy in local dwellers' interactions and tactics. With its history of community development and activism, the neighborhood is the prime site in which the informal occurs. Presence and informal networks of trust are fundamental to building validation in social interactions within this realm. Antagonists that undermine the informal are institutions and actors that abide by formal norms of legitimation. *Población* activists also consider antagonists other actors who take advantage of institutional arrangements, such as drug dealers and depoliticized artists. The threat that antagonists' actions pose to the survival of the informal fuels protective mobilization.

### 1.3.4 Decentralized Protagonism

Until now, I have theoretically explained how collective identity feeds mobilizational citizenship by activating contentious politics through different symbolic mechanisms that I have called agentic memory, mobilizing belonging, and mobilizing boundaries. However, an alternative citizenship can develop if activists use these mechanisms of mobilizing identity to advance their protagonism. Protagonism must be examined in micro-mobilization processes, that is, in the face-to-face relational dynamics leading to mobilization within SMCs (Gamson 1992). At this level of micro-mobilization, protagonism involves activists recognizing each other as community members. While particular leaders may emerge – because they have more knowledge, experience, networks, or access to mobilizing resources than others in the group – the success of building protagonism depends on a sense of leadership becoming accessible to other activists as well. In other words, activists are socialized to exercise protagonism and thus to conceive of themselves as valid initiators of collective action and agents of rights-claiming. For this to occur, exchanging and acquiring political capital at the level of micro-mobilization is essential.

Bourdieu thought of political capital as a set of resources conceptually located in the intersection between social and symbolic capitals (Bourdieu 1991; Swartz 2013). Social capital refers to the use that we make of our social relations to achieve our goals in a collective environment. In his words, social capital is "the aggregate of the actual or potential resources which are linked to possession of a durable network of more or less institutionalized relationships of mutual acquaintance and recognition" (Bourdieu 1986, 21). On the other hand, symbolic capital should be understood as the collective recognition of honor, social standing, and legitimacy. Thus, it provides people with symbolic power, which means the ability to create social categories with an impact on other people's social positioning. As the state acts as an apparatus that regularly creates and legitimizes normative social categories, it is the principal (but not the only) locus of symbolic power in our societies (Swartz 2013).

Political capital results from the interaction between these two forms of capital because it refers to the tangible or intangible resources by which social actors mobilize support from others. This support can be seen as directed toward a candidate or a political party, if one is concerned with electoral or partisan analyses (Swartz 2013; Joignant 2019). However, my focus here is on political capital's ability to mobilize people and resources as support for a movement's leader, a cause, or a community (Bénit-Gbaffou and Katsaura 2014). This is the case of community leaders in the urban margins. The resources mentioned here are diverse and not restricted to financial means; they include a person's charismatic traits (Weber 1978), their identity, their history or fame, and their skills to catalyze action (Ganz 2010).

Like all other forms of capital, political capital can be transmitted, acquired, and lost. The incorporation of political capital mobilizes others and builds leadership as it promotes an agent's trustworthiness, credibility, and social standing in a particular context of social action (Casey 2005; Ganz 2010). The micro-dynamics of political capital determine what is considered legitimate and what is not in order to activate collective action in a particular community or group. In the urban SMCs analyzed in this book, in which informal networks prevail, political capital is what gives legitimacy to local informal leaders. As Bénit-Gbaffou and Katsaura (2014, 1808) argue in studying underprivileged urban South Africa, community leaders draw their legitimacy from "various forms of collective popular consent ... and they represent their followers, as they have been given a (formal or informal, explicit or sometimes tacit) mandate by them."

Political capital is, therefore, both collective and individual. SMCs increase their political capital when the idea of acting collectively to overcome grievances or change their reality becomes more plausible, legitimate, and desirable in people's minds. Financial means, elite allies, and the use of successful collective action frames may promote this idea. Also, particular activists may be more skillful than others at using resources to promote mobilization. They may be particularly savvy at, for example, reframing interactions with institutions as unjust. They may also be especially effective public speakers, as well as able to access useful political networks and financial resources to boost collective action. By doing this, these activists will individually accumulate political capital to informally or formally legitimize their position as community leaders.

Decentralized protagonism advances mobilizational citizenship because, on the one hand, it uses mobilizing identity to construct an alternative form of political incorporation, and on the other hand, it promotes face-to-face micro-mobilizing dynamics that spread political capital, decentralize leadership, and sustain mobilization over time.

As individuals become locally valid agents of mobilization and identity transmission, they disperse this political capital among community members through socialization. This dynamic promotes autonomy and leadership among community members, both collectively and individually. Furthermore, by adhering to this mobilizing identity, activists will proudly embody its promotion of political consciousness and self-determination. As political socialization spreads across different local groups, the SMC will become more diverse. Activists' efforts to reach younger neighborhood dwellers are crucial. Offering identity and political capital to young people promotes the emergence of new leaders who will sustain collective action through mobilizational citizenship in the future. Decentralizing protagonism will then result in a highly horizontal organizational structure. This is not to say that the process of erecting specific activists as leaders is avoided. In fact, specific people able to make strategic decisions and channel resources in order to activate others' mobilization are essential to sustaining collective action (Hanisch 2001; Morris and Staggenborg 2004). Yet, these specific leaders will only promote the decentralization of protagonism if they transmit political capital among other current and potential activists.

I borrow Gamson's (1992) model for the study of mobilizing acts to suggest that protagonism becomes decentralized through the transmission of mobilizing identity in at least three types of micro-mobilizing encounters: organizing, reframing, and divesting acts. These encounters socialize activists and potential activists. *Organizing acts* promote collective action in group meetings or other private situations. They are usually not public and do not involve interactions with authorities. Decentralized protagonism in these occasions results from highlighting activists' position as worthy bearers of mobilizing identity both as a collective and/or individually. Mobilizing identity symbols will be transmitted through relatively structured socializing strategies (formative activities, workshops, talks, debates, etc.) or through more informal socialization (stories of the past, improvised discussions, designing slogans, etc.). *Población* leaders, for instance, tailor a substantial proportion of their local initiatives to children in the neighborhood. These events seek to expand the children's cultural and political awareness. This tactic follows a long-standing tradition of political socialization developed by the left and other political groups, and emulates the children camps in which they themselves received political training during the 1980s.

Through *reframing acts*, collectives interpret events they experience as unfair, oppressive, or threatening. Often, mainstream accounts of these events will clash with how activists understand those same events. Yet, through those interpretations, activists performatively reaffirm identity symbols and promote unity. This reframing process often occurs progressively and involves several encounters. The resulting sense of injustice works as a call to action that activates strong emotions of resentment. Moreover, this resentment grows when reframing acts confirm relational settings of past oppressive experience. Consequently, the highly emotional reaction that these acts often trigger among SMC members makes activists' assimilation of mobilizing identity symbols more likely. Activists in Chile's urban margins, for instance, tend to reframe interactions with the police or the military as highly oppressive because these institutions trigger memories of human rights violations during the dictatorship. Those interactions are thus opportunities for newer, less experienced activists to learn mobilizing identity symbols and tactics. They learn how to interpret interactions with authorities as "repressive" and engage in actions to react against that repression. *Divesting acts* usually follow reframing acts and tend to be public encounters that disrupt norms of interaction, especially with authorities. Activists in these situations strongly agree in their interpretation of events, which promotes their strict cohesiveness. In this context, they experience any challenge to their interpretation of events as a moral transgression. In other words, activists will interpret as a moral threat an intervention that disagrees with how they decode a conflicting situation with authorities.

As I explain above, decentralizing protagonism builds a sense of incorporation among community members. In other words, by engaging in contentious politics, local activists become protagonists of community-building. This sense of community should be understood beyond our traditional framework of the nation-state. In addition to their national community, people who develop mobilizational citizenship may engage in imagining political community as the city, the neighborhood, historical SMCs, or global communities. However, decentralized protagonism is not only an opportunity for people to become valid agents of community production and reproduction, but also a chance of self-producing an unconditional sense of political incorporation. The leadership that decentralized protagonism produces allows activists to create new initiatives of collective action. In Chile's urban margins, for example, local leaders and groups of activists tend to emerge in different areas of each neighborhood. They hence act as gatekeepers and enablers of mobilization in those zones. They coordinate actions in each zone, liaise with local gangs and drug dealers, and make some resources available for other activists. With these actions, they gain the trust of families residing in that area. While this collective action follows the local mobilizing identity, it also expresses the innovations developed by new generations, genders, races, and other interconnected identities. Much like Isin's (2008, 2) "acts of citizenship" – that is, "collective or individual deeds that rupture social-historical patterns" – these initiatives will challenge the dynamics of interaction that exclude community members from entrenched cultural and political institutions.

## 1.4 THE BUILDUP OF MOBILIZING CAPABILITIES

Through mobilizational citizenship, the SMC in a neighborhood will provide residents with a locally validated exit to structural and interpersonal mechanisms of political exclusion. Their passionate defense of mobilizational citizenship is, therefore, expectable. This dynamic explains why, although highly diverse, neighborhood SMCs will be ready to react with great cohesion when their identity and community are under threat (Dolgon 2001; Van Dyke 2003). Neighborhood organizations involved in mobilizational citizenship will also be able to take advantage of contexts that provide critical opportunities to advance broad democratization.

However, mobilizational citizenship's decentralization dynamic and territorially based identity make joint action particularly challenging, especially when it comes to collaborations across the urban margins. Consequently, it is not sufficient to trigger the swift, collaborative action required for supporting large-scale protests and broad political change. Mobilizational citizenship will only allow activists to react in unison to large threats and opportunities when it has sustained collective action long enough for those activists to develop the necessary capabilities that make coalition-building more likely.

Reportedly, the prior production of networks is a powerful predictor of people's participation in events of protest (Knoke and Wood 1981; Lim 2010; Hong and Peoples 2020). Through its enduring collective action, mobilizational citizenship allows activists to develop these links both within their SMC and more broadly in their neighborhood. When network-building expands within the neighborhood, beyond the local SMC, it increases the community's mobilization potential (Klandermans and Oegema 1987). In other words, it makes it more likely for neighborhood residents who do not regularly participate in the local SMC to engage in public protests when other conditions are favorable and when they are invited to join those events of mobilization. Furthermore, mobilizational citizenship allows activist networks to progressively grow and extend across the urban margins. These connections can even reach other movements beyond segregated neighborhoods, such as trade unions, student associations, and feminist organizations. SMCs may also attract activists from other, less active communities in the urban margins who want to engage in alternative citizenship-building. Additionally, as newer generations bring updated resources and knowledge to their performance of mobilizational citizenship, the SMCs' tactics diversify and multiply.

To engage in large-scale protest, organizers at the urban margins will also need to build the capabilities required to participate in broad coalitions. The ties developed through mobilizational citizenship will allow brokers within local organizations or SMCs seeking to create future collaborations to establish relatively stable and trustworthy bridges between groups (Bystydzienski and Schacht 2001). For these ties to facilitate broader coalition-building, they will need to expand beyond the neighborhood. Additionally, in all cases, they will need to create "free spaces" in which those links can evolve. As Polletta (1999) describes them, free spaces are events, situations, or locations of voluntary participation and cultural exchange in which people feel detached from authorities' oversight. These settings bring people together to develop the ideas that will fuel their collective challenges and, in turn, their joint mobilization. Aware of this kind of spaces' importance, *población* activists have made efforts to take control of community buildings in their neighborhood. They also organize land repossessions, which are coordinated occupations of squares, soccer pitches or other sites used for community-building and mobilizing. Organized every year, fundraising events, music festivals, and neighborhood anniversaries also function as free spaces. These settings work as platforms of interaction, collaboration, and network-building in which activists and leaders from different SMCs can create ties. They are also spaces in which neighborhood activists may meet organizers from movements beyond the urban margins.

These ties provide local activists at the urban margins with the informal access to resources needed to act in collaboration, thus increasing the plausibility of coalition-building (Almeida and Stearns 1998; Chung 2001). Activists' use of self-management to find the required resources for mobilization has become increasingly frequent in *poblaciones*. Part of this tactic involves complementing resources from different organizations within the neighborhood's informal networks when coordinating local events or initiatives.

Cohesive identities and similar cultural traits also make coalition-building more likely. The different components of mobilizational citizenship, as well as its strong emphasis on community construction, foster cohesive mobilizing identities within SMCs in the urban margins. Simultaneously, mobilizational citizenship gives local organizers a sense of autonomous engagement and freedom, which will allow them to create cultural links across communities. This tactic has been described as a threat to collaborations across class, racial, and ethnic divides in middle-class and feminist movements (Lichterman 1995; Roth 2010). Yet, while some of those dynamics may be at play in the urban margins, a relative class and racial interrelatedness between activists in impoverished urban zones should be expectable. Despite their commitment with their local SMCs, for instance, feminist and hip-hop groups in *poblaciones* have developed increasing networks beyond their neighborhood whereby they exchange ideology, collective identity symbols, and tactics. Feminist organizations from different *poblaciones* coordinate meetings and organize boycott campaigns to hold perpetrators of sexual abuse accountable. Similarly, rappers organize music festivals that gather singers and bands from the urban margins across the country. These events have become hubs of cultural exchange for young *población* activists.

As I show in later chapters of this book, población activists used these built-up capabilities to have pivotal roles in key protest events during the highly influential 2011 student demonstrations, both in the urban margins and in central urban areas. Later, they became particularly involved in the No+AFP movement (named in opposition to the companies managing the private pension scheme, Pension Funds Administrators, or AFP in its Spanish abbreviation), and in November 2016 a group of población organizations participated in large-scale disruptive protests and riots against Chile's privatized pension system. Población organizations have also had an active role in the feminist movement that has grown throughout the past decade. These mobilizations were fundamental to Chilean democracy because they created momentum for the outburst of riot-style, country-wide protests that erupted in October 2019. These were massive and often violent protests that disrupted most services and strongly challenged the entrenched political elite for over four months. In the weeks and months after the protests exploded, *poblaciones* like Lo Hermida responded quickly and efficiently in activating networks and resources for large-scale action. They spearheaded the creation of urban territorial coalitions, carried out urban land invasions, implemented disruptive tactics, and engaged in violent clashes with the police. These neighborhood activists also created healthcare fronts that aided wounded protesters and liaised with the Chilean Institute for Human Rights and other NGOs to document police brutality. These protests obtained widespread support in the population and triggered a democratic process that will redraft Chile's political constitution through a highly inclusive constitutional convention (see Chapter 2 for details).

## 1.5 THE FAILURE OF MOBILIZATIONAL CITIZENSHIP

Typically, mobilizational citizenship fails to develop in the urban margins. Around the world, regimes politically exclude the underprivileged. Multiple barriers obstruct the urban poor's ability to make decisions about their habitat and shape their own communities. Their depoliticization and demobilization are the expression of this political exclusion. Consequently, the urban underprivileged become unable to activate contentious politics, which prevents their participation in national and local systems of democratic development.

In this process, political institutions not only undermine underprivileged residents' macro-level political opportunities, they also discourage their public engagement and social mobilization through micro-political strategies of depoliticization. To accomplish this goal, political institutions implement governance tactics that affect the availability and control of political capital for the development of contentious politics. This means that governance socializes local dwellers to impact the resources by which mobilization becomes legitimate.

As I argue in Chapter 3, the micro-dynamics of political exclusion in dictatorial and post-dictatorial underprivileged urban Latin America ultimately consist of the external control of political capital at the local level. Political institutions exercise this control by: (a) withdrawing mobilizing resources; and (b) shaping from the outside the local dynamics of political legitimacy. This conceptualization of political exclusion extends beyond cultural and political processes in urban Latin America. Fueled by labor precariousness, urban segregation, criminalization, and government assistance programs, over the past 60 years the urban underprivileged have suffered a process of increasing political exclusion across middle- and high-income economies (Wilson 1990; Wacquant 2008). Urban marginality in these societies, too, has suffered the erosion and external control of political capital.

The withdrawal of mobilizing resources – including financial, infrastructural, and human resources – is a fundamental step to diminishing political capital in the urban margins, and thus to accomplishing their demobilization. This is, in part, why activists' connections with elite allies willing to support their mobilization are so important (Piven and Cloward 1977). Resource withdrawal is usually a strong deterrent of contentious politics (Jenkins and Perrow 1977; Davenport 2015). This is what the urban poor experienced in the Chilean process of regime change during the late 1980s and early 1990s. The loss of support – either from elite allies, from other influential political networks, or by losing financial resources – discourages activists, as their goals seem less plausible. This makes collective action less legitimate, which in turn diminishes political capital. Also, community and movement leaders derive much of their legitimacy and credibility from their access to elite networks and resources (Lapegna 2013; Bénit-Gbaffou and Katsaura 2014; Ganz 2016). In a scenario of exclusion and demobilization, the heterogeneous networks connecting local organizations with external and different actors – what Putnam (2000, 20) calls "bridging social capital" – are undermined. Furthermore, as mobilizing resources are depleted, it is likely that fellow activists in the community will question local leaders' legitimacy. Since the resources by which these activists constructed, accumulated, and shared political capital at the grassroots level are no longer available, their ability to sustain a sense of protagonism and leadership fades away.

Depleting the urban margins of political capital also includes undermining their human resources available for mobilization. In their seminal work on poor people's collective action, Piven and Cloward (1977) explain how government officials use concessions to manipulate underprivileged activists and reincorporate movements into noncontentious collective action or into more traditional systems of political representation. This tactic involves reintegrating movement leaders into stable institutional roles and excluding the claims of those activists considered to be more radical and contentious. Isolated and deprived of resources, the more radical leaders tend to lose credibility beyond their closest group of followers. Finally, while government concessions do not make structural changes to the poor's social position, they discredit contentious politics among potential supporters and movement activists. The government builds an image of being caring and effective at solving people's problems. Political capital is consequently eroded both within and outside the movement, as activists' claims and tactics increasingly lose legitimacy among potential supporters. Once movement leaders leave grassroots organizations to take institutional positions or join partisan political projects, the local dynamics that once fueled micro-mobilization become dislocated.

This withdrawal of resources is complemented by elite agents' external shaping of legitimacy dynamics in the urban margins. In other words, politicians or state agents will seek to influence who, when, and under what conditions neighborhood organizers may (or may not) increase their local legitimacy. The prior erosion of mobilizing resources in those communities makes it easier for those external elite political agents to exercise control over the remaining political capital. Through public policies that ultimately stigmatize the urban margins, state bureaucrats in the United States, Europe, and Latin America have repeatedly reproduced this dynamic of political capital control (Wacquant 2008; Castañeda 2012).

State agents stigmatize the urban underprivileged as delinquent, savage, and antisocial people. The result is bureaucratic, dominant discourses, policies, and assistance programs that discipline the poorest of society by pushing them to the margins of democracy (Feagin, Peterson, and Jencks 1991; Jargowsky 1997). Social policy implementation, therefore, acts as the state's socializing tool to rectify behaviors on the basis of dominant cultural and economic standards. In doing so, the state socializes underprivileged urban dwellers to delegitimize indigenous, local identities and behaviors, framing them as not complying with mainstream standards of "civility" (Wacquant 2009). Stigmatization therefore undermines autonomous political capital construction and mobilization in urban underprivileged areas. Empowering neighborhood initiatives that assert unconditional belonging and build leadership on the basis of autochthonous, oppositional identities are easily criminalized or excluded as a threat to state-sponsored notions of civility (Wacquant 2008; Wacquant, Slater, and Pereira 2014).

These mechanisms discourage collective action and affect communities across the urban margins. Through the development of mobilizational citizenship, some of those communities overcome these exclusionary forces to sustain contentious politics. Yet, most neighborhoods in the urban margins react passively to these entrenched, marginalizing mechanics of citizenship-building. In these cases, agentic memory fails to develop. Regularly, people will face events that challenge the cohesiveness or continuity of community-building over time. The urban poor often experience displacement or gentrification. The recent Chilean dictatorship represented a dramatic and violent disruptive event for *población* dwellers. Many of them could hardly conceive of their communities as one and the same before and after the coup d'état in 1973. Many community leaders were persecuted and killed. Regular raids conducted by the military affected local dwellers. The dictatorship modified the name of neighborhoods and their roads in many politicized *poblaciones*, and organized a large-scale relocation program that pushed underprivileged families to the urban peripheries. Keeping a sense of historical continuity within underprivileged communities was very difficult. In this context, mobilizing identity symbols from the past was no longer a valid resource to inspire collective action in the present, which precluded the development of agentic memory.

Simultaneously, local leaders in these communities become more exposed to networks of political loyalty led by elite political agents – local representatives or political party members. These networks will provide them with legitimacy within their communities and access to privileged connections with institutional political actors. As Lapegna (2013) reports, these interactions often expose these community leaders to pressure, which results from their need to simultaneously obtain validation from those elite political agents and from their fellow neighbors. To successfully respond to these loyalty networks' demands, community leaders learn to accumulate and compete over political capital at the grassroots level. Their regular interactions with partisan tactics of political competition will also train them to become savvy political capital monopolizers in their neighborhoods. As a result, they will not be available to provide a political socialization to other community members. In this context, recovering symbols from the past and transmitting a mobilizing identity within the community will not be possible, and agentic memory development will remain sustainably precluded.

## 1.6 CONCLUSION

This chapter provided this book's theoretical background. It defined the concept of mobilizational citizenship and explained its components. Mobilizational citizenship explains how activists in the urban margins develop an alternative type of political incorporation that sustains grassroots-level mobilization regardless of their political marginalization and contingent events. This sustained mobilization provides underprivileged urban activists with the knowledge, networks, and resources to protect their community and engage in broader processes of social change.

The analytical framework that I created for this concept described the development and dynamic interaction of four dimensions. The first three of them – agentic memory, mobilizing belonging, and mobilizing boundaries – advance a collective identity that promotes contentious politics, namely a mobilizing identity. As activists instrumentalize this mobilizing identity through encounters of socialization that spread its symbols within organizations and among other community members, they develop decentralized protagonism, the fourth dimension in the framework. The expansion of protagonism makes activists empowered agents of community-building and allows the emergence of new leaders that will contribute to maintaining mobilization over time.

Applied to the case of *poblaciones*, this framework explains how community empowerment survives the legacy of dictatorial rule and exclusionary democratic transitions to later contribute to expanding democracy. It is also a contribution to the field of citizenship studies. While a substantial number of studies in this area address the interaction between citizenship-building and mobilization, their core concern so far has been providing the evidence to back emerging citizenships. This effort has successfully complemented the formal and liberal emphasis of dominant approaches to citizenship in the fields of politics, sociology, and anthropology. However, this body of work has not yet provided an analytical account capable of examining diverging developments of politicization and mobilization. This is where the mobilizational citizenship framework becomes handy. Finally, the framework adds to social movement theories of collective identity and political opportunities that fall short of explaining enduring mobilization dynamics in the context of strong political exclusion and high social inequality. Although comparatively extreme in many cases, the sense of marginalization experienced by *población* dwellers is increasingly closer to that of minorities struggling to expand their rights in an increasingly unequal and diverse world.

Chapter 2 delves into Chile's urban margins. It presents a historical account of *poblaciones*' development and mobilization since the 1960s with a focus on the communities acting as this book's core case studies. The chapter includes key arguments to explain the development of mobilizational citizenship since the democratization process in the 1980s.

# 2

# The History of Mobilization in Chile's Urban Settings

## 2.1 INTRODUCTION

This chapter provides the historical background to the development of mobilizational citizenship in underprivileged urban Chile. It addresses the events that shaped the sociopolitical configuration of *poblaciones* throughout the country while simultaneously looking at the specific case studies in Santiago that this book focuses on, the neighborhoods Nuevo Amanecer and Lo Hermida. Combining primary and secondary sources, the chapter covers the period from the mid-twentieth century through to the large wave of protests that erupted in Chile in late 2019. In doing so, it makes several key arguments.

First is the idea of prior mobilization. This notion refers to a variety of forms of collective action that operated in the decade before the coup d'état in the urban margins. This experience of collective action instilled the notion of what I call "a socialist project of society" in underprivileged urban communities that has functioned as activists' ideal reference point for their mobilization in the past four decades. Chapters 3 and 4 examine the role of this socialist project in the development of mobilizational citizenship in *poblaciones*.

The dictatorship's powerful ability to disrupt people's sense of community in *poblaciones* is also addressed here. Military authorities violently intervened in the urban margins by persecuting and killing activists, organizing raids, changing the names of neighborhoods and roads, politically reorganizing cities, and forcefully displacing many urban residents. My process tracing highlights this fundamental historical factor in the diverging developments of citizenship among urban communities.

The chapter also introduces case study variation by showing that different events in urban communities during the democratization process of the 1980s led to different results. In the wave of protests against the dictatorship in the 1980s, radical political groups on the far left entered Lo Hermida and a few other mobilized *poblaciones* to train local dwellers on subversive tactics and coordinate disruptive protests. This tactic transmitted a mobilizing identity to active local dwellers. This mobilizing identity would become the source of mobilizational citizenship in these neighborhoods, thus allowing the survival of collective action over the years. In contrast, more moderate leftist political party activists reached most demobilized *poblaciones* in those years and installed a top-down, managerial leadership approach. Nuevo Amanecer is an example of this dynamic. This process led to the demise of mobilization in most communities in the urban margins after the democratic transition.

My arguments unfold chronologically in four periods. Each of those periods begins by describing sociopolitical events in Chile's urban margins in general and then delves into the particular historical developments in the case studies under analysis, the neighborhoods Nuevo Amanecer and Lo Hermida.

First, I look at collective action in *poblaciones* in the years before the 1973 coup d'état. I describe the collaboration between urban dwellers and political parties in widespread land invasions and the tactics implemented by the more radical leftist political factions in the urban margins. Second, the years of the dictatorship are covered, from 1973 to 1990. I show how the dictatorship interrupted community development and undermined mobilization in underprivileged urban communities. I describe how mobilization reemerged in *poblaciones* after a few years of deactivation, and I also explain the engagement of leftist militants and party activists in urban protests against the authoritarian regime in the 1980s. I suggest that while many of those activists developed managerial leadership in some *poblaciones*, some of them produced subversive roles in other urban communities. Third, I address the events in underprivileged neighborhoods during the return to democracy and in Chile's post-democratic transition, between 1990 and 2006. These years were largely characterized by the demise of mobilization. Yet, I highlight how Lo Hermida is among other *población* social movement communities that, against the odds, sustained collective action in those years. Finally, I look at the role of the urban margins in Chile's new wave of mobilization, from 2006 through 2020. In these decades, mobilizational citizenship allowed *población* activists to build the autonomy, knowledge, networks, and resources to support large-scale protests. I thus show their critical role in the massive, game-changing mobilizations that erupted in Chile in late 2019.

## 2.2 PRIOR MOBILIZATION AND THE SOCIALIST PROJECT (1960–1973)

Throughout the first half of the twentieth century, Chile enjoyed a stable democracy[1] with a representative party system, unlike most other countries in the region (Valenzuela 1989). Social and political engagement generally occurred with the involvement of political parties, which then channeled local organizations' demands to the state (Garretón 1989). The mobilization of the urban poor grew from this collaboration between local activists and political party representatives.

As rural–urban migration increased, the proportion of urban dwellers living in poor, vulnerable, and unhealthy conditions also grew. Initially, urban informal settlements were called *callampas* (mushrooms) because they grew in an improvised way, often exposing people to dire living conditions. Progressively, however, coordinated groups of families seized urban land in collaboration with political parties on the left. These settlements became known as *tomas* (takeovers). While they gave underprivileged families accommodation in the city, they were also a method of demanding social housing from the state (Espinoza 1988; Garcés 2002; Hidalgo 2005). As political engagement evolved in these settlements, the *movimiento de pobladores* emerged. *Tomas* grew as urban hubs of leftist activism, concentrating political networks and influential leaders. Created by Communist Party (PC) activists in the late 1940s, the settlement La Legua, for instance, quickly became one of the most prominent centers of leftist mobilization in Santiago (Garcés 2002, 339). Similarly, La Victoria was a land seizure organized in 1957 that turned into a symbol for poor people's mobilization in Chile and a stronghold of Communist urban activism (Cortés 2014).

As an increasing number of parties began to support land invasions, *pobladores* put huge pressure on government authorities and eroded their governance. The most politicized *tomas* were called *campamentos* (camps). *Campamento* communities often sought a great deal of autonomy from national authorities. They organized locally run committees to deal with

---

[1] Chile did have some undemocratic interruptions in this period. Democracy was briefly paused during a civil war in 1891. Later, from 1924 to 1932, economic crises led to the quick resignation of four consecutive presidents.

daily matters and services such as safety and security, healthcare, nurseries, and urban development. Dwellers in *campamentos* regularly participated in protests to demand their housing rights and had highly politicized leaders.

While initially support for *tomas* came only from leftist parties, the Christian Democrats (DC) also began to help squatters in the 1960s. This boosted the party's popularity among more conservative – but still center-left-leaning – underprivileged urban residents. With an emphasis on service provision, the DC had in fact been one of the first parties to electorally target the urban poor and had strong political support in marginal areas. The DC's move was in line with broader support that different sections in the Chilean Catholic community were already giving to the urban poor. Since the 1950s, the Jesuit charity Hogar de Cristo, for example, had given food and emergency infrastructure to new *tomas*. Several Catholic priests also publicly defended squatters in front of authorities determined to evict them.

President Frei Montalva's government implemented the Popular Promotion program in 1964, which encompassed a set of measures to deal with marginality and poverty. The program created a network of legally recognized neighborhood organizations promoting local development in underprivileged areas, that is, *juntas de vecinos* (neighborhood councils), *centros de madres* (mothers' centers), *centros juveniles* (youth centers), and *clubes deportivos* (neighborhood soccer clubs) (Garcés 2002). During Pinochet's dictatorship, this formalization of neighborhood associations would allow increased governmental oversight over local community organizers.

Additionally, Frei implemented a program called *Operación Sitio* (Site Operation). This policy gave poor families access to urbanized lots with very basic social houses. The program encouraged families to build and expand their own houses. Although it initially emerged as a disaster-alleviation program for the 1965 earthquake, Site Operation became a highly effective housing policy as it gave over 51,000 lots to poor families between 1965 and 1970 in Santiago alone (Hidalgo 2004b, 220).

Mobilization in the urban margins increased to unprecedented proportions by the end of the 1960s. The spectrum of political support for *tomas* widened. It included the Popular Unitary Action Movement (MAPU) – a small leftist political party that splintered from the DC – and even some right-wing politicians. Underlying prior mobilization in politicized *tomas* were many dense political networks on the left that connected underprivileged dwellers with other grassroots activists, militant political leaders, political party members, institutional agents, and political authorities. Despite these networks' diverse ideological positions, they all shared the goal of pursuing a *socialist project of society*. This shared leftist project strongly emphasized economic redistribution and located underprivileged people at the center of political action. It was the framework that motivated mobilizations and legitimized disruptive tactics such as invading urban lands. At the same time, the project connected people's future livelihood expectations with their first experiences of collective solidarity and social cohesion in the *toma*.

The passionate and politicized activists in those years saw this socialist project of society as a cohesive framework whose core goal was to achieve *poder popular* (popular power). Popular power is created through grass-roots organization, and, according to Marxist theory, this may lead to a new institutional order (Lenin 1974). A socialist society would have a government whose authorities belonged to the working class and enjoyed no special status or benefits. Furthermore, workers would collectively own the property of production in this new society, that is, industry, production machines, and land. According to the Marxist tradition, capitalism is built upon historical events that have violently dispossessed workers of their means of livelihood and production. Actions that sought to retrieve land and companies from their capitalist owners were therefore needed to achieve a socialist and fair society. These actions were understood as *recuperación* (repossession tactics). Adhering either partially or fully to these ideas, many politicians and a great deal of left-wingers started supporting urban land seizures, the expropriation of private land, or the nationalization of companies in the late 1960s. In this socialist society, workers would not depend on company owners or landlords to manage the country's production. Rather, workers would use *autogestion* (self-management) to maintain industrial production and land exploitation.

While some activists on the left fully adhered to these notions and passionately opposed capitalism, others had a more moderate stance and were only attracted by the redistributive quality of that socialist project. In all cases, however, this project of society represented a more prosperous future for the lower classes and therefore shaped underprivileged urban dwellers' livelihood expectations. Additionally, as they participated in *tomas*, built their own houses, and helped each other improve their settlement, many of those dwellers felt that they were protagonists in a larger process of social change.

One of the most radical proponents of these ideas was the MIR, which began organizing urban land invasions in the late 1960s. Its work deserves closer inspection, as it was the most influential and well-organized political group supporting the mobilization of the Chilean urban poor up until 1973.

*Campamentos* created with the MIR's support and coordination were considered to be at the forefront of the dwellers' movement in those years. These settlements enjoyed high mobilizational potential: They had very well-trained leaders and an organized internal structure (Schlotterbeck 2018).

The MIR was a Marxist-Leninist party self-identified as a vanguard to empower the lower classes to advance a socialist revolutionary process (Pinto 2005). The MIR gathered several groups that, disenchanted with electoral politics and inspired by the Cuban experience, broke off from their parties to seek new, more radical political avenues. While the MIR developed as a leftist guerilla with violent means and revolutionary goals, most of its work promoted people's engagement in radical participatory politics at the grassroots level (Sandoval 2014; Schlotterbeck 2018). In its first years, the MIR concentrated its efforts on recruiting politicized students in Valparaíso, Concepción, and Santiago. However, the movement failed to create support among indigenous people and rural organizations. Additionally, its presence was weak among trade unions – a sector in which the Communists and Socialists were much stronger. Nonetheless, by the end of the 1960s and beginning of the 1970s, the MIR was able to expand its political work at the grassroots level by supporting and coordinating urban land invasions, and by organizing the *campamentos* that emerged as a result of those invasions.

In these settlements, MIR militants sought to develop popular power. In other words, they produced autonomous systems of local, grassroots organizing that opposed the state's hierarchical power structures (Pinto 2012). Consequently, in collaboration with *campamento* dwellers, the MIR organized a sort of mini-society in each settlement, meant to work as a model for the socialist revolution at the local level. Every block in these settlements elected a representative leader among local residents. Additionally, groups of *pobladores* known as "fronts" were in charge of community welfare; one front provided basic healthcare services for neighbors and another ran a kindergarten for local children. Fronts also acted as fire-fighters, coordinated basic food provision, and guarded the settlement to defend it against retaliations from the police, external petty thieves, and groups that might want to steal their land.

The MIR's first large land seizure was Campamento 26 de Enero, created in early 1970. This settlement gained public attention because it was the first where the MIR's urban political strategy was implemented. Local dwellers regularly participated in protests and even occupied government buildings to assert their housing demands. Campamento 26 de Enero quickly became the MIR's model for future mobilizing strategies and urban policies. Additionally, by organizing the Provincial Urban Dwellers' Congress[2] in this *campamento*, the MIR disseminated its grassroots strategies among urban activists across local organizations and political parties (Garcés 2002, 412).

The MIR became an illegal organization after its militants began kidnapping wealthy members of the elite to fund their initiatives through ransoms in 1969. They carried out clandestine operations and created informal, secret networks within political parties. This underground type of work made the MIR a particularly appealing and influential movement among the leftist elite. The popularity of the MIR ensured the spread of its policies from *campamentos* to many other leftist informal settlements across the country.[3]

Salvador Allende was elected president in 1969. He was supported by a coalition of leftist political parties called Popular Unity (UP).[4] While many politicians supported urban invasions, the previous government had officially rejected *tomas* because they represented a threat to its ability to govern. However, Allende declared social housing a right for every family, and publicly supported informal settlements with the aim of upgrading them. Due to Allende's support, *tomas* increased sharply in 1970.[5] In the years that followed, mobilization in the urban margins grew and sometimes reached a state of political frenzy. The urban dwellers' movement became larger and more influential. In those years, *población* community-building emerged largely from people's experience of collective action, especially in their land seizures and protests over social rights. Activists and local dwellers often named their neighborhoods, roads, and squares after famous leftist figures.

Simultaneously, parties began a fierce competition to develop leadership among *pobladores* and obtain resources from the state to improve living conditions in shantytowns. Upon assuming his mandate, Allende implemented an intensive socialist reform. He nationalized large-scale companies,

---

[2] This congress involved a large meeting in which leaders from different informal settlements in the Santiago province reflected on recent events and agreed on the movement's future policies.

[3] Examples of other organized informal settlements that implemented similar initiatives in the 1960s and early 1970s are La Victoria, Herminda de la Victoria, Lo Hermida, Villa O'Higgins, Sara Gajardo, La Pincoya, La Bandera, La Legua, Ché Guevara, Violeta Parra, Cardenal José María Caro, Villa Francia, and Yungay.

[4] The Popular Unity included the Socialist Party, the Communist Party, the Radical Party, the Social Democratic Party, the Independent Popular Action, and the Popular Unitary Action Movement.

[5] Until 1968 Santiago saw a yearly average of 10 land seizures. This figure increased to more than 220 with Allende's victory in 1970 (Ducci and Fadda 1993).

increased labor protection, intensified land reform, raised minimum wages, and implemented inclusive programs for the most marginalized sections of society. Although Allende set out an ambitious plan to solve the social housing problem, Santiago's informal urban dwellers increased in his mandate and reached 500,000, or 17.9 percent of the city's population (Santa María 1973, 105–6).

### 2.2.1  Case Studies (1970–1973)

The two *poblaciones* analyzed in this book – Nuevo Amanecer and Lo Hermida – emerged and developed as almost identical communities in Santiago's urban margins between 1970 and 1973 (see Table A.1.1). Both played an active role in this process of prior mobilization. Their time of emergence, political factions, methods of creation, socioeconomic composition, and community development were also very similar. In fact, because of the strong similarities and shared political networks, leaders often called these two settlements *poblaciones hermanas* (sister neighborhoods). They were created in 1970, in Santiago's eastern outskirts, as part of the land seizures boom that Allende's victory produced (see Figure 2.1). The substantial distance from the city center and lack of urbanization meant both settlements were disconnected from networks of transportation and other urban services. These were MIR-led communities[6] that became part of a network of contentious neighborhoods adhering to a more radical interpretation of popular power.

Nueva La Habana (only later called Nuevo Amanecer) was created on November 1, 1970, in the district of La Florida. Only a couple of months earlier, in late July, the MIR had coordinated three land invasions in Santiago, in private plots of land belonging to the Pontifical Catholic University (PUC), the University of Chile (UCH), and the Catholic Church. The MIR was quick to organize the 1,880 families in these *campamentos*. Together with local dwellers, MIR leaders established community discipline statutes that forbade domestic violence, theft, and alcohol abuse, and created security and healthcare fronts, and a soup kitchen. In addition, they organized protests demanding housing rights. During the entire month of August, *campamento* residents carried out marches, occupied public buildings, and even held a hunger strike. By the

---

[6] As I explain later, Lo Hermida had a more complex political composition, which also included sections of the land invasion coordinated by Socialist, Communist, and Christian Democrat activists.

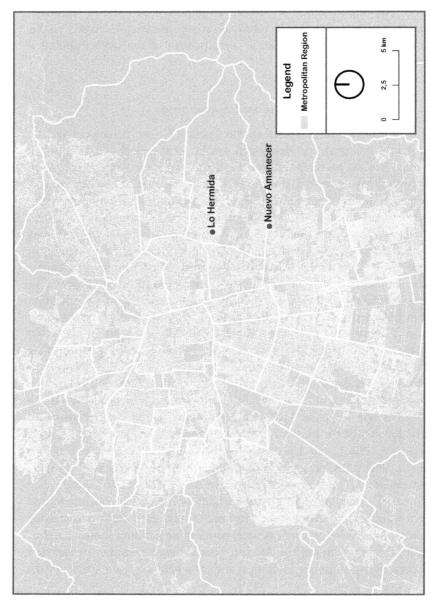

FIGURE 2.1 Map of case studies located in Santiago. Source: Made by the author.

end of August, authorities from both universities (PUC and UCH) and the Ministry of Housing and Development had negotiated a solution for these communities, together with squatters and MIR leaders. The *campamento* residents were given temporary plots in the east of the city (Cofré 2007). The new informal settlement – Nueva La Habana – was home to around 1,700 families. They would be able to receive land tenure and build their own houses in adjacent land, which would soon be equipped with urban infrastructure and services (see Figure 2.2). The government provided the funding and building materials. Out of the 500 workers hired for this building project, 300 were unemployed local dwellers. As my interviews show, this project was seen as evidence of an auspicious future for families in Nueva La Habana. However, the building works would only continue until September 1973.

Lo Hermida was created at almost the same time in 1970, in the district of Ñuñoa, also in the eastern periphery of Santiago. That year, the government had initiated a Site Operation program that was planned to transform agricultural lands in the eastern periphery of the city into space for 6,000 basic houses. Negotiations between union leaders and DC members agreed that those houses would go to families from workers in the companies Tucmon, Implatex, Pollak, and Sello Sur (Reyes 2011). The project evolved in phases, from east to west, in the areas known as Lo Hermida and Lo Arrieta.

In mid-August, however, housing committees coordinated by the Socialist, DC, and Communist parties invaded the project's remaining land. Squatters continued the occupation of the land on the west, in spite of the apple, peach, and alfalfa crops that covered much of it. By the end of that month, another group of families coordinated by the MIR had invaded the adjacent land to the south of the settlement, resisted eviction and began erecting emergency dwellings. This group of settlements was eventually called Lo Hermida, and its residents subdivided it into four zones. The section of lots given to 2,000 families by the Operation Site program constituted zones 1 and 2. The first phase of invasions was considered zone 3, and the final and larger portion of the settlement, under MIR leadership, became zone 4 (see Figure 2.3). Neighbors subdivided these latter two zones into smaller "*villas,*" corresponding to the different housing committees and the particular political factions that organized the land invasions. Committees named their *villas* after leftist politicians and revolutionary references. Despite these subdivisions, Lo Hermida's community grew more cohesive and emulated most of the organizing methods implemented in Nueva La Habana. Additionally,

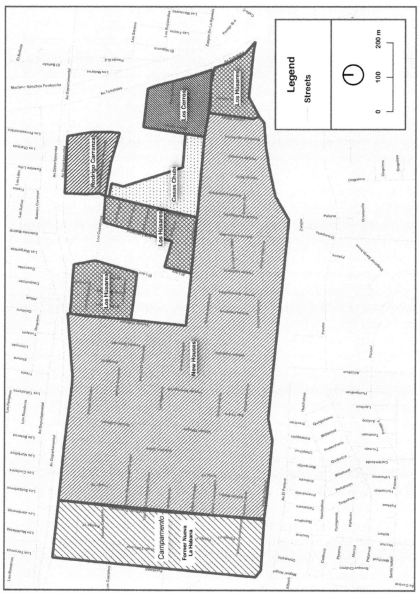

FIGURE 2.2 Map of Nuevo Amanecer divided by *villas*. Source: Made by the author.

FIGURE 2.3 Map of Lo Hermida divided by zones and *villas*. Source: Made by the author.

after erecting basic houses in their lots, squatters also carried out protests to demand urban services, land tenure, and social housing.

Controversial events of unrest marked community life in these two *poblaciones*. In 1972, for instance, a group of local residents in Nueva La Habana tried to lynch a man accused of sexually assaulting a female teacher. After a chaotic situation, community organizers acted as a popular tribunal and agreed on obtaining a psychiatric evaluation of the man's mental liability before bringing him to the police (Cofré 2007). In Lo Hermida, a violent police raid killed a local leader and unleashed intense protests in the neighborhood. The MIR released a nation-wide declaration denouncing the event and Allende himself addressed dwellers in Lo Hermida to express his regret over the incident (Punto Final 1972).

### 2.3 MOBILIZING UNDER DICTATORSHIP (1973–1990)

In September 1973, Chile was thrust into a brutal 17-year-long dictatorship that impacted dwellers, activists, and militants in the urban margins. Between 1973 and 1990, Chile's dictatorship implemented a drastic plan to eliminate those involved in left-wing activism. The military dictatorship saw the left as a subversive threat to the government; famous for its cruelty, it exiled around 200,000 people, killed, and disappeared another 3,065, and tortured over 40,018 of those clandestinely detained (Rojas-Corral and Shaftoe 2021).

The military government imposed stringent limits on people's political participation. In the months after the coup, most civil society organizations were dissolved through intimidation and persecution. Authorities banned leftist media outlets and confiscated their properties and equipment; their journalists were detained or sent into exile. Furthermore, the military authorities implemented a 15-year-long curfew, legally banned leftist political parties, dissolved congress, and severely restricted labor unions' activities, including collective bargaining and strikes.

#### 2.3.1 Community Disrupted

Despite acts of resistance in some communities, it only took the military 48 hours to take control of the whole country. The dictatorship quickly released a most-wanted list of leftist political leaders, and organized raids in all of the mobilized *poblaciones* searching for leftist leaders, common delinquents, guns, and subversive material. Through the disproportionate use of violence, random killings, and the arbitrary detention of tens of thousands of *población* residents, these raids spread terror among urban dwellers (Moya, Videla, and Balladores 2005; Bruey 2009). As my interviews confirm, many underprivileged urban dwellers witnessed the police detain or violently beat people in public places. Moya, Videla, and Balladores (2005) report that persecutions, arrests, and torture targeted the urban poor in large numbers (see also Hechos Urbanos 1987, 5). Many members of leftist political parties and local leaders who coordinated mobilization in *tomas* were arrested or fled the neighborhoods, seeking refuge in exile or in other areas where they could go unnoticed.

These events occurred in the weeks and months after the coup and indicated a swift, radical shift in the state's policy regarding the political engagement of the urban poor. Analyzing the impact of the dictatorship in two mobilized *poblaciones* in Santiago – La Legua and Villa Francia – Bruey (2018, 77) writes, "[T]he post-coup process of political and economic change represented for many a traumatic rupture with previous lived experience." Upon its establishment, the dictatorship severely frustrated the expectations of a substantial portion of local dwellers and activists. As my interviews indicate, the socialist project of society in which these communities had engaged was abruptly interrupted. On the one hand, political activists and militants took a more ideological outlook of this new scenario. The military was erasing the ideals, values, and plans that they had passionately struggled for. For Silvia Leiva, an MIR member and local dweller in Nueva La Habana, for instance, the dictatorship "interrupted [the community's] self-management, the autonomy that the Chilean society was developing ... a process of collective solidarity" (Inostroza 2013). On the other hand, for less-politicized local dwellers, the dictatorship meant the destruction of promises of livelihood prosperity formulated by socialist narratives at the time. These narratives, promoted by leftist activists and authorities, had, on many occasions, promised and justified the delivery of social housing to those residing in informal settlements (Garcés 2002). After the military coup, however, urban dwellers in *poblaciones* across the country faced eviction and violence. Pinochet's dictatorship brought great uncertainty to the urban underprivileged. These disrupting policies continued in the following years, and ultimately dislocated the sense of community that prior events of collective action had forged in the *poblaciones*.

State policies repressed and controlled dissidence within *tomas*, which increased fear and distrust within neighborhoods. Furthermore, soon after obtaining power, the dictatorship replaced the democratically elected mayors with loyal appointees and eliminated municipal elections.

The new mayors also replaced local-level leaders running neighborhood councils, mothers' centers, and soccer clubs in each settlement with others considered more loyal. These designated local leaders worked as control points for the regime. Henceforth, neighborhood organizations contributed to people's deepening sense of distrust and fear during the dictatorship (see Valdés 1986, 14–15).

As a way of justifying the human rights violations it was committing, the dictatorship and the mainstream media publicly criminalized left-wing mobilization as terrorism. This propaganda tactic contributed to stigmatizing underprivileged communities that were widely known for their contentious politics. In line with this stance, the dictatorship renamed *poblaciones* and roads that glorified revolutionary experiences, and after 1976 it forbade naming public spaces after any leftist symbol. Government authorities instead named parts of the city after rivers, mountains, and local flora and fauna (Hidalgo 2008). Along with many others, the Ché Guevara and Fidel Castro shantytowns, for example, were renamed Santa Anita and General Baquedano (Hidalgo 2008). According to my interviews, this policy contributed to alienating *población* dwellers who were proud of their neighborhood.

Furthermore, the dictatorship's economic reforms produced a recession that severely impacted the lower class and damaged community-building in the urban margins further. Average unemployment rates grew to three times higher than those of the 1960s, reaching a critical 31.3 percent in 1983. In the midst of the crisis, in 1983, almost 50 percent of heads of households in some underprivileged urban areas were unemployed, and a further 21.6 percent were only employed in temporary or unstable jobs (Hardy 1986a, 8). This included those in the government's underemployment emergency programs: the Minimum Employment Program (PEM) (1975–1988) and the Occupational Program for Heads of Household (POJH) (1982–1988).

The dictatorship's economic plan included its new Urban Development National Policy (PNDU), which reorganized Santiago and other cities across the country. Implemented in 1979, this policy stimulated private investment by liberalizing urban land, eliminating restrictions for urban expansion, and privatizing construction companies. Also, a new subsidy system supported companies involved in the construction of social housing (Sugranyes 2005). An additional decree, in 1981, split and incorporated several districts in Santiago, thus adding 17 new municipalities to the city. The PNDU contributed to the segregation of cities and the further marginalization of the urban poor. Between 1979 and 1985, this policy allowed the implementation of a government plan that forcibly relocated approximately 150,000 informal residents to social housing in the urban peripheries. Unprepared to receive such an influx of residents, destination zones became extended and densely populated urban areas that reproduced poverty and vulnerability (Labbé and Llévenes 1986; Morales et al. 1990). Some informal settlements were able to avoid relocation, because either the UP government had given them land tenure, they were already located in low-value zones, or their leaders at the time were favored by the local military authorities. The housing subsidy system targeted families and not communities. Urban communities were often dislocated into lots and houses in new housing complexes were given to families coming from different parts of the city. These moves often disregarded the needs of homeless families in the adjacent communities. The spirit of collective public engagement that had prevailed in the allocation of housing for the urban poor in previous governments was largely ignored by the dictatorship (Sugranyes and Rodríguez 2005).

However, this issue was not limited to the years of dictatorship. The democratic governments after 1990 kept the housing subsidy system in place and accelerated the production of social housing. Whereas a yearly average of 45,000 houses were built by the dictatorship, the new democratic governments built well over 100,000 houses a year (Arriagada et al. 2004, 187; Rubio 2006, 203). Across *poblaciones*, this housing policy has resulted in countless frictions within and between urban communities over the last 40 years. My fieldwork in Santiago's urban margins is, in fact, plagued with stories of hostility between previous settlers and newcomers. Often, it seems, previous residents were frustrated by the distribution of houses built in their vicinity. For example, residents in the neighborhood Mamiña II in the Puente Alto district were attacked with sticks by an angry mob of neighboring residents a few days after they moved into their new houses in the early 1980s. In El Castillo, in La Pintana district, residents welcomed newly relocated neighbors with what current residents call "night wars" (fights with sticks and stones at night). Since the dictatorship, such relocations have become a challenge for community-building all over the city. This experience of violent disruption undermined urban dwellers' community-building and created a sense of historical discontinuity in *poblaciones*.

### 2.3.2 The Reemergence of Mobilization

Despite these unfavorable conditions, around 1976 civil society began to reemerge in underprivileged urban areas. With the support of the Catholic

Church's Vicariate of Solidarity, *pobladores* created local associations for their defense against the dictatorship's human rights violations. Soon after, collective subsistence initiatives reappeared and expanded across *poblaciones* (Razeto et al. 1990; Oxhorn 1995). Run by local dwellers and supported by the Vicariate of Solidarity, these organizations provided basic services for the community. Often, local residents coordinated their efforts by creating or joining *Comunidades Cristianas de Base* (Grassroots Christian Communities, CCB). CCBs expanded across Latin America in those years as grassroots organizations that emerged from local Catholic parishes to promote community development and protect people against poverty and state violence (Valdivieso 1989; Hewitt 1993). *Ollas comunes* (community kitchens), for example, gave food to the poorest families in the settlement. Urban dwellers also organized *comprando juntos* (cooperative supply acquisition groups), which involved a group of families buying groceries wholesale to get lower prices, and *bolsas de trabajo* (employment groups), to collectively help the unemployed. In addition, they created *arpilleras* (burlap sewing groups) composed mainly of women who created patchwork weavings that depicted their daily realities of repression and poverty. By selling these pieces of art outside their settlement, *población* women were able to support their families. Also funded by the Vicariate of Solidarity, residents organized different activities for children in the neighborhood. Young people learned leadership skills by acting as monitors in *colonias urbanas* (children's camps). These camps included games, competitions, workshops, and even summer trips that became valuable experiences for children in underprivileged neighborhoods in those years. Eventually, housing committees also reappeared in the political sphere, and continued to demand their social rights. Besides providing economic support, subsistence organizations were also a way of exposing and denouncing the consequences of the dictatorship's economic policies.

In the years that followed, *población* organizations expanded their networks and strengthened people's sense of solidarity. *Pobladores*, therefore, began to protest more directly by participating in mass demonstrations organized in the centers of cities. Political parties had begun regrouping underground, and supported many of these protests. As Bastías Saavedra (2013, 204) reports, protests sharply increased through the late 1970s and early 1980s. The government's repression strengthened activists' sense of cohesion (Schneider 1995). People responded with marches, hunger strikes, and occupations to demand the release of arrested protestors, thus increasing mobilization further.

The dictatorship created a new political constitution in 1980 that gave more power to Pinochet. The realization that Pinochet was consolidating and formalizing his role alarmed civil society. Unrest in Chile grew, and in May 1983, widespread demonstrations erupted after mining unions called for a national strike. In the urban peripheries, local residents organized marches and blocked streets with barricades, in open acts of public disobedience.

Despite the dictatorship's cracking down on protestors, large-scale, country-wide demonstrations continued in the years that followed. In this wave of national protests, political parties to the center and the left working underground joined *población* mobilizations in support. Collective action thrived in the urban margins. Underprivileged urban dwellers were able to expand their informal networks of activism and participate in initiatives implemented in *poblaciones* across the nation. They marched in the streets, clanging pots and pans, and held hunger strikes. They also barricaded the avenues nearby their neighborhoods and organized sit-ins in public buildings to protest human rights abuses. Young groups of *pobladores* looted supermarkets, the offices of the Minimum Employment Program, and other public buildings (Schneider 1995, 161). Protests in *poblaciones* often included violent confrontations with the police. Groups of underprivileged dwellers organized as *comandos* (defense groups) and covered their faces to fight the police with sticks and stones. In parallel, community development organizations, like soup kitchens, groups of *arpilleras*, children's camps and neighborhood cooperatives, continued to operate in the urban margins. These actions could only occur with the help of external allies – the Catholic Church, NGOs, and political parties – that provided mobilizing resources, including money, networks, political knowledge, tactics, and training. Local parishes, for instance, often acted as safe spaces in which party activists could meet local dwellers to organize demonstrations. These resources promoted local leadership construction, empowerment, and political identity development among local dwellers.

In these years, center and left-wing political parties that joined with *poblaciones* were part of two different coalitions. A more moderate group of parties led by the DC formed the AD, and the more radical parties created the Popular Democratic Movement (MDP).[7] Both political camps

---

[7] The parties in the Democratic Alliance included the Christian Democrats, Social Democrats, Radicals, Liberals, Republicans, and moderate factions of the Socialist Party. The Popular Democratic Movement comprised the Communist Party, Leftist

opposed the dictatorship and strived for the return of democracy. However, while the AD sought a legal and peaceful democratic transition, the MDP aimed to reestablish democracy by overthrowing the dictatorship. The AD, therefore, interpreted the national protests as a collective expression of grievances that would be able to erode the military's popularity and attract international support. In contrast, MDP activists understood the national protests as the beginning of a revolution that would evolve to ultimately rebuild the Chilean state. They adhered to the socialist project of society that grew and evolved during the 1960s and early 1970s. Consequently, the new regime envisioned by the MDP was built on popular power and the working class's control of industrial production and the state. The MDP complemented these political notions with insurgency tactics.

The more radical protests in the urban margins were part of what MDP parties called the Politics of Mass Popular Rebellion (PRPM). The PRPM included a diverse set of violent and nonviolent tactics to resist military repression, destabilize the dictatorship's institutional order, and motivate mass mobilization. Because the goal of MDP parties was to advance a large-scale popular uprising, following the examples of Iran and Nicaragua, their politics of rebellion were in direct interaction with the wave of national protests that the rest of Chile was experiencing.

The PRPM were promoted in *poblaciones* in the late 1970s, when the MAPU created a set of "Resistance Committees," also known as the "R," which were groups of party members who implemented short-term, disruptive propaganda initiatives to undermine the dictatorship's public legitimacy. For example, they painted murals, made banners, and handed out anti-dictatorship pamphlets. They also coordinated more disruptive actions, such as burning tires to build street barricades. They organized quick, small demonstrations in public spaces, during which groups of activists shouted slogans against the dictatorship and then dispersed into the crowd after a few minutes (Acevedo 2014). Simultaneously, brigades of PC members with military training, called "Zero Fronts," began carrying out PRPM tactics. They implemented large-scale, disruptive forms of protest and sabotage, which made the PRPM publicly known. In November 1980, for example, they disrupted the electricity supply in the cities of Santiago, Valparaiso, and Viña del Mar for several hours by bombing a high-voltage tower (Pérez 2013, 247).

Revolutionary Movement, the Christian Left Party, Popular Unitary Action Movement, and a more radical faction of the Socialist Party (the PS Almeyda).

During days of national protest, *pobladores* joined PRPM actions by carrying out acts of civil disobedience and sabotage, including banging pots and pans after the curfew, blocking roads, displaying anti-Pinochet banners in public places, handing out leaflets, and creating power outages. Militants trained in war and guerrilla tactics contributed to the MDP's PRPM strategies through military operations aiming to erode the power of the national armed forces. These militants belonged either to armed wings of political parties – such as the PC's Manuel Rodriguez Patriotic Front (FPMR) – the MAPU's Lautaro Youth Movement (MJL), or the MIR.

The FPMR emerged as an armed group under the PC's Military Commission in 1983. It gathered party militants leading the Zero Fronts – who had obtained military training in the late 1970s – and members who were returning to Chile after years of training and fighting abroad.[8] Similarly, a group of MAPU militants returned to Chile after their military training abroad to join the party's Military Commission. According to Acevedo (2014), this commission had already recruited and trained a substantial number of *población* youths to strengthen the R. By the early 1980s, some groups in the R had radicalized their initiatives, which included attacking banks in Santiago with Molotov cocktails. Created in 1982 by the MAPU, the MJL included these militants. What made the MJL different from other groups was its focus on underprivileged youth as opposed to older adults. The MJL's formal mission was, in fact, to "become a model for the youth ... [by] promoting mobilizations and struggles for the defense of young people's key demands, and [giving] social and political power to the underprivileged youth" (Moyano 2010, 397). The MJL was, therefore, meant to represent young *pobladores'* specific demands, needs, and political orientations. The MJL would later prove to be very effective in recruiting young, disenfranchised urban dwellers to join their struggle.

The PC also created the Manuel Rodriguez Militias (MR).[9] Like the MAPU's R, these groups gave citizens the opportunity to develop PRPM

---

[8] A group of Communist Party militants were sent to Cuba and Russia to receive military training in 1974. After that, a portion of them were sent to support the Popular Sandinista Army's fight against Somosa's government in Nicaragua. For more details see Bonnefoy, Pérez, and Spotorno (2008) and Bravo (2010).

[9] Their name in Spanish was *Milicias Rodriguistas* (Manuel Rodriguez's Militias). They were bureaucratically positioned under the Communist Party's Military Commission and their official role was that of "Territorial Operative Forces."

at the grassroots level. The groups included students, workers, and young *población* dwellers, and their work involved boosting mobilization, promoting the radicalization of protests, and carrying out minor acts of subversion. Their actions included, for example, protecting *población* communities from police violence, barricading roads, attacking the police with Molotov cocktails, and identifying and detaining military informants who were posing as protestors during demonstrations. Famously, the MR also conducted *recuperaciones*, which were operations in which militants delivered goods that they stole from private companies to underprivileged people. Militants saw these operations as opportunities to rectify the unjust dispossession that the capitalist bourgeoisie had imposed on the poor. A famous series of acts of *recuperación* involved MR militants storming private grocery distribution trucks on their way through *poblaciones* to steal the food and give it to the people in the neighborhood.[10] In their public declarations, the FPMR militants would often invite people to join the MR in order to participate in their struggle. Therefore, while the MR were under the PC Military Commission's command, people often categorize them as a section of the FPMR.

After 1986, the political scenario began to favor peaceful action. The economic recession and social unrest that had affected Chile throughout the 1980s had undermined the regime's legitimacy, both domestically and internationally. As a result, and in an effort to regain legitimacy, Pinochet legalized opposition parties, and agreed to negotiate the terms in which this transitional process could begin with AD politicians. The MDP parties and movements, however, were excluded from these dialogues. Fearing their further political isolation, most parties in the MDP abandoned their PRPM. As many militants in the FPMR and the MJL insisted on continuing their military and revolutionary endeavors, both the PC and the MAPU decided to break with them.

A constitutional plebiscite was organized to take place in October 1988, asking citizens to choose between the continuation of the dictatorship ("Yes" vote) or a new democratic regime based on free elections ("No" vote). Center and left-wing parties created the new Concertación de Partidos por el No, a coalition of parties supporting the No Campaign, that obtained international support and organized a full-fledged electoral campaign. In contrast, many MDP members rejected the very principle of

---

[10] One of these operations in the neighborhood La Victoria in 1986 was televised by the show Edición Impacto on the network Chilevisión.

the plebiscite as, in their view, it politically validated the authoritarian regime and its constitution.

The No Campaign mobilized civil society and had a particularly strong presence in *poblaciones*. Parties devoted their full efforts and resources to this campaign and managed to bring many grassroots leaders on board. The No Campaign won the plebiscite with nearly 56 percent of the votes, after persuasively branding their campaign in a way that connected democracy with "joy" and "happiness." The resulting election in 1989 saw the DC candidate, Patricio Aylwin, come into power.

### 2.3.3 Case Studies (1973–1990)

The military coup d'état in 1973 was a surprise for urban dwellers in Lo Hermida and Nueva La Habana. In the following 17 years of military rule, the dictatorship would strongly disrupt *pobladores'* sense of historical continuity and community in both neighborhoods.

Very soon after the coup, the main MIR leader in Nueva La Habana, Micke, gave his last speech to local dwellers and left the neighborhood. He was eventually killed by state agents in Valparaiso in 1975. Most other political leaders in these communities left the neighborhood to hide and escape military repression. Both neighborhoods were violently searched by the police and the military. Rumors suggesting that the military would bomb Lo Hermida and other mobilized *poblaciones* sparked alarm among residents. The state's control and the fear that it produced in residents dismantled local organizations.

State authorities also instructed the renaming of the settlement Nueva La Habana. Socialist leader Mr. Castillo decided in a meeting with a few other residents on the new name: Nuevo Amanecer (New Dawn). The politically charged names of *villas* in Lo Hermida were also replaced,[11] and roads in both neighborhoods were named after neutral, geographical features (e.g., Afluente, Voclán Osorno, and Descabezado Chico). In addition, later, in 1981, the government split the district of Ñuñoa as part of the large administrative reform it was implementing. Located in the eastern

---

[11] The *villas* in Lo Hermida's zone 3, Lulo Pinochet and Asalto al Cuartel Moncada, were renamed as El Duraznal and Los Copihues. The *villas* Vietnam Heroico, Guerrillero Manuel Rodríguez, and Trabajadores al Poder, in zone 4, became Yungay, Simón Bolivar, and La Concepción.

portion of that division, Lo Hermida became part of the new Peñalolén district. These changes made historical continuity difficult for local residents. Since events of prior mobilization had occurred in a community or in a place with a different name to that of the present, connecting these events with current experiences became especially challenging.

Furthermore, between 1973 and 1976 Nuevo Amanecer experienced a neighborhood expansion that would disconnect people further from their past collective project and frustrate their livelihood expectations. Supported by the MIR and state authorities, local dwellers had been building a social housing complex next to their informal settlement, which was meant to accommodate them in the future. However, the military authorities assigned most of those new houses to external families who were considered a priority when it came to social housing applicants. A portion of neighbors in the *campamento* whose housing installments were up to date at the Housing Corporation (CORVI) were also given houses in the new settlement.[12] Most Nueva La Habana residents remained in the *campamento* living informally in wooden emergency housing, sharing latrines, and experiencing low living standards. Although the whole area was called Nuevo Amanecer in 1974 and the informal settlement was later improved and urbanized, the division remained for community members and increased people's sense of historical disruption. To this day, in fact, local dwellers refer to the eastern extension as *"casas nuevas"* (new houses) and to the original settlement as *"campamento"* (camp/shanty town) (see Figure 2.2).

Similar events would later occur in Lo Hermida. In the late 1980s and into the early 1990s, a number of new settlements accommodating people from different zones in the city were installed in the south-east of the neighborhood. These became known as the *villas* Aquelarre, El Parral, and Lago Vichuquén (see Figure 2.3). Although these new houses created some local conflicts, they did not pose a proper threat to Lo Hermida's sense of continuity because, as I will argue later on in this book, a strong mobilizational identity had already become established in the neighborhood (see Chapter 4).

As in most other *poblaciones*, people reactivated local organizing in the mid-1970s with the support of the Catholic Church and some NGOs.

---

[12] In those years the families applying for social housing paid installments to the Housing Corporation, a government agency in charge of researching, managing, and funding social housing provision.

A local CCB in Lo Hermida organized the first community kitchen in 1975 to feed children whose families were affected by the growing unemployment and poverty. In both *poblaciones*, neighborhood chapels worked as community centers where local dwellers organized survival initiatives, leisure activities, and political meetings. Each chapel in Lo Hermida, for example, held a community kitchen; they eventually fed over 1,400 people every day (Aillapan and Poch-Plá 2017, 85). Community parties, children's camps, and groups of *arpilleras* were also organized at Jesús del Señor, the central chapel in Nuevo Amanecer. Groups of local dwellers defending human rights emerged in the chapels of both neighborhoods as the first properly political organizations. Several youth groups in Nuevo Amanecer created Chacón, an organization that regularly met in the local chapel and provided community assistance to other *población* residents. They used resources given by the Catholic Church to, for instance, fix the roofs of the poorest houses in the neighborhood. Another group of young local dwellers also created the Grupo Juvenil de María (Mary's Youth Group, GRUJUDEMA), which was more concerned with organizing events to boost the community's sense of tradition and identity.

In Lo Hermida, a group of residents created the Cristo Joven Community Center, which complemented the work carried out at chapels by providing healthcare services, working skills training, and childcare. Later, in order to manage international aid coming to Lo Hermida, *pobladores* and missionaries created the Missio Foundation.

In the early 1980s political party members began to reappear in both *poblaciones*. In those years, new youth associations emerged in Nuevo Amanecer. Formally, these groups belonged to the chapel's *Pastoral Juvenil* (Youth Ministry). Although the *Pastoral* was designed to give young people the experience of evangelization and charity, members were mainly secular, including many nonreligious local dwellers and party activists. The latter often came from outside the neighborhood to coordinate local initiatives.

Despite their reemerging connection with party activists, Lo Hermida and Nuevo Amanecer had so far kept MDP militants at bay. Because they were understood as "MIR territory," these two communities seemed especially dangerous to leftist militants and activists (Interview July 30, 2017). During the dictatorship, formerly MIR-led urban communities were controlled by local informants and state intelligence agents that the dictatorship had assigned or infiltrated into neighborhood organizations. In addition, the extermination of MIR militants by state agents in the first decade of the dictatorship, as well as the scarce presence of PC and MJL members in these *poblaciones*, made for weak neighborhood support networks for MDP militants.

An incident in Lo Hermida in 1982, however, opened a window of opportunity that prompted the entrance of Communists into the *población*. In July that year, the San Carlos Canal riverbed collapsed, turning several parts of the neighborhood into a large swamp, destroying houses, and causing a sanitary emergency (see Díaz 2013). The flooding laid bare the dramatically poor conditions that characterized Lo Hermida at that time. Latrines all over the neighborhood overflowed, drawing attention to the lack of sewage treatment facilities. As a result, an influx of aid personnel from the Catholic Church and NGOs came to the area to help the community and support the reconstruction of damaged infrastructure. Chapels served as collection points and health centers, and the number of local community kitchens grew quickly in order to aid the affected residents (Aillapan and Poch-Plá 2017, 85). The frenzy of the disaster and the arrival of external people into the neighborhood gave Communist militants the chance to enter local organizations unnoticed by authorities and neighbors. Soon after, several other political groups belonging to the MDP also took advantage of the flood as an opportunity for undercover militants to infiltrate Lo Hermida organizations in the early 1980s. These included the FPMR, the MJL, and, to a lesser degree, the MIR and a group of radical Socialist militants.

Organizations in Nuevo Amanecer acquired a stronger political role after the national protests of 1983. Left-leaning party members increased in the neighborhood and came to the chapel to coordinate initiatives with the local population. In this context, emergent local social leaders began to interact with party activists. For security reasons, party membership was generally kept secret, as anyone could be a potential *sapo* (snitch). However, community leaders generally knew who belonged to a party and who did not. The most influential political leaders coordinating protests in Nuevo Amanecer – and therefore those in charge of implementing party decisions at grassroots level – belonged to the Christian Left Party (IC), and moderate factions of the MAPU and PS. There were also several DC activists and only a few PC members. In other words, most of them adhered to the AD's political project.

In contrast, when the national protests began in 1983 radical political leaders belonging to the MDP were already operating in Lo Hermida. Although AD party activists were also present in the neighborhood, MDP militants managed to recruit and train local dwellers to create a dozen local militia cells (MR) that coordinated disruptive actions. As I argue in

Chapters 3 and 4, AD party activists developed a managerial type of leadership that sought to control and contain mobilization in Nuevo Amanecer with a top-down approach. Conversely, MDP militants in Lo Hermida used a subversive leadership that reconnected collective action with the symbols that had shaped the left's socialist project of society during prior mobilization in the 1960s and early 1970s. Both communities participated actively in anti-dictatorial protests. In Lo Hermida, however, local activists also organized PRPM tactics and often engaged in clashes with the police.

### 2.4 THE CHALLENGES OF THE NEW DEMOCRACY (1990–2006)

The Concertación ruled during the first two decades of democracy, with the right-wing coalition, Alianza por Chile, as its political opposition. Although often internationally considered a model transition, Chile's new democratic regime had strong limitations (Delamaza 1995; Moulian 1997; Huneeus 2014). Before leaving office, Pinochet activated a set of restrictive laws,[13] the so-called *leyes de amarre* (binding laws), limiting the new government's ability to modify the norms regulating key matters of national interest. These laws reduced threats to the military, boosted the elite's economic privilege, and undermined people's substantive access to democratic participation. Most of these laws were constitutionally protected, which meant that they could not be modified without a substantial proportion of right-wing votes in congress. Pinochet's constitution also created a Constitutional Tribunal that was able to veto legislation already approved by congress. These legal locks protected the

---

[13] These norms prohibited congress from requesting an investigation into crimes committed by any military organism. They also precluded the new administration from replacing public servants, giving the Aylwin government the authority to appoint only 400 new government employees, while the dictatorship kept over 30,000 political appointments in government institutions. Furthermore, these laws limited the control of the president over the military, gave significant autonomy to the Chilean Central Bank, and created a binominal electoral system that gave more power to the two largest political coalitions and overrepresented the right-wing in congress and local governments. With these laws, Pinochet also gave himself considerable power to elect mayors across the country. The constitution further included several norms that restricted Chile's democratic development. The constitution created the National Security Council, which allowed the military to keep a strict oversight over the new civilian rule. After 1989, the constitution also mandated the nonelected appointment of nine designated senators – selected by the president, the National Security Council and the Supreme Court – and the appointment as life-long senators of the former Chilean presidents Augusto Pinochet and Eduardo Frei. For more details see Angell and Pollack (1990) and Valenzuela (1997).

endurance of legislation that made social services attractive markets for national and international investors in areas such as urban connectivity, public education, healthcare, and environmental planning.

The Chile that the Concertación had to deal with in 1990 was just reemerging from the great economic crisis of the 1980s. Since then, Chile has become more prosperous and stable. Constitutional amendments and new legislation gradually did away with several binding laws, thus widening Chileans' access to political and civil rights. Although slowly, the state also advanced in prosecuting the human rights abuses that occurred during the dictatorship through two truth commissions in 1991 and 2004.[14] The dirt roads and latrines that used to be symbols of poverty in informal settlements were progressively replaced with pavement and sewage systems. A yearly average of over 121,000 new houses were built between 1990 and 2018 using the government's subsidy system, and several other state programs allowed underprivileged dwellers to refurbish or build new neighborhoods.

### 2.4.1 Excluding the Urban Poor

Despite these efforts, Chile's substantive democracy was slow to develop. Constitutionally designed by the dictatorship to secure the oversight and dominance of the armed forces over civil authorities, the National Security Council saw its power removed only in 2005. Similarly, a group of institutionally appointed senators[15] created by the dictatorship's constitution remained in congress until 2006. In addition, Chile has remained a deeply unequal country. The income of the richest 20 percent of Chileans is 10 times that of the poorest 20 percent. While these circumstances undermined the ability of most Chileans to fully engage in politics, the democratic transition exposed the urban poor to exceptional levels of political exclusion. These conditions contributed to the demobilization of the urban margins.

In the democratic transition, most *población* organizations were abandoned by external supportive entities. Those political parties that had

---

[14] For further details on the National Commission on Truth and Reconciliation (1991) and the National Commission on Political Imprisonment and Torture (2004) see Hiner (2010), Sepúlveda (2014), and Rojas-Corral and Shaftoe (2021).

[15] The constitution of 1980 designed a senate that included directly elected members (26), members appointed by the National Security Council, the Supreme Court and the president (9), and former presidents, who got life-long appointments as senators. Only two life-long senators reached the chamber, Augusto Pinochet and Eduardo Frei.

previously coordinated and funded anti-dictatorship protests quickly stopped their assistance to underprivileged neighborhood organizations.[16] Additionally, party members prioritized electoral politics exclusively and neglected *población* activism (Posner 2004). The Catholic Church also withdrew its support for *población* mobilization. Local *población* parishes that previously acted as spaces of protection against military repression increasingly excluded secular collective initiatives after 1988. The Church's funds for poverty alleviation and protest also ended, and progressive priests who had supported and led local contentious actions in their *población* parishes were relocated (Drogus and Stewart-Gambino 2005). International NGOs also withdrew funds and support from local cooperative organizations, civic education workshops in *poblaciones*, and grassroots democracy development projects.

The structure of the state and its urban policies further segregated cities and marginalized *poblaciones*. The democratic governments continued liberalizing urban land after 1990 and did not substantially reform the social housing subsidy system that had segregated urban poverty during the dictatorship. Neglected and stigmatized by the state, neighborhoods in the urban outskirts were concentrations of poverty and were poorly equipped with social services, connectivity, security, and green areas. Reports by the media, state agencies, and think-tanks portrayed these neighborhoods as areas colonized by gangs and drug dealers. In a context in which public spaces could be dangerous and violent, many *población* dwellers saw public engagement and mobilization not as areas of successful citizenship and cooperation, but as potentially frustrating and harmful actions (Skewes 2005; Rodríguez et al. 2012). In addition, the stigmatization of these neighborhoods as zones of criminality, incivility, anomy, and poverty undermined underprivileged urban dwellers' self-esteem, as well as their appreciation for their local community. Thus, residents often distrusted their neighbors and were more dedicated to trying to leave these neighborhoods than to engage in community organizing (Dammert 2004; Dammert and Oviedo 2004). This scenario made engaging in collective action very costly in the eyes of *población* residents. In this context, the spaces and resources that local authorities provided for initiatives in these neighborhoods became often perceived by local dwellers as the only safe opportunities for participation.

---

[16] Reportedly, the PS Almeyda, whose help was key for *población* activists under the dictatorship, began discouraging mobilization after they joined the Democratic Alliance in the mid-1980s (Muñoz Tamayo 2017).

Furthermore, the Chilean state remained a highly centralized structure, which also undermined the inclusion of the urban margins. Although since the dictatorship more responsibilities have been given to local governments and local deliberative citizen councils were created,[17] the Chilean state did not make substantial strides in distributing power to localities.[18] As Posner (2008, 139) explains, the Chilean state developed as "an institutional edifice that represented the interests of the [central] national government at the regional, provincial, and local levels." The Chilean central government hence developed as a technocratic machine that grew increasingly insulated and detached from local-level demands (Flinders and Wood 2015). In contrast, local governments fostered an image of closeness with and commitment to the population because they were the ones channeling resources to neighborhoods, implementing social programs, and promoting participation. In this context, municipalities had little real political power, allowing for very restricted forms of participation. Participatory programs reached localities with concepts, development standards, and policy agendas that were predefined at the central level. This scenario shaped people's mindsets in the urban margins, thus creating a collective sense of marginality and political exclusion in those neighborhoods.

### 2.4.2 Some Exceptions

Despite this hostile scenario, mobilization survived in those urban communities where radical groups had developed subversive leadership tactics under the dictatorship. Local activists in these *poblaciones* used the legacy of those radical groups to create an alternative form of political incorporation that this book calls "mobilizational citizenship." These active communities could be found in neighborhoods like Villa Francia and Población Santiago (Estación Central district), José María Caro (Lo Espejo and Pedro Aguirre Cerda districts), Lo Hermida (Peñalolén district), La Pincoya (Huechuraba district), Juanita Aguirre (Conchalí district), and La Victoria (Pedro Aguirre Cerda district) (Lock 2005; Finn 2008; López-Morales 2013; Molina and Molina 2015; Escoffier 2018).

---

[17] These were the *Concejos de Desarrollo Regional* (Regional Development Councils) and the *Concejos de Desarrollo Comunal* (Municipal Social Development Councils).

[18] This is despite the democratization of municipal councils in 1992, of mayors in 2004, and of regional governors in 2021.

These neighborhoods held a diverse, informal network of organizations that regularly carried out activism in their respective underprivileged communities. During the 1990s, local organizers continued coordinating neighborhood development initiatives, such as soup kitchens, community parties, employment and food supply cooperatives, children's camps, and groups of *arpilleras*. Several of these actions had helped local communities cope with deprivation and social exclusion during the dictatorship. Yet the country became more and more economically prosperous in the 1990s and intensive social policies made substantial strides in tackling poverty. Consequently, these tactics survived over time because people saw them as a way of protecting their local sense of community and collective identity. Residents in these neighborhoods also continued mobilizing over human rights and social housing.

Additionally, every year following the democratic transition, on 11 September and 29 March, disruptive demonstrations have erupted in different parts of the city to protest the dictatorship's human rights violations and mark the violent protests that were staged against the dictatorship during the 1980s. These actions have included marches, bonfires, roadblocks, and confrontations with the police. Depending on the year, these protests sometimes involve occupations and clashes with security forces in a few universities, and marches organized by human rights groups in the city center. They have been more regular, numerous, and violent in those contentious neighborhoods that remained active in the urban margins.

Organizations in mobilized *poblaciones* also began supplying protests beyond their neighborhood with leaders, informal networks, information, repertoires of contention, ideological underpinnings, and resources. Reportedly, for example, the mobilizing capabilities of activists from the *población* La Victoria were instrumental in blocking a new masterplan that threatened underprivileged communities in the district of Pedro Aguirre Cerda in 2005. Promoted by the local government, the masterplan was meant to widen roads and rezone urban land in order to attract middle- and high-rise tower projects to the district. Underprivileged residents therefore feared gentrification and evictions. La Victoria activists led a coalition of organizations from the neighborhoods José María Caro, El Esfuerzo, and Nueva Lo Valledor. Leaders used a TV station created by La Victoria activists to spread information on the problem and conduct public interviews with experts and stakeholders. Through workshop methodologies they had implemented in the past, La Victoria leaders created awareness and fostered cohesion among community leaders from the other neighborhoods (López-Morales 2013). The coalition also employed connections with NGOs and architects that La Victoria activists had established in past years to learn about urban planning, build leadership skills and draft a bottom-up alternative master plan proposal (López-Morales 2013). A group of organizations in the section of the *población* José María Caro within the Lo Espejo district faced a similar conflict in 2006. They also created a network of organizations and managed to push the local and central governments to include them in the decision-making process behind the new master plan (Parraguez 2012).

### 2.4.3 Case Studies (1990–2006)

With the accelerated expansion of Chilean cities, both Lo Hermida and Nuevo Amanecer became better incorporated within the urban perimeter. As urban services and connectivity expanded, these neighborhoods became less isolated, and their residents could better access other areas in the city. In the one and a half decades after the democratic transition, different government programs improved these neighborhoods' equipment and infrastructure. In these areas, the state invested in paving roads, replacing public lightning, and improving public spaces. It also built or refurbished local police stations and health centers; community buildings and neighborhood libraries; soccer pitches and squares. Residents' daily experience in these *poblaciones* therefore improved substantially in this period.

In 1991, Carmen, an experienced community leader, along with a few adolescent residents in Nuevo Amanecer, initiated literacy courses with adults, as well as workshops with local children. Inspired by the legacy of the MIR, they promoted community and political engagement. Several local families demonstrated their trust in and commitment to the new democratic regime by actively participating in these activities. "It seemed to me that people were putting their fear [of state repression] aside ... there were new feelings of openness," the leaders told me (Interview, October 13, 2014a).

A few months later, several local organizers coordinated the neighborhood's founding anniversary celebration for the first time since the military coup. They set a stage on one of the roads to display a few shows in front of all neighbors on November 1, the date Nueva La Habana was created. While Carmen was introducing the first performance in front of the audience, a group of young people with covered faces and holding shotguns and pistols suddenly came on stage. They greeted the *población* on behalf of the MIR. Scared of engaging in activities that might result in conflict, residents began to fear Carmen and other local organizers. This nascent attempt to develop neighborhood contentious organizing was therefore quickly quelled.

In the years after the democratic transition, other local organizations in Nuevo Amanecer developed in close connection with the municipality as well as with center and left-wing political party representatives. Local organizers therefore engaged in the same demobilizing dynamics that affected most communities in Chile's urban margins during those years. Neighborhood councils and local soccer clubs became dominant, stable associations in the *población*. Housing committees grew in the area in those years coordinating large groups of families living as *allegados*[19] and applying for the social housing subsidy. Development committees of only a few dozen families also appeared in the neighborhood in order to coordinate local residents' access to smaller subsidies that funded neighborhood infrastructure improvements.

Carmen and a few other local organizers ran the neighborhood council located in the oldest area of the *población* – the formerly MIR-led settlement that residents call *campamento*. They used the organization to attend to the needs of other local dwellers. Much of their work involved making connections and channeling resources coming from the PS and the municipality to the local community. In the early 2000s, however, this neighborhood council ended its operations after a dispute between two local leaders left a pending debt with the municipality. Authorities legally banned the organization while waiting for payment and the council has remained closed since then.

Organizations devoted to local service provision also existed in Lo Hermida, but the local community evolved differently in the 1990s. The neighborhood inherited deep political tensions from the dictatorship years. A few neighborhood councils, for instance, continued to be run by right-wing leaders who had been loyal to Pinochet's government. Parallel to these formal organizations were a set of other groups composed of local dwellers who had participated in revolutionary actions in the 1980s with the goal of overthrowing the dictatorship. They were committed to keeping *población* mobilization alive, despite the recent change of regime, and continued to defend the socialist project of society.

---

[19] These are people or families who do not have a home of their own and live in overcrowded conditions in other people's homes (often relatives). This experience regularly hinders people's privacy and personal development.

Disappointed with the market-oriented policies implemented by the Concertación and the privilege that the right-wing and the military enjoyed after the dictatorship, these activists grew highly skeptical of Chile's mainstream political class. They only continued to collaborate with the PC because they saw it as a party that would not betray their ideals. Some of these activists created a community development center that organized children's camps, public Christmas celebrations, and the neighborhood's anniversary. Others also coordinated neighborhood soccer clubs, groups of *arpilleras*, and a few community kitchens. In the late 1990s, organizations led by youths who had learned about Lo Hermida's mobilizing identity in local soccer teams or children's camps began to multiply. They all saw local community development as the backbone of political engagement and transformative social change. Several of them were devoted to the creation, spreading, and self-education of local art and culture. One of them was Murgarte, which became a hub for youths learning jugglery and other circus technics. Others, with a more explicitly political goal, defended the dignity and autonomy of *pobladores*. The Alex Lemun organization, for example, carried out workshops on social justice and human rights in land occupations within the neighborhood that they called "*recuperaciones.*" Unlike in Nuevo Amanecer, a shared sense of deep admiration for past radical political groups survived across age groups in Lo Hermida.

Lo Hermida's mobilizing capabilities reached other parts of the city on different occasions in the 1990s. The two largest land invasions since Chile's return to democracy were a result of this dynamic. The *toma* Esperanza Andina in 1992 mobilized over 790 homeless families from different parts of the district of Peñalolén in eastern Santiago; they invaded land, created a democratic system of local decision-making, built emergency houses, and mobilized in order to access the deeds to the land and public services. In these early years of democratic rule, this settlement rejected collaborating with political parties because community leaders wanted to avoid all possible political co-optation (Figueroa 2003, 2–3). It was the first large-scale mobilization by the urban poor that managed to defy the newly appointed democratic authorities (Salazar 2012, 185–90). Later, in 1999, another large land seizure took place in the district of Peñalolén. Around 1,900 families, formerly living as *allegados* in the district, invaded private lands and demanded access to social housing. This land seizure became known as the Toma de Peñalolén and was featured repeatedly on the television news and in newspapers. The *toma* was an act of protest against what underprivileged families saw as the government's segregationist housing policies, which invariably allocated social housing in the urban peripheries. After years of negotiations, a group of moderate *toma* leaders reached a deal with authorities for nearly half of the squatting families to be relocated into houses in a different area of the same district. These leaders had developed links with center and left-wing Concertación political parties. A group of leaders representing almost 1,000 families and closely linked to Lo Hermida's organizations, however, rejected partisan collaborations and insisted on getting social housing in the same place as the *toma*. Authorities reacted to what they understood as these leaders' highly rigid and radicalized position by relocating most of these families to different areas of the urban outskirts. Countless families in these *tomas* had been *allegados* and belonged to housing committees in Lo Hermida, and several of their leaders had either belonged to Lo Hermida's community or were in direct communication with the neighborhood's organizations. My interviewees in Lo Hermida's SMC thus recall the many times in which they brought supplies to squatters and discussed mobilizing tactics with the *toma* leaders. Most people in the Toma de Peñalolén were relocated to social housing in other parts of the city between 2006 and 2008.

## 2.5 THE REAWAKENING OF CIVIL SOCIETY (2006–2020)

In the past decade and a half, Chile has seen sustained economic growth and poverty has decreased steadily. Material conditions have consequently continued to improve in *poblaciones*. Yet, the country's achievements evolved along a restrictive notion of democracy. Institutional politics became increasingly dominated by an upper-class elite with little empathy with ordinary citizens. As people became more educated and informed, they demanded a stronger voice on policy decisions. But the mechanisms by which Chile's centralized political administration addressed those demands repeatedly frustrated citizens. Both main political coalitions, Concertación and Alianza por Chile, lost credibility among the population because their elitism and highly liberal economic policies did not seem to take on board people's real-life concerns.

Furthermore, the predominance of market-oriented policies added increasing precarity to people's experience of Chile's economic success. Inequality and employment flexibility remained very high. The pension system created by the dictatorship began to show its inability to sustain the growing numbers of elderly people falling below the poverty line. Chileans' individual indebtedness increased to alarming rates after 2009

(González 2018), which heavily affected the opportunities of thousands of first-generation higher-education students who had to pay bank loans after ending their studies (Disi 2018). Disappointed, youths continued to withdraw themselves from formal politics and began to vote less and less (Luna, Zechmeister, and Seligson 2010). These new generations were detached from the debates that shaped the politics of dictatorship and transition. In addition, the middle class grew in size and began to seek a more open and meritocratic society (UNDP 2017). After almost two decades of post-transitional political exclusion, the young middle class was ready to open new avenues of political engagement.

### 2.5.1 Protests

Protests organized by high-school and university students were the first to express this new collective sentiment. In 2006, the Pingüino Movement, named after students' penguin-like black and white school uniforms, occupied hundreds of schools, and organized marches of over 100,000 people in the main cities. The protests sought structural reform, which included modifying the constitutionally protected Organic Education Law (LOCE). Although the negotiations eventually frustrated students, they managed to increase awareness in the population and obtained high levels of public support. Students mobilized again in 2011. This time, university students joined secondary school students. They argued that only by eliminating structures that incentivized profit-making in education would the system improve its quality and become properly inclusive. Students demanded that free, quality education be considered a social right, which required changing the constitution. The movement held 23 large protests in Santiago and other major cities across the country between May 2011 and September 2013 (Donoso 2016). The public, again, showed its widespread support for students' demands, with 79 percent approval among those surveyed in October 2011 (Cooperativa 2011). The state's ongoing inability to provide solutions eroded politicians' legitimacy further. Then-President Piñera's administration saw its public approval rate progressively decline. In an attempt to regain their popular support, political parties created new coalitions. In 2013, the Nueva Mayoría brought together the parties formerly in the Concertación plus the PC, and the right-wing Chile Vamos replaced Alianza por Chile. Parliament would eventually pass the Education Inclusion Bill, which forbade profit-making through the educational system, and eliminated the selection of students in state-funded schools as well as parental fees.

Along with the student mobilizations, collective action became increasingly regular from 2006 onwards, fueling a growing sense of empowerment in the population. Subcontractors, students, indigenous groups, LGBT+ organizations, feminist groups, and environmental movements have spearheaded a wave of protests that are impacting people's sense of political incorporation (Escoffier 2017b; Somma and Medel 2017). As Chile's political process became more and more elitist and disconnected from the grassroots, these mobilizations increasingly evolved detached from political parties (Somma and Bargsted 2015; Disi 2018).

Organizers in *poblaciones* that had remained active since the dictatorship joined this general wave of political engagement. Feminist and environmental organizations became increasingly active in these neighborhoods. Several young *población* residents who had acquired political training in their neighborhoods developed leadership roles within student organizations. Following the struggles of urban dwellers in Esperanza Andina and Toma de Peñalolén, an increasing number of *allegados* started to demand access to good-quality social housing in their district of origin. Organizations like the Movement of Underprivileged Dwellers in Struggle (MPL), Housing Movement for Dignity, and Ukamau emerged after 2006 (Rodríguez 2020). They created a movement coalition called Underprivileged Urban Dwellers' National Federation (FENAPO), which increased their coordination and visibility. In their need to influence government authorities, they became more informed about housing policies and organized demonstrations beyond their neighborhood boundaries (Pérez 2019). The Ukamau movement, for instance, was created in 2010 by a group of leaders in the Población Santiago. These activists had previously received training from organizations that persisted in their *población* since its community rebelled against dictatorial rule under Communist leadership in the 1980s. The movement used *autogestion* to learn and carry out the bureaucratic procedures involved in social housing provision. Its activists contacted and received help from universities and architects. Belonging to FENAPO also helped these activists learn from others in similar situations and exercise more pressure on authorities. After almost a decade of conflicts with reluctant governments that prioritized land profitability over people's access to decent housing, Ukamau managed to acquire and build a large housing project in the same district for over 400 families (Paulsen-Espinoza 2020). Yet, in their quest for more institutional influence, several of FENAPO's organizations engaged in electoral politics and created branches outside their neighborhoods. Some of their leaders joined political parties and aimed to expand their reach to the country level. This move increasingly detached them from their SMCs of origin and created conflicts with many *población* organizations that fiercely opposed institutional politics.

In parallel, locally based neighborhood organizations in mobilized *poblaciones* have continued promoting political awareness, shaping cultural norms, and strengthening community-building. Their rejection of corporatist politics has grown stronger, which means that they usually avoid collaborating with political parties and engaging in formal institutional procedures. SMCs in these *poblaciones* involve local networks of dynamic and well-connected neighborhood organizations. While some of them are formally recognized by the state,[20] most organizations in these neighborhoods are informal and do not belong to any institutional registry. State-recognized organizations are usually neighborhood councils, local development committees, housing committees, and soccer clubs. These organizations can access state funds, may be eligible for other state benefits, and have the right to take part in local state-managed decision-making processes like participatory budgeting programs. Informal organizations, on the other hand, either do not need state benefits, hold ideological convictions that prevent them from legitimizing formal institutional procedures, or are simply transient associations that serve a specific initiative. These include, for example, arts organizations, the more radical local groups, and committees coordinating specific local events. These organizations maintain a relatively cohesive collective identity that mobilizes *población* residents to continually foster a sense of community and promote political awareness. In *poblaciones* with active SMCs, neighborhood activists utilize these diverse types of organizations to challenge oppressive cultural norms, resist institutional abuse, and sometimes even organize protests to hold authorities accountable.

Unlike in most demobilized *poblaciones*, in which local participation is dominated by residents in their 50s and 60s (usually female residents who spend most of their time in the neighborhood because they are not employed or have flexible jobs), in mobilized neighborhoods local organizing involves a substantially wider age-range. In politicized *población* organizations, older and more experienced activists collaborate with the local youth. As I highlight in detail later, despite the organizations' emphatic defense of horizontal power interactions, those activists who have more experience, knowledge, and access to resources than others

---

[20] Local organizations are recognized by the state once they obtain "legal personality," a bureaucratic procedure at the local municipality.

tend to act as informal leaders. A casual and informal leadership training system allows younger activists and newcomers to learn shared collective identity symbols, tactics, and strategies.

Only a few organizations in these SMCs obtain their funds by participating in competitive local government grant schemes. Most of them either use their own members' private resources or organize local crowdfunding events (*autogestión*), such as neighborhood parties or soccer competitions. Furthermore, many *poblaciones* with a politically active past celebrate their anniversary with a public event on the date of their creation. The many activities involved in gathering the resources to organize larger events add to the neighborhood's vibrant and dynamic community. After organizing several *peñas* (crowdfunding community parties) throughout the year, a local group of rappers, for example, coordinated a large concert that brought artists from different parts of Santiago to the neighborhood. This event worked as a campaign against police repression both in *poblaciones* and in Mapuche communities.

Organizations in mobilized *poblaciones* have also continued to expand their reach beyond their neighborhood boundaries. Individuals with passionate political inclinations and the desire to engage in contentious politics, but living in less active neighborhoods, often join local organizations in mobilized *poblaciones*. This gives them the opportunity to acquire mobilizing identity symbols, network, and learn about *población* tactics. Organizers in these mobilized *poblaciones* also coordinate events that bring activists from different parts of the city together. These include *población* anniversaries, commemorations, and neighborhood concerts. In addition, these organizers often provide support for community-building initiatives in neighborhoods with a smaller but motivated activist contingent.

The endurance of mobilization in these communities has allowed local organizations to develop increasing mobilizing capabilities for the display of both peaceful and disruptive collective actions. In early November 2016, for instance, a network of particularly radical *población* activists participated in riot-style, violent protests that interrupted a peaceful mass demonstration organized by the No+AFP movement. Beginning in the early hours of the morning, individuals with covered faces took to the streets, using burning tires, sticks, and other debris to block Santiago's arterial transit routes. In many other main cities, they built barricades, halting the flow of traffic. These citizens staged violent confrontations with the police and controversially set fire to several public transport buses, in public displays of protest. In Santiago, Valparaiso,

Concepción, Talcahuano, and other urban centers, daily life was severely disrupted. SMCs in mobilizing *poblaciones* would display these tactics, networks, and resources in the country-wide mass protests that erupted three years later.

In mid-October 2019 high-school students organized fare-dodging protests in a few of Santiago's metro stations. These disruptive actions occurred for several days in a row and were a reaction to a recent public transportation fare increase. Several other prices of basic goods had increased in the recent months, and comparisons posted on social media placed average Chilean living costs as higher than that of several other much richer countries. In public declarations, authorities repeatedly ignored people's hardship and discontent over the increase of prices (La Tercera 2019). When interviewed by CNN about the metro fare, for example, the Minister for Economic Affairs advised people to get up earlier in order to catch the off-peak fare (CNN Chile 2019). Over the course of a week, violence escalated rapidly. Metro stations in the city center began closing their doors earlier and the police exercised force to stop and detain students. As images of police brutality spread across social media, many other student and non-student protestors joined the mobilization. In large groups *población* activists went to their nearest metro station and dodged the fare to support protests against the government.

On October 18, unrest increased to unprecedented levels. Protestors and clandestine groups completely burned 20 metro stations and damaged many others (Somma et al. 2020). The president responded by ordering a curfew and a state of emergency that brought the military in to guard the streets of Santiago. But the conflict did not subside. Instead, people continued protesting and defied the curfew by banging pots and pans in the streets at night. The next day, countless supermarkets and shops were looted, and the security forces cracked down emphatically on both rioters and peaceful protestors. This mobilized people further. Many middle-class neighborhoods and *poblaciones* without a collective action tradition, or where its few local activists had previously participated in other mobilized neighborhoods, experienced an outburst of local engagement. Diverse, impromptu groups emerged in these neighborhoods ready to defy authorities through collective action. Mobilization spread across the country.

Simultaneously, the mobilizing capabilities developed by *poblaciones* where contentious politics had endured for the past 30 years allowed their local organizers to take a leading role in the process. These communities were better prepared to coordinate mass protests because their activists had built strong collective identities, leadership skills, and informal networks. Organizations in these *poblaciones* created local assemblies in order to produce joined, contingent demands, coordinate protests, and protect each other. In only a few days, these assemblies coalesced into larger territorial coalitions called *cordones* (cordons), which incorporated those more recent and improvised local associations from other neighborhoods. These *cordones* were able to deploy peaceful and disruptive collective action in larger portions of the city. Eventually, Santiago's Coalition of Territorial Assemblies emerged; this was a supra-organization devoted to coordinating the *cordones* across the city.

The brutal violence exercised by the police and the military shocked the population, radicalized protestors, and motivated more mobilizations. This repression affected both violent and peaceful protestors, and it included illegal detentions and extra-legal beatings; shooting hundreds of protestors in the face and torso with metal pellets; firing tear gas cans inside healthcare centers and other buildings; destroying memorials and impeding rescue teams from helping injured protestors. Evidence also indicates that the police's water cannons, repeatedly used to control demonstrations, contained a toxic substance that burned people's skin (Cortés, Martínez-Gutiérrez, and Jiménez 2021). As protests expanded into the urban margins, police repression began to affect local communities within their own neighborhoods. In *poblaciones* the police carried out violent raids, teargassed apartment blocks, intimidated leaders, ran over local residents with police cars, and carried out beatings.

Daily protests continued for weeks on end, despite President Piñera announcing several social measures that included freezing public transportation fares, increasing the minimum wage, supplementing pensions for the lowest households, and increasing taxes for the super-rich. People's rejection of the government endured and on October 25, the largest demonstration ever reported in the country gathered around 1.2 million peaceful protestors in Santiago's city center. At the edge of peaceful protests like this one, individuals covering their faces regularly engaged in clashes with the police. These protestors became called the *primera línea* (first line) and orchestrated well-coordinated attacks. A first group formed a protecting line using self-made shields. Others prepared Molotov cocktails or gathered stones and placed those weapons near another group who threw them at the police. Finally, a group of volunteers waited on the side to aid the wounded. As my interviews indicate, a substantial proportion of these first-line protestors either belonged to neighborhoods in the urban margins or had prior experience of mobilization in *poblaciones*. After a month of daily peaceful and violent demonstrations, members of congress devised an agreement that kick-started a process leading to the redrafting of Chile's political constitution. Peaceful demonstrations decreased in scale and became disconnected from first-line protestors, who continued mobilizing and clashing with the police in the city center almost every evening (Somma et al. 2020).

In April 2020 the COVID-19 pandemic health crisis brought intense economic hardship to *poblaciones*. A large number of *pobladores* under precarious and informal employment saw their income disappear in only a few weeks. Those activists who had been coordinating protests in the months before turned to help those fellow community members in need. They organized fundraising campaigns and created hundreds of community kitchens that fed the poorest families.

## 2.5.2 Case Studies (2006–2020)

As public engagement and mobilization increased in Chile during these years, the contrasting developments of civil society in Nuevo Amanecer and Lo Hermida became particularly evident. Most organizations in Nuevo Amanecer continued to understand their work as service provision and were populated by people over 50 years old, most of whom were women. Furthermore, organizers remained close allies to political representatives and collaborated especially with politicians from the Socialist Party. Exceptionally, an additional neighborhood council that emerged toward the east of the neighborhood and a few community leaders heading development committees in *villa* Los Húsares changed their collaboration with political parties depending on more pragmatic tactics. Hence, as the right-wing coalition took La Florida municipality in 2011, these local leaders joined political networks headed by politicians on the right. In this context, the youths in Nuevo Amanecer were largely disconnected from the neighborhood's public life. Those who engaged in collective action did it through joining local gangs that were often involved in dealing drugs and exercising violence to protect their turf.

However, a few exceptions to these dynamics developed in these years. In the early 2010s, two groups of youths developed community-building initiatives and revived the neighborhood anniversary. One of these groups, La Casita Periférica, sought to bring back the Month of María – an important event for the *población* in the 1980s – organized art workshops with children and neighbors, and participated in ceremonies and meetings in a Mapuche community nearby. La Casita Periférica is an organization of local residents in their 20s and early 30s. After receiving some training on ideology and leadership from activists external to the *población*, La Casita Periférica began organizing occasional art workshops with children and the yearly neighborhood anniversary celebration. Another youth organization created a street band that played in community events in Nuevo Amanecer and other *poblaciones*. Both of these groups rejected collaborating with political parties and with most other local organizations, but did not organize protests or acts of collective defiance.

The actions of a housing committee called Don Bosco could be seen as another exception in the neighborhood's generally acquiescent political landscape. For two years, families in the Don Bosco housing committee waited for a plot in which their subsidized housing could be built. Getting no answers from authorities and in an act of spontaneous defiance, in early 2013 these families stormed a social housing project next to their *población* and occupied the houses under construction. Families in the Don Bosco committee organized protests to pressure authorities. They also developed political tactics and collective action frames that highlighted their quest for dignity in the city (Pérez 2018). Several Don Bosco leaders even joined FENAPO to support a larger coalition of organizations demanding social housing. Yet, once families in the committee obtained their subsidized houses in the proximities of their *población*, obtaining the majority of their short-term demands, their collective action became mostly deactivated. The absence of a mobilizing identity among local organizations in Nuevo Amanecer prevented the Don Bosco committee from drawing on the neighborhood's symbolic resources to sustain mobilization over time.

In Lo Hermida, in contrast, a numerous and diverse set of organizations developing contentious politics continued growing alongside those concerned with service provision. Several organizations defied the elitism of upper-class art through workshops on hip-hop and folklore. Organizations also coordinated *recuperaciones de terreno* (land reappropriations) in the neighborhood. In other words, local residents occupied squares or buildings in the *población* when building projects from corporations, private investors, or the municipality threatened community control of the area. Activists in Lo Hermida regularly organized protests to react to national or local issues, which included commemorations, marches, roadblocks, and clashes with the police.

While mobilization flourished in Lo Hermida, a key neighborhood council deactivated in Nuevo Amanecer during this period, thus epitomizing the neighborhood's dislocated organizational life. Socialist political representatives had especially close connections with a small group of female organizers in the neighborhood council of the oldest part of the *población* – that which is still called *campamento*. Because of this area's past as a stronghold of MIR activism, this council could be understood as that with the highest mobilizing potential in the area. However, in the mid-2000s these neighborhood council leaders engaged in disputes over benefits provided by political patrons. The conflict between these leaders escalated and led to aggressive accusations from both sides over financial malpractice. Consequently, the municipality refused to update the neighborhood council's legal personality, and the organization has remained inactive since then. The other neighborhood councils in the area stayed close to local politicians and devoted their attention to providing services for the local community.

Conversely, Lo Hermida experienced the opposite dynamic in those years. Appointed by government authorities during the dictatorship, a group of right-wing leaders running the 18th neighborhood council, located in the neighborhood's first zone, had remained in charge of the organization for decades. Used to this council's disconnection from local, leftist networks of cooperation, local activists, and residents did not bother to participate in its periodic elections. Right-wing council leaders had gained the loyalty of a few local residents who repeatedly elected them. In the mid-2000s, a group of youths in their 20s collaborated with a few older and more experienced leaders in order to democratize and reappropriate this neighborhood council. By calling for the *recuperación* of that organization, this group of leftist activists summoned the collaboration of other local community organizers. Only after two consecutive elections in which they canvassed and organized events to increase voting in the neighborhood did these activists manage to win all the seats in the council.

This victory made available a set of additional resources for local organizations. The new leaders in the council got to manage a community building in the neighborhood and obtain financial support from the municipality. They were able to take part in participatory funding events coordinated by the government and could access information on authorities' decision-making. By running the council, these leftist leaders also became part of a local governance network that included the police station, municipal agencies, NGOs, and other similar neighborhood organizations in the district. Local activists have continuously won the neighborhood council's seats since then, thus making the council's building a vibrant hub for local organizing and community events. Furthermore, they inspired several other groups who more recently carried out similar *recuperaciones* in other neighborhood councils within Lo Hermida. These two examples show the stark contrast between the development of mobilizing capabilities in Lo Hermida and Nuevo Amanecer at this time.

Simultaneously, in the mid-2000s, a group of radical community leaders in Toma de Peñalolén strengthened their cohesion after several years of failed negotiations with the local and central governments. Most of them originally belonged to Lo Hermida and demanded social housing in the same district. They were also frustrated with the lack of support they were receiving from the PC, formerly a key ally of *población* organizing. As government concessions and conflicts split the broader coalition of organizers in Toma de Peñalolén, this group of leaders decided to create a new movement that could summon housing committees in the district and push for social housing policy reform. In 2006, they founded the Movement of Urban Dwellers in Struggle (MPL), which included six assemblies of *allegados* in Lo Hermida and other *poblaciones* in the district (Guzmán et al. 2009).

MPL leaders would passionately use the notions of self-management and popular power they had learned within *población* organizations in Lo Hermida to design their tactics. They replaced the management and building agencies involved in the development of new social housing projects with community-run organizations. They also complemented their previous knowledge on housing policies with the technical support from university students and academics. Regular critical pedagogy workshops ensured their cohesive community, sense of empowerment and self-training over time. In addition, MPL activists and their affiliated *allegados* coordinated numerous protests to demand houses in their district of origin and more inclusive social housing policies.

After only a few years, MPL activists had created a network of organizations that extended across Santiago and reached several urban groups struggling for improved living conditions in other Chilean cities. FENAPO resulted from these actions. In this way, the MPL contributed to expanding Lo Hermida's mobilizing culture beyond the neighborhood. Furthermore, in 2008 MPL activists obtained a seat in Peñalolén's municipal council. This event gave local organizations in Lo Hermida access to information on the policies being discussed in the local government. The electoral political ambitions of several MPL leaders eventually led to heated conflicts with other neighborhood organizers and partially isolated the MPL within Lo Hermida. But it remained an impactful organization both at the district and city levels.

Additionally, in 2011 Lo Hermida organizations together with a few other groups within the district coalesced into the Peñalolén Council of Social Movements (CMSP). The CMSP coordinated actions of protest against a new masterplan designed by the municipality. The conflict mirrored that experienced by *población* organizations six years earlier in the Pedro Aguirre Cerda district. In this case, however, the CMPS organized a petition for a referendum that got the support of over five percent of the district's electorate. The mayor was thus compelled to submit the regulatory plan to a popular vote. Although both the municipality and the CMSP carried out fierce campaigns, the new masterplan was eventually rejected in the referendum (Hölzl 2018). The *población* organizations' victory demonstrated their ability to work together in order to defend their community.

In mid-October 2019, several groups of activists in Lo Hermida went to their nearest metro stations, joined high-school students in their fare-dodging protests and engaged in violent confrontations with the police. Protests and violence escalated rapidly on the 18th of that month. While the government prepared a state of emergency and curfew that would come into effect on that day and last for over a week, leaders from the main organizations in Lo Hermida met to discuss a joint reaction to the situation. They created Lo Hermida's Territorial Coalition (COTLH). Besides a few right-wing and non-politicized local groups, most organizations in the *población* joined the coalition. The COTLH had two main goals. It produced a long list of demands to be brought in front of authorities and created links with other organizations in neighborhoods close by. Its core intention was to expand its reach and create a larger coalition that could coordinate actions and develop demands in the whole of Santiago's eastern side.

In the following days, similar coalitions emerged in other neighborhoods of Peñalolén. Organizers in *población* La Faena, who had learned about activism in Lo Hermida and other neighborhoods, created two other coalitions and joined the actions planned by the COTLH. Similarly, another group of organizations in the area, known as Peñalolén Alto, also joined the COTLH's work. They exchanged information, protected each other, and coordinated disruptive protests within the district. Soon after, Lo Hermida organizers met other *población* activists and created the Grecia Cordon, a broader alliance that gathered together associations in *poblaciones* and other neighborhoods across

Grecia Avenue in the central and eastern parts of Santiago. This cordon allowed the organization of larger and more visible actions. For example, to demonstrate against police brutality, the cordon produced an installation in which numerous representations of bloodied eyeballs were hung or drawn along several kilometers of Grecia Avenue. It also coordinated large-scale protests, which included numerous and simultaneous roadblocks that greatly disrupted people's mobility in the city. The meetings held by the Grecia Cordon allowed Lo Hermida's activists to interact with community leaders in other mobilized neighborhoods, like those from Villa Frei and Villa Olimpica. These connections provided them with information and valuable discussions on current political matters. In mid-November, as politicians discussed a forthcoming constitutional convention, for instance, the cordon gathered the varied positions of its several territories, held discussions, and reached agreements on a joint political stance on the matter. The cordon continued to hold regular meetings and carry out demonstrations until the end of 2019. In addition, several groups of young protestors in Lo Hermida joined the "first line" and combined their *población* activism with regular participation in disruptive protests and clashes with the police in the center of the city.

On October 26, an additional conflict erupted in Lo Hermida. After a march to demand social housing in the district, several housing committees entered the Cousiño vineyard adjoined to the *población* and occupied part of its land. The police violently repelled squatters using teargas, firing pellets, and physically removing them from the vineyard's premises. Enraged, more protestors and neighbors in the area reacted by throwing stones and yelling slurs at the police. As Rasse (2019) reports, violence escalated further when local dwellers who approached the police station located in Lo Hermida were denied information about those detained in the incident. Videos that circulated widely through social media showed the police retaliating by teargassing households in the area, carrying out raids, and conducting extra-legal beatings of young local residents presumed to be involved in the protests. These events created a conflict that led to daily riot-style protests and attacks against the local police station. People built barricades near the station and threw stones and Molotov cocktails. In order to attend to the dozens of affected and wounded residents that these clashes produced every week, a brigade of volunteers installed an emergency healthcare service in the 18th neighborhood council building and a few other points of the *población*. Another group of volunteers provided legal counseling to those detained. Daily confrontations around Lo Hermida's police station continued until mid-December 2019.

Instead of coordinating and actively engaging in mobilizations from the start, organizers in Nuevo Amanecer had a reactive approach to this wave of protests. Furthermore, in line with the neighborhood's organizational structure, this reaction was segmented by age groups. Those organizations populated by older leaders (over 50 years old) faced the protests with fear. Indeed, a couple of days after the protests began, the quick spread of lootings gave many people a strong sense of chaos and vulnerability. Fearing attacks or theft, neighborhood council leaders got in touch via WhatsApp with other local organizers in the nearby neighborhoods of Santa Teresa and Alto Macul to set up a network of mutual reporting and aid.

As the protests evolved, younger groups in the *población* decided they did not want to miss out on the demonstrations. They gathered in the central square, Plaza Los Palos, and organized a march that combined artistic and political representations. Several of them participated in a batucada group that gathered people from different parts of the district. Furthermore, together with other organizers in *población* Los Copihues, in the La Florida district, these youth groups in Nuevo Amencer coordinated the creation of a large mural in support of the mobilizations. Aware of the *población*'s past of political activism and inspired by the large-scale protests, a few leftist political organizers and agitators got in touch with these youths to seek their support in more disruptive tactics.

After a few weeks, the legitimacy of protests increased in the neighborhood as a result of the endurance of mobilizations, the persistent brutality of the police, and the loss of informal jobs among many local dwellers. Therefore, neighborhood councils, soccer clubs, and housing committees in Nuevo Amanecer, as well as many other local residents with no prior participation in organizations, joined initiatives of collective action. Local organizers sporadically attended meetings in assemblies and cordons that emerged within the La Florida district, which gave them access to networks and information about acts of protest in the area. They coordinated three community kitchens in the neighborhood and participated in a large march in the district that included many other local organizations in that part of the city.

The COVID-19 pandemic struck both *poblaciones* in March 2020. The resulting economic recession strongly affected many residents in these neighborhoods. Local activists, therefore, set up several soup kitchens to help feed the growing number of residents in poverty.

## 2.6 CONCLUSION

This chapter examined the historical events underlying the development of mobilizational citizenship in *poblaciones* from the 1960s through to early 2020. In doing so, it looked at the diverging development of mobilization in this book's case studies, Nuevo Amanecer and Lo Hermida. As I show, these two cases are representative of a broader reality among underprivileged neighborhoods. Despite persistent marginalization, the urban poor were able to shape their political role to their advantage in collaboration with political parties on the left throughout most of the twentieth century. Over the years, the underprivileged dwellers' movement effected policy changes and advanced the recognition of rights for the poor. Importantly, however, it also created a tradition of mobilization that still survives in parts of the urban margins, based in long-standing repertoires of collective action and a mobilizing identity.

The urban underprivileged have endured precarious conditions over time. The state persistently refuses to engage with their demands. Consequently, they often resort to collective action that borders on the illegal. Through land invasions, the urban poor have protested and pressured authorities to supply affordable housing. Political parties on the left and the Catholic Church had become key allies in these endeavors by the end of the 1960s. This chapter calls this period of high collective action before the coup d'état of 1973 – in so many *poblaciones* – "prior mobilization." It describes how a socialist project of society began shaping the political aspirations and livelihood expectations of many underprivileged urban dwellers in this period. As a result, urban communities built a sense of unity and purpose.

The military dictatorship, however, disrupted these processes of community creation. It violently repressed activism and implemented a stringent package of liberal economic policies that further marginalized and fragmented the urban poor. Mobilization in *poblaciones* would only reactivate after several years of authoritarian rule had passed. As my case studies demonstrate, those more radical political groups on the left developed a subversive leadership in communities like Lo Hermida while coordinating anti-dictatorship protests in the 1980s. These events transmitted a mobilizing identity to local activists that became the seed of mobilizational citizenship. In contrast, more moderate leftist political parties produced a top-down, managerial interaction with grassroots organizers of *poblaciones* like Nuevo Amanecer in these years.

The urban policies of post-dictatorial Chile continued to segregate and marginalize the urban poor, and collective action declined. Mobilization has survived in some neighborhoods, like Lo Hermida. In these *poblaciones*, flexible networks of activism are embedded in local communities that share a relatively cohesive collective identity, as well as many tactics and goals. Their mobilization tends to reject liberal and formal systems of political incorporation. For this reason, *población* organizations tend to reject collaborating with political parties and other institutions. Instead, they mobilize to promote collective identity and strengthen community. This enduring collective action over the past four decades built the knowledge, networks, and resources needed for *poblaciones* to support the massive widespread protests that erupted in Chile in late 2019. Organizations in Lo Hermida created a cohesive coalition that was able to quickly coordinate protests across neighborhoods and districts.

Chapter 3 analyzes the case of Nuevo Amanecer to examine how mobilizational citizenship failed to emerge in many urban communities. Organizations in these areas have developed an acquiescent participation in public matters that is generally reluctant to challenge institutions and authorities. Consequently, they engaged in Chile's recent wave of protests in a reactive capacity, only when the generalized legitimacy of the demonstrations and the loss of credibility of the government made participating in mobilizations a common practice.

# 3

# The Demobilization of the Urban Margins

In this chapter, I draw on over a year of ethnographic research in *poblaciones* to explain their demobilization. I pay special attention to Nuevo Amanecer. Despite its potential to sustain contentious organizing after the democratic transition, Nuevo Amanecer echoed most other *poblaciones* and demobilized. A number of large-scale social and political processes shape the micro-level dynamics that undermine mobilization and politically exclude communities at the urban margins. In Chapter 1, I drew on the main theories of collective action and urban marginality to place the notion of political capital at the forefront of my analytical explanation of demobilization. I use the work of Piven and Cloward, Davenport, Ganz, and Wacquant, among others, to suggest that political exclusion in underprivileged urban communities results from the institutional withdrawal and external management of their political capital. In other words, what discourages mobilization at the urban margins is a set of tactics that political institutions use to influence which resources people utilize and how they use those resources to build leadership and legitimize collective action at the local level. I claim that this intervention occurs, firstly, through the withdrawal or denial of support for mobilization by parties and other political entities. Secondly, state authorities and other institutions implement systems of collective decision-making that control political capital in underprivileged urban communities.

Using this framework, I will now begin my comparative endeavor. The paired comparison I develop focuses on two very similar urban communities that experienced different mobilizational outcomes: Nuevo

Amanecer and Lo Hermida. These neighborhoods are located in analogous areas of the city, and their spatial configuration, criminality rates, and socioeconomic levels are also similar. They were originally formed through land invasions coordinated by the MIR and other political parties in 1970, and enjoyed high levels of mobilization in their first years of existence. These communities understood their experience of the military coup in 1973 and the subsequent dictatorship as a violent interruption of people's political projects and livelihood expectations. Similarly to many active, leftist communities in the urban margins, Lo Hermida and Nuevo Amanecer were severely repressed by the dictatorship. The two communities were also very active in the pro-democracy national protests of the 1980s.

Despite the ways in which they are similar, these two communities developed differently after Chile's democratic transition. In line with a general demobilization across Chile's urban margins, Nuevo Amanecer organizations abandoned contentious politics. In contrast, mobilization has survived for the past 40 years in Lo Hermida.

I argue that urban communities in Chile's urban margins have reacted in at least two ways to processes of demobilization. On the one hand, a few exceptional *poblaciones* resist those systems of political exclusion through sustained community organizing. These communities mobilize to challenge unfair institutions and promote an alternative type of political incorporation. They have developed what I call *mobilizational citizenship*. I directly address this phenomenon in my study of Lo Hermida in Chapters 4, 5, and 6 of this book. On the other hand, most communities in the urban margins demobilized because they reacted passively to these systems of exclusionary governance. In these *poblaciones*, governance socializes the urban poor to normalize their behavior and discourage contentious politics. Importantly, the way I choose to frame my study is that, rather than encountering an absence of participation in these places, I actually witnessed an acquiescent collective action that is docile and servile to elite, institutional interests.

In this chapter, I focus on the case of Nuevo Amanecer to discuss how mobilizational citizenship has failed to gain traction in some areas since Chile's return to democracy. I explain how, along with Nuevo Amanecer, most other *poblaciones* reacted passively to the several challenges they faced in the democratic transition. Most influential community leaders in *poblaciones* like Nuevo Amanecer engaged in sustainable networks of political loyalty with politicians from the AD who supported grassroots collective action during the 1980s. As young party activists, during the pro-democracy national protests (1983–1986) these politicians managed and promoted the mobilization of urban dwellers, and the referendum campaign in 1988. Loyal, durable interactions between politicians and local leaders emerged out of these years of protest. As I explain in this chapter, these relationships shaped community leaders' approach to the past and allowed the dictatorship's disruptive impact to endure over time within communities. This dynamic has therefore prevented agentic memory-building and the development of mobilizational citizenship. Furthermore, these interactions evolved throughout the 1990s and 2000s to become networks of clientelism and political socialization that taught local leaders to compete over political capital at the local level. The result is the community's inability to activate mobilizational citizenship. Instead, these political networks feed local leaders with what I call "alleged protagonism." In other words, these political loyalties provide them with a sense of worthiness and local legitimacy while simultaneously excluding them from policy decisions. While local leaders' tactics often facilitate people's access to public resources, they also advance the external intervention of political capital in the neighborhood, thus perpetuating broader dynamics of political exclusion in the urban margins.

I begin the chapter by explaining the demobilization processes experienced by *poblaciones* in the past decades. I outline how political institutions and external elite allies have withdrawn and controlled political capital in those neighborhoods since the democratic transition, thus discouraging contentious politics. I then delve into the specific dynamics of political capital that explain why organizers reacted passively to those demobilization processes in most neighborhoods. I develop this argument in three sections. First, I examine the historical developments that led to Nuevo Amanecer's demobilization, including the disruptive role of the dictatorship in people's memory-building. I also investigate how local leaders engaged in networks of political loyalty in the 1980s. Second, I use an ethnographic lens to study political loyalties in Nuevo Amanecer in detail. I explain the way in which they evolved to become clientelist relationships, and how local leaders obtain a sense of alleged protagonism in those interactions. Third, I show how these networks have socialized community leaders to promote their accumulation of political capital at the neighborhood level. I explain that this dynamic deactivates collective initiatives, encloses spaces for collective action in the neighborhood, and thus prevents the development of mobilizational citizenship.

## 3.2 DISCOURAGING COLLECTIVE ACTION IN *POBLACIONES*

Key to this book's framework is the notion of political capital. I define it as the tangible or intangible resources by which social actors mobilize others' support. These resources include all the means that enable and motivate people's support for a leader, a cause, or a community, including economic resources or a person's charisma, fame, identity, and social connections. In underprivileged neighborhoods, political capital refers to the means by which community leaders develop legitimacy to mobilize others. Political capital can be acquired, lost, and transmitted (Bénit-Gbaffou and Katsaura 2014). I use this definition here to argue that political institutions and elite potential allies discourage people's engagement in contentious politics in excluded urban communities by externally controlling local-level political capital. To exert this control of political capital, these agents begin by withdrawing resources from mobilized communities. Then, they manage the access to political capital and shape its exchanges within those communities. This control allows external agents to deactivate contentious politics by influencing the dynamics of political legitimacy within neighborhoods.

These factors were at play in Chile's *poblaciones* during the democratic transition and the decades thereafter. First, elite allies removed their supporting resources from contentious initiatives in *poblaciones*. Around the year 1990, political parties, the Catholic Church, and many NGOs that had hitherto supported collective action in *poblaciones*, abruptly withdrew their financial, social, and human resources (see Chapter 2 for additional details). The loss of elite support in *poblaciones* made neighborhood activists perceive goals as less plausible, thus contributing to a delegitimization of mobilization in this new scenario. Furthermore, *población* leaders experienced the loss of social validation in their neighborhoods as they lost access to the elite networks and resources that had hitherto legitimized them. The withdrawal of resources consequently eroded political capital in the urban margins. The new democracy also deprived *población* leaders of many of their middle-class mobilizing networks, which further diminished political capital in those neighborhoods. A substantial proportion of middle-class activists in formal and well-established civil society organizations – for example, university student federations, trade unions, alternative media networks, NGOs, and human rights organizations – obtained positions in the central government during the 1990s.[1] Their new roles as public servants required former activists to be loyal to government directives, which ruled

[1] 51 percent of the civil servants in Delamaza and Ochsenius' (2006, 472) sample (100 central government employees hired between 1990 and 2000) had previously belonged to civil society organizations.

out their support of contentious initiatives in *poblaciones*. They consequently abandoned their support of local leaders pursuing mobilization in the urban margins (Delamaza and Ochsenius 2006). These dynamics further undermined political capital in the urban margins.

Second, authorities and elite potential allies managed to intervene and shape political capital within underprivileged neighborhoods. The 1990s consolidated the state as the only source of participatory funds in *poblaciones*. Since then, neighborhood organizations had to compete over scarce grants for the promotion of local participatory initiatives, which were managed by local governments. By giving these funds only to activists willing to align their initiatives with government standards, the state has exercised control over which initiatives and *población* leaders enjoyed more legitimacy. In turn, activists pursuing contentious politics became generally excluded from those resources (Greaves 2002; Posner 2008; Koppelman 2016). Despite these challenges, several urban land seizures carried out in the 1990s in the urban margins demanded housing rights, as well as the expansion of social rights. However, authorities reacted by framing the liberties gained by Chile's return to democracy as a concession, as a great success that had to be protected, even if many of the grievances of the urban poor persisted. Therefore, government officials and party representatives publicly condemned *población* mobilization as "endangering democracy" and as "anti-democratic" (Hipsher 1996, 283). With this tactic, state agents managed to delegitimize mobilization by convincing many *población* activists to see protests as actions that destabilized the new democracy. Those leaders who insisted on pursuing mobilization did so at the expense of their elite connections. Many times, this challenge to the government's public rhetoric also invalidated leaders among fellow activists and potential challengers who agreed to support a more "stable democracy."

Local governments have also played a role in controlling political capital within *poblaciones*. Chile's strong administrative centralization has shown central government policies as off-limits for most *población* organizers' demands. This phenomenon has shaped their expectations and prevented their making networks of activism that extended beyond the district to pursue overarching, politicized struggles. As a result, municipal authorities were in a privileged position to teach *población* residents about what they considered appropriate forms of participation. Reportedly, municipality agents frame their interactions with urban dwellers as opportunities to "teach" people about "responsible citizenship" (Greaves 2004, 210) and "responsible participation" (Escoffier

2017b, 55). They also exclude and isolate contentious organizations. This institutional disciplinary instruction delegitimizes contentious neighborhood initiatives among both leaders and local dwellers and allows municipalities to build a durable informal bloc with docile local organizations in the district.

These different dynamics of political capital management and demobilization have affected the urban margins as a whole in Chile for the past three decades. But why have so many communities reacted compliantly to these policies and systems of interaction while others resist demobilization? Based on the case of Nuevo Amanecer, the next sections in this chapter explain the micro-dynamics of political capital that prevented the development of mobilizational citizenship in *poblaciones*, therefore consolidating their demobilization.

### 3.2.1 Disrupting Politicization and Memory-Building

In the 1960s and early 1970s, *población* community-building emerged largely from people's experience of collective action, especially in their *tomas* and protests over housing rights. I call prior mobilization this collective action before the coup in 1973. In those years, leftist narratives outlining a socialist project of society served as a discursive framework for people's community development in the urban margins. That project pursued strongly redistributive policies through popular power, thus situating underprivileged communities at the forefront of social progress. These narratives organized urban dwellers' expectations about the future, as well as their motivation to participate in mobilizations. As I explain in Chapter 2, however, the dictatorship violently disrupted this political progression in the urban margins. Activists and local dwellers had, for example, named their *poblaciones*, roads, and squares, after leftist famous figures. Nuevo Amanecer was initially called "Nueva La Habana," and squatters in Lo Hermida used names like Vietnam Heróico (Heroic Vietnam) and Guerrillero Manuel Rodríguez (Combatant Manuel Rodríguez) to call the *villas* they created in their land invasions. But after 1974 the dictatorship would decide to change all these names to avoid their commemorative references to leftist ideology. This disruption imposed by the new authoritarian regime was therefore also a challenge to communities' sense of identity and cohesion.

My interviews indicate that protests during the dictatorship in some cases allowed communities in the urban margins to update and legitimize the mobilizing symbols that articulated prior mobilization. These were neighborhoods where subversive political leaders belonging to the MDP exercised considerable influence among local community members (see Chapters 2 and 4 for details). In those cases, communities created a sense of historical continuity that connects prior and current mobilization, thus allowing a new, alternative form of political incorporation to develop (see Figure 3.1). I call that novel type of politicization "mobilizational citizenship." In most *poblaciones*, however, mobilizations against the dictatorship were coordinated by more moderate party activists on the center and the left. These party members exercised a managerial leadership in these areas that did not update symbols of prior mobilization among local dwellers. The sense of historical discontinuity promoted by the dictatorship's policies, therefore, endured in these communities and made them react passively to the processes of demobilization unfolding in post-dictatorial Chile.

## 3.3 THE ORIGIN OF POLITICAL LOYALTIES IN NUEVO AMANECER

I suggest here that moderate party activists on the left and center belonging to the AD exercised a style of managerial leadership to conduct the anti-dictatorial national protests in many *poblaciones*. This tactic was key to sustain communities' sense of historical discontinuity. Party activists controlled protests and created political loyalties among *población* leaders. They did not, however, train local dwellers on political concepts and identity. Therefore, these parties could not encourage people's reconnection with identity symbols of prior mobilization.

Only a few leftist party activists survived dictatorial repression and remained in Nuevo Amanecer after the coup in 1973. They were from relatively moderate factions of the left. In the subsequent decade these political forces in the opposition, human rights movements and other types of local organizations would grow in number and power, both in Nuevo Amanecer and across the country. Youth groups emerged in the neighborhood using the resources and spaces provided by the local chapels to assist a strongly impoverished community. Soon after, political party activists entered those groups to coordinate anti-dictatorial protests and gave them a clearer political purpose.

As the wave of anti-dictatorial protests began in the early 1980s, Nuevo Amanecer's local chapel became a center for activism and the neighborhood gained a vibrant political environment. People of different age groups mingled in the daily tasks of organizing activities. Human

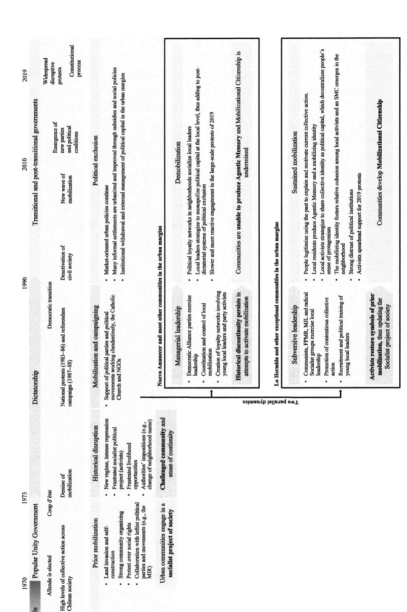

FIGURE 3.1 Case studies' evolution timeline. Source: Made by the author.

rights groups organized visits to detention centers, community kitchens served food every day (mainly to children), and *colonias urbanas* organized workshops and games for young people and children. Older participants taught younger ones; *colonias urbanas* offered charity, entertainment, and leadership skills for children. In contrast to the dictatorial restrictions that routinely confined people to their private lives, the chapel provided a free, open, and protected space. Many residents (especially the young people) felt they could develop a public role through their participation in the church. People from many different backgrounds mixed in this space. According to one former resident who belonged to *colonias urbanas*, "At the chapel, our differences were erased, even the bad young guys (*los cabros más malandras*) were there, and we all participated together" (Interview, October 13, 2014b). Many of the neighborhood residents that engaged in protests and developed community work at the chapel at that time are still *población* leaders today, running, for example, development committees, neighborhood councils, and soccer clubs.

Political party leaders from the AD came to Nuevo Amanecer's chapel in the 1980s and led initiatives of activism. They belonged to the Socialist, MAPU, and the Christian Left parties. Political parties coordinated meetings, marches, printing and distributing pamphlets, and making barricades. Former local party activists explained to me that parties tended to work under strict hierarchical command.[2] Party activists responded to top-down decisions made by specific party leaders. As one former leader told me, "Things were coordinated by the head of the party and then the orders went downwards" (Interview December 13, 2014). Hierarchical commands and coordinating actions occurred in very brief meetings. To ensure security, secrecy was crucial; working underground protected both party activists and residents, as public knowledge of other people's party membership was a potential danger that could deter residents from confidently attending the chapel. At the same time, gossip and stories gave residents an idea (although not necessarily validated) about who belonged to a party. This relative secrecy allowed closer interaction between local residents and party activists, enabling party activists to mingle with and influence local leaders and residents in Nuevo Amanecer.

The reputation of bravery and underground work of party activists made them appealing figures to *población* residents. "Belonging to a party

---

[2] In her study on these protests against the dictatorship, Bravo (2017, 192), for example, describes how political parties punished members who disregarded hierarchical commands.

back then was really dangerous ... you admired those who were in parties because they were the ones taking the biggest risks" (Interview October 22, 2014), remembers an interviewee. Furthermore, party members had uncontested access to political networks and resources, and were better trained in public engagement tactics than most *población* residents. Consequently, they generally ensured positions of leadership for party activists in *población* organizations and in initiatives at the chapel. Despite their influential role, these party members were not committed to recruiting *población* dwellers to increase party ranks. Rather, they exercised a managerial leadership that was concerned with articulating and controlling mobilization, and not with identifying and training politically skillful residents. According to Schneider (1995), most Chilean party activists on the center and the left had traditionally subordinated the interests of *pobladores* to those of the party. As she points out, party activists saw developing empowerment at the grassroots level as disconnected from larger party policy and planning. Consequently, these parties persistently avoided recruiting *población* activists into their ranks. Politically training *población* dwellers or incorporating them in party policy decision-making processes was, therefore, excluded from these parties' repertoires.

While party planning failed to incorporate non-partisan local dwellers, hierarchical party commands progressively influenced grassroots politics in Nuevo Amanecer. Neighborhood leaders realized, for instance, that party members influenced other participants, pacifying and deactivating protests in the mid-1980s. In fact, influenced by party activists, the chapel's Youth Ministry board promoted a conciliatory discourse among Nuevo Amanecer participants. Reportedly, these tactics were used by moderate center and leftist politicians across the country (Bastías Saavedra 2013). The Christian Democrats also implemented a clear strategy to isolate and discourage the more radical activists. These tactical changes expressed the AD's attempts to increase its political leverage in its talks with the right-wing military authorities and in its disputes with its more radical counterpart on the left, the MDP. In demonstrating its ability to control protests, the AD boosted its public credibility and governability (Tironi 1990).

Pablo, a former participant at the local church, explained to me that before 1986 there were debates between young residents regarding the aim of national protests: "Some supported the idea of overthrowing the military government through insurgency ... I remember that one would hear things like 'we will all build an unbreakable chain and the government will fall'" (Interview October 13, 2014b). However, according to Pablo, the newly elected Youth Ministry board at the chapel established a new and much more conciliatory discourse in 1986. The new board supported the AD's work to secure a national democratic referendum and rejected calls for the violent confrontations with the dictatorship. Several former participants at the local chapel confirmed this information (Interview October 13, 2014c; Interview December 29, 2014). Influenced by political parties, chapel board members sought to contain people's motivation to protest, requesting that they "pick the consensus" (Interview October 13, 2014c).

These years of national protests were critical in establishing a bond between neighborhood leaders and political party activists. Political parties provided nationwide coordination, thus enabling local leaders (and residents more generally) to become protagonists of social change during a period in which Pinochet's authoritarian government precluded collective political engagement. This experience was a seminal one for large numbers of disenfranchised young *población* dwellers. For the first time in their lives, they were engaging in institutionally recognized actions that would shape Chilean politics. AD activists were able to manage and modulate this widespread sense of inaugural protagonism across the urban margins.

My comparative analysis shows that party activists did not take full advantage of this context of social protest to train local dwellers. These intense and sustained mobilizations provided an ideal platform to teach young *población* leaders about strategies of mobilization, leftist ideology, and concepts. However, political parties did not intend to recruit local dwellers. Hence, they also did not engage in training tasks and provided little political socialization to *población* activists. Had these parties devoted energy to socialize neighborhood activists, they might have restored identity symbols of prior mobilization. As a result, they would have prevented the endurance of the sense of historical discontinuity that prevailed in Nuevo Amanecer and many other similar urban communities since the coup d'état, in 1973.

Soon after the legalization of political parties in 1987, the AD established a campaigning branch in a house next to Nuevo Amanecer's central square. That would be the coalition's local coordination center for the 1988 No Campaign and the 1989 presidential campaign. The branch house allowed neighborhood leaders to openly develop political activities for the first time. In contrast with what I observed in Lo Hermida, my interviews in Nuevo Amanecer categorically show that local center-left-wing leaders were fully committed to AD's political project. As a current leader recalled, "Back then, all the youths here went to work at the No branch, even the most leftist [radical] ones ... we all wanted to get back to democracy" (Interview October 13, 2014a).

As I was able to corroborate, most of the current Nuevo Amanecer leftist leaders worked for the No Campaign in 1988. Through activities that included meeting at the AD branch, handing out pamphlets, painting murals, and informing other people through word of mouth, Nuevo Amanecer residents consolidated their sense of protagonism in national politics. By advancing the AD's political project, local residents again obtained a sense of agency and citizenship. As a current leader and former No campaigner put it, "I fell in love with the work that we were doing at the [AD] branch" (Interview December 12, 2014). In Lo Hermida, in contrast, many young leaders (who also remain leaders to this day) opposed the negotiations that AD politicians undertook with the military authorities to lead a democratic referendum and a peaceful transition. By that time, national protests had been able to restore symbols of prior mobilization in *poblaciones* like Lo Hermida, thus reactivating activists' commitment to the socialist project of society that had previously organized mobilization in the urban margins (see Figure 3.1).

Nuevo Amanecer residents saw parties deploying convincing national communication strategies, greater resources, and significant manpower in the No Campaign (Otano 1995, 64). During these years, center-left party activists progressively established networks of political loyalty in the *población*. In fact, many local current leaders continued to work for politicians they first met during the referendum campaign. "I have been working for political campaigns since the No [Campaign]" said Javier, a current leader at a neighborhood council, now in his 60s. Like him, many others campaigned for politicians throughout the 1990s and 2000s. But political networks of loyalty installed by politicians do more than just serve campaigns; these networks also equip local organizations with information, political contacts, and systems of informal redistribution. The *Red de Iniciativa Ciudadana* (Network for Active Citizenship) was, for example, a Socialist web of political loyalties that grew from the 1990s through the mid-2010s in La Florida district. Although it was weakened and disarticulated in the late 2010s, this network connected members of parliament, other local politicians from the Concertación, and leaders from many *población* organizations in the district.

## 3.4 POLITICAL LOYALTY NETWORKS

Since the democratic transition, several Nuevo Amanecer neighborhood leaders have established allegiance to local politicians. Many *población* leaders support specific politicians, work in their campaigns, and have a strong interest in using any opportunity to boost those politicians' image in the community. During an interview, for example, one of those leaders criticized the group of youths who were organizing the neighborhood's anniversary celebration for purposely rejecting municipal funding for the event (Interview October 22, 2014). Because it attracts a large crowd, the *población* anniversary is potentially an opportunity to boost the mayor's image locally or to increase other politicians' political capital. If the organizers had accepted the municipality's offer to fund the anniversary, they would also have had to accept advertisement promoting the mayor and his administration in the event. To boost their popularity and secure reelection, mayors tend to provide municipal resources for large community events in exchange for shows of support and advertisement in those events. Loyal to the mayor's interests, the leader I was interviewing expressed her dissatisfaction at being unable to profit from the event.

I argue that the strategic attitude deployed by that leader should not be understood in isolation. It is common practice for neighborhood leaders that have engaged in sustained political loyalty networks since the democratic transition to insist on using collective initiatives in the neighborhood to pursue the individual monopoly of political capital. For decades, those networks have exposed these *población* leaders to partisan tactics of political competition. They have thus learned to compete over political capital accumulation in order to increase their personal legitimacy in the neighborhood.

Having already discussed the historical roots of political loyalty, I will now engage with my ethnographic fieldwork to address two ways in which *población* leaders engage in political loyalty networks: clientelism and false protagonism. I will show how community leaders become socialized in these two types of political interaction.

### 3.4.1 Clientelism

My interviews and observations in Nuevo Amanecer suggest that politicians often reciprocate *población* leaders' political loyalty by providing them with rewards. These rewards target loyal local leaders who help maintain politicians' popularity in the neighborhood and help them campaign. Rewards also sometimes reach a group of local dwellers that remain loyal to that leader, either voting for their political candidate or by collaborating in political campaigns. The rewards usually involve privileged (and faster) access to public services and goods. Given this dynamic, people also expect that their political loyalty will be repaid in this way. Students of politics (Hilgers 2012; Stokes et al. 2013) call politicians engaged in networks of clientelism, *patrons*. The citizens who receive resources in exchange for their political support are called *clients*, and those who connect and mediate the relationship between these two agents – clients and patrons – are *brokers*. Neighborhood leaders in Nuevo Amanecer often act as political brokers.

In my fieldwork, I also encountered other residents who are disconnected from these political networks, and only see the work of local organizations from a distance. Some of them judge the functioning of these political dynamics as unfair and call local leaders *"apitutados"* (Group Interview November 17, 2014), which refers to people who receive undeserved benefits from privileged contacts.

In his work on Latin American clientelism, Auyero (2000, 2001) examines grassroots networks in Argentina's shantytowns. He demonstrates that loyalty in clientelist relationships results from the capacity of those connections to provide survival resources. The rampant poverty and large unemployment in Argentinian shantytowns by the end of the 1990s left informal networks bereft of their subsistence provision. With the exhaustion of local solidarity-based survival networks, neighbors resorted to Peronist clientelist networks to access food and medicine. Auyero describes the distribution system of goods, food, and medicine provided by the municipality of Cóspito and managed by local brokers from Villa Paraiso, a shantytown in Buenos Aires. This system constitutes a complex, yet organized structure, involving patrons, brokers, and clients.

Clientelism can also be found in Chilean *poblaciones*. Although similar to Auyero's description, the type of informal redistribution in Santiago's *poblaciones* is less systematic and structured. It is also less visible and less regular than in Villa Paraiso's case because it is highly opportunistic. However, we can still speak of clientelism because, as the following paragraphs will demonstrate, the interaction between politicians, brokers, and clients constructs an association between political loyalty and the expectation of privileged access to resources. This is not to say that all *población* leaders belong to networks of clientelism. Indeed, many of them keep political allegiance to specific political patrons and only engage in clientelist exchanges when the opportunity arises.

The example of Ana, one of my informants in Nuevo Amanecer, demonstrates how local leaders have been politically socialized in their engagement in networks of loyalty and clientelism. Ana grew up in Nuevo Amanecer. She is now in her thirties and has had several part-time jobs in the last few years. She also runs workshops for women, both from the *población* and from wealthier areas of the city, who want to learn crafts. As she proudly told me, demonstrating the quality of her work, "I make the upper class women come all the way to the *población*" (Interview October 28, 2014).

Ana's parents fought against the military during the 1980s; later, her mother began campaigning for local politicians during the No Campaign in 1988. Since then, her family has become connected to local party politics. Ana has always felt a great attachment to her neighborhood. Since she was a girl, she learned about communitarian life and developed close bonds with her community. Her parents and her neighbors taught her the importance of solidarity and of helping others, and she eventually became embedded in the *población*'s networks. Simultaneously, Ana grew up learning the nuances of party politics: "All the campaign launches in this area were here in my house – presidential campaigns, mayoral campaigns, all of them … everyone [every politician] that was running for something came to start their campaign here" (Interview October 28, 2014). Ana explained to me that, with one of the largest populations among Chilean districts, La Florida, is highly regarded by politicians. Nuevo Amanecer, she said, was one of the main strongholds of the Ex-Nueva Mayoría[3] in La Florida.

As a young woman, Ana began to work in campaigns for different politicians. She learned the craft of campaigning and expanded her network of contacts, among both neighbors and politicians. Proving to be skillful, she soon became the campaign manager for one of the major politicians in that zone. Ana explained that her political socialization was facilitated by Socialist politicians working in that area: "[T]hey [politicians] trained me politically from the Socialist side, I learned everything about how to behave, what one has to know, everything about how [electoral] politics works" (Interview October 28, 2014). She identifies both herself and her mother, as "*maquineras*" – people who have become very skillful at imposing their will and influencing others at grassroots level with electoral political aims.

A politician involved in one of the campaigns that Ana led hired her as a civil servant with the municipality. "That was part of my political job," she said (Interview October 28, 2014). Her political contacts allowed her

---

[3] The Ex-Nueva Mayoría refers to the parties that belonged to the Nueva Mayoría coalition between 2014 and 2018.

to hire a few of her loyal neighbors in the municipality. When I met her, Ana was also helping her mother run a *"comité de mejora"* (infrastructure development committee), which allowed them to apply for subsidies to build and refurbish houses for poor elder residents who were still living in emergency wooden dwellings. In this way, the two women expect to earn the gratitude and trust of those elder local dwellers and their families. Through these solidarity endeavors, Ana and her mother promote themselves as valid, effective community leaders. This validation allows them to also act as political brokers, and informally access additional rewards, either for themselves or for loyal community members. For example, the politician that Ana campaigned for eventually paid her expensive medical bills.

This brief story shows how Ana became a campaigner and broker for one of the main local politicians. Ana's experience is a particularly good example of how political parties socialize people who have the potential to become young *población* leaders. Similarly, most other neighborhood leaders are loyal to a local politician and have learned the ways of party work, just as Ana did.

### 3.4.2 Alleged Protagonism

Politicians also reciprocate local leaders' political loyalty in Nuevo Amanecer by providing them with a false sense of protagonism. Some *población* brokers conceive their allegiance to politicians and parties as a way of supporting the political project that best meets their needs. Leaders understand that participation in organizations is a way of playing an active role in that project. Politicians organized gatherings with supportive leaders of the district. Most of those meetings included sessions in which local leaders could theoretically voice their concerns to higher governmental authorities. These meetings usually brought ministers, members of Congress, or high-level executives at state agencies to the neighborhood to listen directly to people's concerns. Being invited to large meetings to discuss local issues with the most important national authorities gave attendees a strong sense of privilege and importance. However, this perceived capacity to influence decisions or hold authorities to account is deceiving.

By the end of 2014, La Florida's health system was experiencing a number of issues. The service was deficient, and most health centers lacked enough doctors. The newly built Hospital of La Florida concentrated most complaints thanks to its extensive service and infrastructure issues. A few politicians from the same coalition planned an event to bring the Health Minister to the district so that residents could discuss their complaints directly with him.

On a Saturday morning in October 2014, a large tent installed next to the hospital welcomed community leaders from all over La Florida district. As I realized later, only supportive, loyal community leaders had been invited. Young party representatives and hired staff arranged the event and coordinated the activity; important politicians and the Minister would arrive later. When community leaders came into the tent that morning, the procedures for the discussion had already been planned and set up. Attendees received a folder containing documents summarizing the issues up for discussion. In these folders, the dysfunctions of the local health system were divided into topics. Attendees joined groups devoted to discussing each of these topics in parallel during the morning. Pre-assigned representatives led each of the discussions. The session in which I participated was devoted specifically to the hospital's infrastructural problems. The plan was that each group would eventually have the opportunity of presenting and discussing their results with higher authorities, including the Minister for Health.

The group representative took notes and guided the session. The hospital manager was also present to answer questions. Attendees discussed several points regarding the hospital's services and presented a few crucial demands to be told to the Health Minister upon her arrival. Some were especially enthusiastic, and spoke of demanding commitments and establishing realistic dates for improvements to the Hospital. Two ladies sitting next to me during the session seemed even more eager to hold authorities accountable; they said "We should ask the Minister to sign a paper with the commitments" (Field notes October 8, 2014).

Convinced that their ideas would make a difference, community leaders engaged in a two-hour-long detailed discussion about the challenges of the new hospital. As the end of the session approached, the discussion shifted from a collective to an individual and personal focus. A few attendees recounted their own unaddressed problems regarding the hospital's services. Their claims were mainly directed to the hospital manager. One lady spoke of her frustration after endless bureaucratic hurdles that had delayed her treatment for months. The healthcare staff had denied her treatment after sending her back and forth from La Florida Hospital to the Sótero del Río Hospital, in Puente Alto. As others explained similar problems, anxiety grew among participants and the discussion became rather heated.

Confronted with this situation, the hospital manager stood up, pointed to her assistant and told the group, "She will take your details to solve each one of these issues" (Field notes October 8, 2014). Once the session ended, the affected attendees gathered around the assistant to provide their personal details and get solutions to their problems. This experience provided me with evidence that highlights the way that these community leaders have learned that attending these events and making informal demands about private issues offers a means of obtaining personal benefits and solutions generally denied to most people.

As it got closer to midday, the temperature in the tent increased. Participants were tired and groggy. But during the break that followed, I also noticed that their moods remained positive and enthusiastic. Attendees were eager to raise their concerns and discuss solutions with authorities. "It seems that the Minister is arriving soon," a lady I knew from a similar past meeting told me (Field notes October 8, 2014).

The Minister was given a warm reception, complete with multiple hugs and handshakes. After greeting the audience, she delivered a 50-minute speech that promoted political support. The talk used country-wide statistics and exemplary cases to highlight the administration's achievements. She also thanked participants and politicians hosting the event for their work. Finally, the Minister explained that despite the government's efforts and great performance, officials could not solve all national problems promptly. The head of the Eastern Metropolitan Health Service as well as other local politicians delivered similar messages. After several hours of discussions and speeches, the crowd's mood had shifted; people now seemed impatient and exhausted.

After this, discussion group representatives were scheduled to present their results to government officials. Only then would local leaders have the opportunity to be heard. However, before this final session started, one of the organizing politicians warned of the little time left for presentations. There were only a few minutes for each group. One by one, group representatives came to the podium and read some notes. I noticed that most of those presentations had been prepared in advance and reproduced almost word by word the content in leaflets handed to local leaders at the start of the event. The outcomes of the discussions conducted earlier in deliberation groups were largely ignored. Furthermore, as each presentation was repeatedly rushed by organizers, people had no time to discuss with authorities the best solutions to the issues they raised. After 20 minutes of presentations, the organizers closed the event. There was no time for a final discussion, a negotiation of priorities, or for establishing commitments.

While leaving the event, I encountered Rafael, a neighborhood council board member from Nuevo Amanecer that I had met in the neighborhood a few weeks before. I asked him about his impressions of the event as we walked together. He told me about his strong historical loyalty to the organizing political coalition. "I started working in their campaigns at the beginning of the 1990s," he said. He seemed thrilled by the event; he was honored to be invited to an event with the Minister: "It's really a privilege that we have here, that our politicians invite the Minister here" (Field notes October 8, 2014).

Despite the fact that authorities had ignored most of the discussions and the concerns voiced by local leaders that morning, Rafael felt like a protagonist whose words and actions were critical in improving his neighborhood's well-being. Rafael saw himself as a special member of the community, as part of a network of socially engaged leaders with direct access to important politicians. Several other local leaders also spoke to me about this notion of protagonism that Rafael so clearly conveyed. As Ana told me, describing her first years as a broker, "I felt part of a group that was doing great social work, we were making a difference, providing services for people" (Interview October 28, 2014).

This false sense of protagonism has developed over the years as leaders engage in encounters that strengthen their commitment to durable networks of political loyalty. In those networks, they have acquired a sense of worthiness, both for themselves and their immediate community. These repeated interactions with political machines shape local leaders' identity and role in their neighborhood. Local leaders think of their brokering position in the community as gratifying, as one that serves a political project and contributes to the local community's well-being. Aware of how deceiving this role developed by local leaders can be, a few neighborhood residents that regularly do not engage in community organizing, skeptically assimilated this alleged protagonism I have described with the entitlement that royalty provides. "[Community leaders in Nuevo Amanecer] feel as if they were sitting in a throne when they sit in the [neighborhood council's] office," one of them told me (Interview December 12, 2014).

### 3.5 MONOPOLIZING POLITICAL CAPITAL

Several community leaders in a neighborhood usually compete over political capital in the area. They will thus become skillful and fierce political competitors in their neighborhoods. This will legitimize those leaders as effective brokers within political networks.

As I show in the next paragraphs, the dynamics of political capital accumulation prevent local leaders from advancing historical continuity in their community. They could only make prior mobilization relevant for present community members by legitimizing experiences, symbols, and tactics of the past. In other words, current local leaders could only connect past and present collective action by investing their effort in politically socializing other *población* dwellers. Contributing to memory-building would require for leaders to become community mediators or, as Yiftachel (2009) calls them, "cultural agents." In other words, these leaders need to promote narratives of the past as they build trust, support, and involve other dwellers in their practices (McIntosh and Youniss 2010). However, community leaders' persistent attempts to monopolize political capital excludes training or mentoring others. Only in very exceptional, cases – such as Ana and her mother's – would leaders teach other residents their tactics and knowledge. These actions would have to prove useful in boosting the legitimacy of leader's political network. In this case, promoting historical continuity would not allow that.

The anecdote I provide here depicts this dynamic. A land dispute emerged in *población* Santa Teresa, next to Nuevo Amanecer. Several housing committees gathering dozens of families from different parts of La Florida, requested their social housing project to be built in an area called Las Tinajas, in that same district, in their meetings with local authorities. These committees had spent years applying for housing subsidies and arranging their social housing procurement. Yet, their plan was rejected by local authorities over unclear technical issues. Suspecting that municipal officials wanted to use those lots with other means, these families decided to protest by invading a vacant land in the northwest of Santa Teresa. Some months before, municipal planning officials had also rejected a request to erect social housing on that same land by a group of housing committees belonging to the same neighborhood, Santa Teresa. The terrain had topographical issues that prevented building on that land, planning officials argued. After much waiting and many bureaucratic difficulties, the families in these housing committees also decided to mobilize. Coordinated by a local broker who was loyal to high-ranking La Florida municipal officials, the protests that these families organized targeted the squatters and created a heated conflict in the area.

Simultaneously, a local member of Congress organized a *cabildo* in Santa Teresa's central square. This *cabildo* was a large meeting that summoned local dwellers and government officials to discuss issues affecting the area. On this occasion, the meeting included a group of high-ranking authorities from the central government and the local police station. The head of the Ministry's Regional Secretariat for Housing and Urban Development was among them. The meeting created working groups of residents discussing problems such as transportation, health-care, and security. Most squatting families in Santa Teresa attended the *cabildo* and created a working group to specifically deal with their housing provision issue.

In an attempt to obstruct the *cabildo*, Santa Teresa's housing committees organized a counter-rally. Around 250 people marched around the neighborhood and reached the neighborhood main square when the *cabildo* had just begun. A municipal official I had met several days before and who was well-known to many local residents, was present at the rally. The crowd appeared at the square raising banners and chanting "Yes to Santa Teresa! No to those from outside!" referring to the squatters that were occupying the land under dispute in Santa Teresa. For a couple of minutes, the marching crowd stood in front of the square repeating its slogan. Suddenly, the community leader heading the counter-rally took a few steps forward and shouted defiantly toward *cabildo* organizers. She vehemently blamed the member of Congress at the *cabildo* for the social housing shortage in the district and yelled offensive remarks to other community leaders who were collaborating with the event at the square. The municipal official at the rally supported her colleague and also yelled a few discrediting accusations to the member of Congress and the leaders at the *cabildo*.

Once the frenzy of shouts and slogans subsided, *cabildo* organizers invited people in the rally to participate in their meeting. Joining the *cabildo* was the best way to unite and solve the area's housing problem, organizers at the square suggested. Although seemingly confused and undecided at first, most rally participants walked across to the square and joined the *cabildo*. In what seemed like an act of desperation, the rally leader reacted by calling on participants of the *cabildo* to join her protest, but even more of her supporters joined the *cabildo,* leaving her and the municipal official standing on the road, alone. Defeated, the rally leader eventually decided to join her fellow neighbors in the *cabildo*. The municipal official, on the other hand, shouted a few additional insults at the *cabildo* organizers and left. Working groups at the square resumed their discussions and the *cabildo* proceeded normally. Although the *cabildo* allowed housing committee leaders to raise their concerns in front of authorities, further conflicts between local brokers would eventually revert negotiations and extend the quarrel between those *población* dwellers.

Although this may seem like a specific conflict, it describes the extent to which competition over political capital can pervert the relationship between local organizations and political institutions at the neighborhood level. My interviews and observations suggest that these aggressive disputes over local legitimacy are not uncommon between community leaders in *poblaciones*. In fact, I was able to identify at least three tactics used by these leaders when competing over political capital in their neighborhood.

Defamation. Describing the actions of community leaders in Nuevo Amanecer, a social worker that I interviewed at the neighborhood health center explained to me: "[local leaders] are always fighting among themselves ... as soon as one of them leaves [a meeting], the others [leaders] tell you bad stuff about her; and the one who left will later smear other leaders ... and it goes on like this all the time" (Interview October 30, 2014). Indeed, in my interviews, community leaders regularly defamed opposing local leaders and residents. Used to this rhetorical tactic to gain support among *población* dwellers, these leaders often imagined that their gossiping and defamation would also gain my trust and validation. In accusing others of betraying local dwellers or of stealing public funds, local leaders portray themselves as loyal and honest in contrast. Additional questions in my interviews and my knowledge of the community usually revealed those defamations to be unwarranted. Leaders use defamation, however, as a way of legitimizing themselves as valid, effective brokers. In other words, they use this tactic to boost their political capital in the neighborhood.

Self-attribution. Community leaders also regularly refer to collective accomplishments as their own personal success. Community leaders use this tactic to elevate their image as effective community supporters. Like politicians in ribbon-cutting ceremonies, leaders attempt to show that they have accomplished things on behalf of local residents' interests. When describing their involvement in successful applications to access state funding for infrastructural refurbishments or neighborhood projects, local leaders invariably neglected the collective nature of those accomplishments, usually attributing full responsibility to themselves. For example, referring to street-paving programs implemented in the 1990s in Nuevo Amanecer and other *poblaciones*, a local leader promoted himself by telling me "I was the one fighting to get roads paved back then!" (Interview 22 October 2014). Similarly, after years of meetings with community leaders from different parts of Nuevo Amanecer, a participatory budget program built a new community center in a previously abandoned building of the neighborhood. Describing her work in

Nuevo Amanecer, one of the leaders referred to that new center as her personal achievement; "I got (*conseguí*) them to make that center," she told me (Interview October 9, 2014).

Imposition. Community leaders, and especially those acting as political brokers, are highly skillful at what residents call *"pasar máquina."* This means the ability to impose their will in any collective decision-making process at the *población* to the benefit of their political network. In other words, these local leaders will attend neighborhood meetings with the goal of imposing their decisions on others. This tactic, sometimes, includes insulting or discrediting contenders in those meetings. For example, a councilman who attended several meetings for a participatory program coordinated by the municipality in Nuevo Amanecer described how aggressive interactions were by telling me "They [community leaders] almost took each other's eyes out" (Interview October 27, 2014). A young resident who also attended several of those meetings confirmed this impression: "They [local leaders] just said whatever, they even said, like [mean] personal stuff to each other," he told me (Interview November 11, 2014). My inquiry reveals that local leaders see their participation in collective initiatives as an opportunity to advance their own political power in the neighborhood. In other words, many neighborhood leaders understand occasions of community deliberation as instances to legitimize their ability to channel political loyalty and resources toward both, their local group of clients and their patrons. In this way, they boost their political capital and exclude opposing agents from decision-making processes.

These disputes over political capital perpetuate people's sense of historical discontinuity and deepen the mechanics of political exclusion in post-dictatorial *poblaciones*. Following Till (2005), the stability in time that the physicality of the neighborhood provides is not enough to politicize it. Exercises of memory-building need to bring forward people's desire to represent scenes, events, and characters from the past in the present. But the symbols of prior mobilization, which would have the potential of empowering the community, are missing in Nuevo Amanecer. Former MIR leaders remain absent and delegitimized, in a past that is excluded from present neighborhood struggles. Several current community leaders once knew the tactics and symbols by which the MIR challenged the inequalities and injustice experienced by the urban poor. However, their insistence on political capital accumulation prevents them from using these symbols and sharing their knowledge with other residents. The structures of interaction by which community leaders situate themselves as political agents – what Somers (1994) calls "relational settings" – consequently neglect the emancipatory lessons of prior mobilization. In fact, murals, songs, or frames exalting the MIR or prior mobilization were particularly rare in Nuevo Amanecer. Local residents only used MIR symbolism – for example, the red and black colors, the star in the MIR flag, and allusions to the Cuban revolution – on the neighborhood's anniversary. Local leaders may often contribute to people's access to services and goods, but the relational settings they promote in the neighborhood also advance the post-dictatorial dynamics of exclusion in Chile's urban margins. This is because local leaders' struggles over political legitimacy instrumentalize *población* dwellers to advance one of the tactics by which political institutions have demobilized the urban poor in the past three decades, namely the intervention and external management of political capital in the urban margins.

However, community leaders should not be seen as villains. Their behavior demonstrates the pressure they experience in order to achieve a sense of community protagonism in a highly exclusionary political context. Their ability to channel public resources toward their community depends on their sustained validation within political networks that tend to instrumentalize urban communities with electoral goals. In other words, Chile's machinery of democratic local governance makes these leaders' participation conditional on their loyalty to political patrons. They, therefore, embody the exclusionary citizenship regime of Chile's urban margins. Developing a mobilizing identity in this context is particularly challenging.

## 3.6 THE FAILURE OF MOBILIZING IDENTITY

Building an SMC in neighborhoods like Nuevo Amanecer and Lo Hermida requires a set of shared mobilizing symbols that cut across a large portion of local organizations and that will motivate unity in cases of urgent shared grievances. As I argue in later chapters, this is present in Lo Hermida. The dynamics I describe above, however, prevent mobilizing identity symbols from emerging in Nuevo Amanecer.

"Belonging" refers to the solidarity that community members share; it is the "mutual recognition that they are part of a single social unit" (Melucci 2000, 2). Belonging advances mobilization when people acknowledge common issues and attribute their causes to a broader cultural, social, and political system. This realization boosts people's self-esteem. As underprivileged urban dwellers use belonging to reject stigmatizing meanings, they are able to challenge exclusionary, oppressive institutions. As I describe above, instead of uniting to recognize the institutional responsibilities underlying their grievances, local dwellers in Santa Teresa, Nuevo Amanecer, and other *poblaciones* often blame each other.

Simultaneously, communities use mobilizing boundaries to promote differentiation and cohesion through attributions of injustice and the identification of specific antagonists. Just as boundary-making activates shared emotional reactions of anger, it also motivates mobilization. However, my observations in Nuevo Amanecer suggest that instead of advancing differentiation, local organizations attempt to resemble municipal institutions. For example, when asked about their role in the *población*, neighborhood council leaders neglected their democratic function as a grassroots civil society organization, and gave me a list of services and aid they provide in the *población*. They spoke about the neighborhood council's tasks of issuing official residence certificates, responding to neighbors' enquiries, and managing the neighborhood *sede* (local community building). These leaders also described how they coordinate fundraising activities, organize events that bring politicians to their *sede*, and manage the municipality's yearly delivery of Christmas gifts to local children. Procedures in local organizations also imitate formal bureaucratic municipal agencies, further precluding boundary-building. The weekly council's schedule was regular, well-structured, and clearly written down in proceedings and on a public board. It indicated the weekly bookings for each building room and the meetings that the council holds every Monday. Their *sede* was open to the public during office hours, every evening of the week, between seven and ten. This *sede* was also an aesthetic demonstration of how much the council considers itself a public institution; the building was clean, well-maintained, and regularly renovated. Tiles formed an outdoor corridor that extends around a futsal pitch. Doors around this corridor led to offices, large meeting rooms, and storage rooms. Like the municipality, the building is surrounded by fences and has a full-time guard, a neighbor who lives in the building.

Furthermore, this failure of mobilizing identity in Nuevo Amanecer is manifest in local organizations' inability to promote cohesion when engaging in collaborative endeavors. Instead, neighborhood collective decision processes tend to stimulate community fragmentation. For example, community leaders' battles over political capital tend to obstruct the implementation of participatory programs, which are occasions that tailor state resources to strengthen community cohesion.

The Neighborhood Recovery Program's (NRP, also known as "Quiero Mi Barrio") execution in Nuevo Amenecer is a prime example of this issue. This is an urban regeneration program managed by the Chilean Ministry of Housing and Urban Development that refurbishes and builds community infrastructure in underprivileged neighborhoods across the country using participatory budgeting. Implemented in early 2007 in Nuevo Amanecer, the program brought together neighborhood leaders in regular meetings with ministry officials, municipality agents, local police officials, building company architects and engineers, and other stakeholders to agree on the developments to be carried out. Several of the leaders attending these meetings were then acting as political brokers in durable relationships of clientelism, and, thus, saw the NRP as an opportunity to increase their political capital. For example, Ana's mother, Carla, who is a well-known leader and broker in the neighborhood, decided to use those meetings to push for the building of a new square that would benefit a group of local, loyal residents. Referring to them as her "ladies," Carla explained to me how she vehemently insisted on the square during NRP meetings by saying: "I pushed forward the square because it is important for my ladies ... and [by doing that] I also make the people I work with [i.e., a politician or patron] happy" (Interview October 22, 2014). As I discovered later, her tenacity and obstinace in these meetings would eventually allow her to impose her will over others. But as she told me, by pushing her interests forward with such determination she was, in fact, defending her legitimacy within her local network of political loyalty. Since other local political brokers used the same tactic when attending these meetings, the NRP became a stagnant clash of interests, in which aggression escalated. Other local leaders, *población* residents, and stakeholders attending these meetings resented the hostility. Many of them, hence, stopped participating.

This issue contributed to substantially delaying the NRP's implementation. A social worker in Nuevo Amanecer's health center who attended several of the meetings, for example, told me: "going to those meetings was terrible ... there were some people who went there only to crush [people] with a machine (*pasar máquina*)" (Interview October 30, 2014). "We thought that it [the NRP implementation] could explode ... and that all the work we had done would be over," a government official coordinating and supervising the NRP in Nuevo Amanecer told me (Interview October 13, 2017). The program could only move forward once this official and his colleagues decided to lobby local leaders directly by negotiating the neighborhood projects separately with each one of them (Interview October 13, 2017).

Conflicts over legitimacy in Nuevo Amanecer lead to community fragmentation, which affects how local residents think about place-making. In fact, residents, as well as leaders and local politicians, learn to conceive of the neighborhood as multiple small pockets of political allegiance. Local residents describe this notion as the "*color político*" (political color) of particular neighborhood squares, buildings, or organizations. In other words, local dwellers label organizations and buildings depending on their loyalty to political parties or patrons. What residents refer to as "political color" determines how trustworthy and available the different areas of the neighborhood are to organizations and politicians. In fact, community leaders consider neighborhood *sedes* critical assets for the accumulation of political capital. For example, neighborhood council leaders often use community buildings to cooperate in their patrons' political campaigning. Candidates bring cake and drinks to their loyal *sede* to attract potential supporters prior to elections.

In this context, an organization that uses the *sede* to hold one of its events is indicating to the rest of the community that its political allegiance, or "*color politico*," coincides with that of the building. Therefore, community leaders and organizations that want to remain politically impartial in the neighborhood are reluctant to coordinate initiatives in one of the colored *sedes*.

For instance, I witnessed how in late 2014 La Casita Periférica members struggled to decide on whether they should borrow a stage on which invited artists could perform in the *población* anniversary celebration from a politically colored neighborhood council. A fellow *poblador* had failed to deliver on his promise to lend the organization a small stage, and the easiest option was borrowing a modular stage belonging to the largest neighborhood council in Nuevo Amanecer. A couple of La Casita Periférica members emphatically refused to approach the neighborhood council leaders. They did not want to become locally labeled supporters of what they saw as the municipality's political network. But having a stage was essential for the event they had organized, and the funds they had raised with a raffle were not enough to rent or buy it. The group only decided to borrow the stage from the council unwillingly, and after exhausting all of their alternative informal connections within and outside the *población*.

These multiple divisions within the neighborhood reflect a weak neighborhood collective identity and the absence of mobilizing symbols in Nuevo Amanecer. In addition, local leaders' insistence on accumulating political capital precludes any potential opportunity they may have to decentralize protagonism. I have already discussed leaders' disinterest in politically socializing other *población* dwellers.

This tactic is particularly apparent in the case of local leaders' distance from the neighborhood's youth. *Población* young people are often "biographically available" because they usually have flexible jobs and live only a few blocks away from where activism occurs. In addition, they are more drawn to participate in identity-building initiatives than their adult counterparts. In other words, *población* youths have personal circumstances that lower their participation costs, thus making their recruitment for collective initiatives more likely (McAdam 1986; Milkman 2017).

However, Nuevo Amanecer leaders' strong concern with accumulating political capital prevents them from offering opportunities for socialization to the youth. In other words, local leaders are not available to teach the youths about the contents and tactics of neighborhood organizing. Socializing tactics would involve sharing, and not accumulating, political capital, and would be the only possible way of decentralizing protagonism. Community leaders' inability to take advantage of young people's socializing potential can be observed across Chilean *poblaciones*. La Casita Periférica, in Nuevo Amanecer, is also a good depiction of this problem. In fact, my interviews and observations indicate that instead of helping and encouraging La Casita Periférica members, older community leaders regularly undermined their work by excluding them from meetings and making discrediting remarks about them in conversations with other neighbors. In turn, La Casita Periférica avoided collaborating with other local leaders unless strictly necessary. In contrast, several La Casita Periférica members would obtain political socialization at the *ruka* (building of spiritual and medical significance for Mapuche people) located in Nuevo Amanecer, which demonstrates their interest in taking advantage of socializing opportunities. The *Lonco* (tribe chief) and *Machi* (tribe doctor) at the *ruka* welcomed the local youths in regular activities in which they provided training on spiritual matters, Mapuche ideology, organizational tactics, and *Mapudugún* (Mapuche language) (Field notes December 11, 2014).

### 3.7 CONCLUSION

This chapter has focused on my ethnographic work in Nuevo Amanecer in order to examine the causes of social demobilization in *poblaciones*. I show the exclusionary mechanics of citizenship-building in Chile's urban margins. The framework I used to develop my argument pays special attention to community dynamics of political capital development.

In line with similar systems of exclusion in cities across the world, political processes in post-dictatorial Chile shaped local political interactions in underprivileged urban communities by intervening their sources of legitimacy-building. In other words, community leaders in *poblaciones* saw their ability to promote contentious politics undermined by new arrangements of power among elite actors. On the one hand, elite allies and institutions withdrew the support they had given to neighborhood organizing. Consequently, urban communities experienced a sudden sharp decrease in their mobilizing resources, which included human, social, infrastructural, and financial resources. The end of the Vicariate of Solidarity in 1992, for example, was critical in this regard. The Vicariate was a progressive office from the Chilean Catholic Church that defended human rights and helped grassroots mobilizing during the dictatorship. Most community kitchens and children's camps in *poblaciones* received the Vicariate's support. Its closure meant the sudden end of financial and human resources for local organizations. On the other hand, elite actors and institutions discouraged mobilization by externally controlling the dynamics of legitimacy in underprivileged urban communities. Politicians and government officials, for instance, framed contentious politics as a threat to Chile's newly acquired democracy, thus increasing the credibility of moderate *población* leaders ready to withhold their demands for social rights.

The chapter explores the micro-politics of Nuevo Amanecer to explain why so many urban communities reacted passively to these systems of political exclusion. Consequently, the four dimensions of mobilizational citizenship – agentic memory, mobilizing belonging, mobilizing boundaries, and decentralized protagonism – fail to develop. Agentic memory fails because acts of memory-building deepen a disrupted sense of historical community development, thus preventing local dwellers from using the past as a source of agency. My comparative analysis gives a key role to people's diminished sense of historical continuity in those communities. In other words, local dwellers conceive symbols of prior mobilization as disconnected from the present and not a legitimate way to motivate current actions. In this context, memory-building is unable to use events, scenes, or characters of the past to demonstrate the community's ability to subvert oppressive experiences. Mobilizational citizenship is hence hindered in its first steps.

The democratizing process that *población* dwellers had been developing for more than a decade was disrupted by the dictatorship. Pinochet's authoritarian regime crushed the socialist project that had hitherto served as the framework to explain and motivate collective action in the urban margins. The government severely repressed activism and political dissent. Most leftist *población* leaders were persecuted or killed. In addition, the promises made by the UP government were dismissed by the dictatorship. President Allende's pledge included social security and urban services to *población* dwellers. People in the urban margins, therefore, experienced frustration and uncertainty regarding their livelihood.

In most of these *poblaciones,* the pro-democracy national protests of the 1980s were coordinated by moderate party activists from the AD, who fall on the center and left of the political spectrum. These parties exercised a managerial type of leadership in these neighborhoods that did not reconnect local activism with symbols of prior mobilization. People's sense of historical discontinuity, therefore, persisted.

Party activists also created networks of political loyalty with community leaders in *poblaciones.* In the decades after the democratic transition, these political interactions endured and often became clientelist relationships. These networks of loyalty gave community leaders a sense of worthiness and protagonism while also excluding them from public policy decisions. Furthermore, in order to succeed in their role as brokers between local residents and political patrons, these community leaders have had to compete over political capital in their neighborhoods. Consequently, local leaders become unwilling to politically socialize other local dwellers. These dynamics deepen the community's inability to connect with symbols of prior mobilization and promote their passive engagement in systems of political exclusion.

Mobilizing belonging and boundaries fails because the micro-politics of local organizing in Nuevo Amanecer have remained aligned with institutional, mainstream systems of political incorporation. Paradoxically, however, Chile's mainstream mechanisms of participatory governance reinforce political exclusion because they push community leaders to instrumentalize other residents in order to enhance their legitimacy in networks of clientelism. Advancing a mobilizing identity in this context would require sourcing symbols that have retained meaning over time and provide lessons for the development of contentious politics. Yet, as I have argued, community members do not use symbols of prior mobilization for this purpose. Instead of resisting stigmatization by attributing the cause of their grievances to a broader social system, residents use what Wacquant (2010) calls "lateral denigration." In other words, local dwellers use stigmatizing, defamatory language to blame each other for the injustice they suffer. Similarly, instead of advancing differentiating identity boundaries, local organizations try to resemble local government agencies in their internal structure, procedures, and aesthetics.

Protagonism can advance mobilizational citizenship if community leaders transmit mobilizing identity as political capital. This tactic spreads leadership skills among other activists and makes them valid agents of community-building. However, grassroots organizations in Nuevo Amanecer fail in decentralizing protagonism because community leaders are not concerned with training others. Instead, they strive to accumulate and monopolize political capital.

Mobilized, exceptional underprivileged urban communities like Lo Hermida provide a contrasting case to my analysis. Activists in those *poblaciones* produced an alternative type of political incorporation after Chile's democratic transition. This new form of politicization has allowed them to sustain mobilization despite the different institutional systems of political exclusion that I outlined in this chapter. In the following chapters, I use the mobilizational citizenship framework to explain these distinct social and political developments.

# 4

# Memory of Subversion

## 4.1 INTRODUCTION

In this chapter, I trace the processes of history and memory that explain mobilizational citizenship in Chile's urban margins. In the previous chapter, I focused on the case of Nuevo Amanecer to address the phenomenon of demobilization of most *poblaciones* after the democratic transition in 1990. I used the idea of prior mobilization to describe a variety of forms of collective action that operated in the decade before the coup d'état in the urban margins, and currently function as neighborhood activists' initial reference point for initiatives of contentious politics (see Figure 3.1). In both communities acting as case studies in this book, Lo Hermida and Nuevo Amanecer, their urban dwellers' intense experience of prior mobilization had a foundational impact. Through the collective acts to invade urban land and struggle over social rights, people in these *poblaciones* created bonds of collaboration, produced community identity, and built expectations of the future. I also explained how a socialist project of society functioned as a discursive framework for this prior mobilization. This project advanced the empowerment of the working class and strong redistributive policies, thus organizing people's expectation of a prosperous livelihood and political future.

The sense of community discontinuity to which the dictatorship exposed *población* dwellers is a key point of departure between my case studies in this book. By violently disconnecting urban communities' prior mobilization from their experience after the coup d'état in 1973, the dictatorship hindered people's ability to draw on the past to motivate actions in the present. In other words, referring to past collective action became an illegitimate tactic to promote mobilization among current community members. Consequently, most communities in Chilean *poblaciones* were unable to build alternative explanations for the social and political positions they developed after the coup. The managerial type of leadership that AD party activists used during the 1980s to coordinate protests in *poblaciones* did not reactivate or draw on symbols of prior mobilization. In turn, urban dwellers passively engaged in a set of demobilizing political dynamics imposed to *poblaciones* in Chile's democratization process. My process tracing of Nuevo Amanecer in Chapter 3 demonstrates how this sense of political discontinuity endured in the urban margins, thus preventing mobilizational citizenship from developing.

In particular urban communities like Lo Hermida, however, radical political groups coordinating anti-dictatorial mobilizations in the 1980s developed local, insurgent leadership structures. This chapter describes how these radical militants entered neighborhood organizations and developed insurgent leadership to socialize community organizers and reactivate past narratives and tactics of collective action. In the years that followed, connecting present and past identity symbols through initiatives of mobilization has become a key part of *pobladores'* repertoire of contention in Lo Hermida.

I also show activists' commitment to implementing initiatives of self-management to mobilize the resources required for collective action. This is a key tactic sourced from mobilizations of the past. Local activists' relational settings also further advance their sense of historical continuity. In other words, they draw lessons about their relationships with external social actors from the past to shape their current political interactions. This sense of historical continuity is a first step in the development of a community's sense of agentic memory.

The chapter also explains how *población* activists use this sense of continuity as a current platform to performatively re-signify and subvert oppressive events from the past. In this way, collective memory makes community construction unconditional for local dwellers, thus boosting a notion of collective power and agency. Agentic memory advances mobilizational citizenship because it successfully produces and reproduces a political community that extends across the years and is able to empower *población* organizers today. The chapter demonstrates that engaging in *pobladores'* historical struggle is a source of political incorporation and dignity for local dwellers.

This chapter is organized in three steps. I begin by providing additional details on how radical leftist militants entered Lo Hermida's organizations in 1982 and developed an insurgent leadership among local residents.

I examine how in those years they activated a sense of historical continuity within neighborhoods like Lo Hermida. Second, I describe the ways in which activists currently use memory-building in their collective action. Finally, I explain how they create a sense of historical continuity as a platform to develop agentic memory. That is to say, they strategically resort to the past to become empowered in their current social interactions.

## 4.2 THE ORIGIN OF SUBVERSIVE LEADERSHIP

The case of Lo Hermida presents a contrasting historical process to the experiences of Nuevo Amanecer and most other *poblaciones*. Lo Hermida's activists and other community members demonstrate a clear tendency to connect present and past, which allows local dwellers to source identity symbols and relational lessons from the past. According to my process tracing, the origin of this dynamic lies on the subversive type of leadership that political groups exercised in the neighborhood while organizing anti-dictatorial protests in the 1980s. This subversive leadership style managed to politically socialize urban dwellers and update symbols of prior mobilization. As I evidence here, this process linked people's actions in the present with the socialist project of society and the broader long-standing struggle of the poor in the urban margins.

It was political parties on the left operating underground that coordinated and supported civil society's resistance against the dictatorship during the 1980s (Garretón 1989; Oxhorn 1995). However, the PC, together with other political groups on the radical side of the left who also used Communist tactics, developed a closer and more organic relationship with *población* residents. This type of grassroots interaction was the source of subversive leadership in the urban margins.

In the late 1940s, as a reaction to Gonzalez Videla's repressive government, the PC decided to redirect some of its energy traditionally devoted to trade unions to focus on expanding its constituency in *poblaciones*. In this process, "[t]he party emphasized the development of an alternate political culture – linking the collective identity and world view of the poor to that of the party itself" (Schneider 1995, 38). Unlike most other parties, Communists understood the development of their party and the empowerment of grassroots organizations as interdependent (Portes 1976). For decades, their work in trade unions had involved politically training and recruiting grassroots leaders, thus perfecting the tactics of subversive leadership. Consequently, Communist activists' work in *poblaciones* created more democratic interactions and organic connections with local leaders and organizations. With the goal of recruiting *población* dwellers into their ranks, Communist activists provided them with political socialization. They trained *población* dwellers on ideology, militant tactics, and leadership skills (Schneider 1991).

These tactics distinguished Communist activism in the early 1980s, when party activists entered *poblaciones* to coordinate protests against the dictatorship. Taking advantage of the sanitary emergency caused by the 1982 flooding of the San Carlos Canal in Lo Hermida, several leftist militants entered the *población* (see Chapter 2). One of my interviewees, Alvaro, became part of a group of Communist militants who infiltrated the community in Lo Hermida on that occasion. "There was an environment [in which many people carried out acts] of solidarity – and of course we also felt solidarity toward the people [who suffered the flooding] – but we also used the opportunity to get into Lo Hermida," he told me (Interview, July 30, 2017).

Alvaro grew up in a *población* and joined the *Jota* (the Communist Youth) when he was 14 years old. Soon after, he created a party cell in his community and campaigned to support Allende's election in 1970. He would eventually receive intelligence and military training in the Soviet Union and Hungary. During the dictatorship, Alvaro continued working for the party as an undercover militant. He was in charge of organizing propaganda initiatives to challenge the regime and recruiting citizens to participate in acts of resistance against the dictatorship. "The instructions [of the party] were to infiltrate social organizations; to get into neighborhood councils, neighborhood soccer clubs, local churches, or any other organization to start activating resistance [against the dictatorship] from there" (Interview, July 30, 2017). Eventually, in the late 1970s, he was arrested by the National Intelligence Agency (CNI) and held in the Borgoño clandestine detention center, before spending time in prisons in Pisagua and in remote islands off the south coast of Chile.

When he entered Lo Hermida in 1982, Alvaro was a highly trained militant in his late 20s. He and his group of Communist militants entered the *población* camouflaged as a collective of university student volunteers who came to help urban residents affected by the flooding. While his party colleagues joined aid squads and other local organizations in the neighborhood, Alvaro began attending meetings with local residents and NGOs in the local parishes, Espíritu Santo, Pedro Pescador, and Esperanza. "We went as university volunteers, to shovel mud out of the houses, help organizing community kitchens, and help in everything that was happening after the flooding," he explained (Interview, July 30, 2017).

As the militants explored the different neighborhood associations, they began identifying people with potential to be recruited to join the PC. Some local dwellers, for example, had previous political experience in the parties of the left, but were too afraid to engage in public initiatives during the dictatorship. The PC thought that these local dwellers would be more likely to join the resistance against the dictatorship if they obtained some support and protection from the party. In addition, several young residents who had no experience in political matters seemed highly motivated to join the struggle against the regime. After careful observation, these PC militants selected some candidates who they thought they could convince to join them in activities of PRPM.

Alvaro explained the initial screening process: "[W]e observed the person, their role in the community, their dominance, how they influenced others, their sharpness of mind, and how cooperative they are to others" (Interview, July 30, 2017). The selection process also included triangulating the candidate's information with other trusted local residents. In order to avoid recruiting a potential snitch by mistake, party militants also structured the candidate's incorporation process in steps. They were first invited to a meeting to assess their commitment to the party's cause. After that, they were asked to carry out a few secret errands for the party. These first steps were conducted in almost complete isolation from the rest of the local Communist network. Eventually, the new neighborhood recruits would join the party and come together to form a local cell in charge of coordinating and implementing acts of PRPM. Acts of PRPM involved a set of violent and nonviolent mobilization tactics that included actions such as painting murals, building barricades to block roads, and engaging in clashes with the military and the police using stones and Molotov cocktails.

These cells belonged to what the party called the *Milicias Rodriguistas*, or MR, which included the different groups of *población* grassroots activists by which the Communist Party implemented PRPM initiatives (Bravo 2010; Reyes 2016). The most protected places to gather and coordinate protests for these MR cells were in neighborhood parishes. The youth group meetings that occurred regularly in the local churches provided the ideal spaces for older, more experienced militants to connect with younger, inexperienced activists. While these MR cells worked in relative isolation from each other, the new party militants would regularly receive training from other Communist members. Key to their survival was learning the party's organizational procedures to work undercover, which was important to avoid being detected by state security agents. The party taught them about Communist ideology and kept them informed of national events that would not appear in the mainstream media. Sometimes, the new party militants would receive training on how to manipulate firearms. "I taught some of them how to use a gun . . . not because they would often need to fire them, but for their safety, [just in case] they needed to use one to defend themselves," Alvaro specified (Interview, July 30, 2017). Around a dozen Communist cells were created in Lo Hermida in those years. Alvaro's team of Communist militants continued to promote the contentious mobilization of local dwellers in Lo Hermida for many months after the flooding. Eventually, the connections that they created in the neighborhood would become instrumental to coordinate collective action in the national protests that erupted in 1983.

Several other political groups belonging to the MDP also took advantage of the flooding as an opportunity for undercover militants to infiltrate Lo Hermida in the early 1980s. These included the FPMR, the MJL, and, to a lesser degree, the MIR and a group of radical Socialist militants. Like the Communist militants, these political groups exercised a subversive type of leadership when entering Lo Hermida. They initially became well-established in Lo Hermida's first zone, before expanding across the whole neighborhood by socializing, recruiting, and promoting the PRPM among local dwellers.

My interviews indicate that MDP parties' subversive leadership in Lo Hermida also involved broadening their work beyond their party cells to build bridges *between* militant groups, incorporating the rest of the community in their activism, and amplifying their impact beyond the neighborhood. MDP leaders and party members began creating these neighborhood inter-party connections by engaging in local organizations outside of their cells, including those organizations running children's camps or community kitchens. Soon after, other initiatives further fostered network expansion. A group of MIR militants, for example, implemented the Cultural Action Workshop (TAC) that gave leadership training to local community organizers. In these workshops, party and nonparty activists of different ages and backgrounds could mingle and learn about organizational issues such as conflict resolution, gender inclusion, and negotiation skills. The TAC additionally involved literacy programs for community members in which militants also taught political curricula.

In addition, militants from different groups carried out regular secret informal gatherings to discuss current events, ideology, social theory, and philosophy. As one former Socialist militant who regularly attended those meetings told me, "I didn't know which parties they [other attendants] were from . . . I know that one of them was from the *Frente* [FPMR], there was another one from the PC and [another] from the MIR ... each week, one of us prepared a topic and we discussed in the group" (Interview, January 25, 2013). In addition to these initiatives in the neighborhood, these groups gave their members in Lo Hermida access to larger territorial organizations that coordinated the activism of different neighborhoods in the east of Santiago. Neighborhood leaders and activists who had joined a party cell could therefore attend meetings and a yearly congress to participate in policy decisions of the parties of the left to resist the dictatorship at the city and the national levels.

This subversive leadership implemented by parties on the radical left reconnected Lo Hermida's community members with the experiences, behaviors, and rhetoric that had organized their prior mobilization. They did so in three ways, which I outline here.

First, party militants put the poor back at the center of political action. As I explain in detail earlier in this book, parties on the left strongly supported different types of prior mobilization tactics, thus making the poor the protagonists of their own struggle for rights. The party policy of recruiting and training in *poblaciones* during the 1980s brought this commitment to empowering the urban underprivileged back to the center of attention. For example, the mass uprising that MDP militants planned – aiming to topple the dictatorship – was intended to be led by subversive urban and rural communities. In fact, Lo Hermida was among the communities that these militants declared as "liberated territories" (Pérez 2013, 270). These were politically conscious communities that radical militants on the left identified as the foci of subversion. In these *poblaciones,* revolutionary groups were present in high concentration, and local residents were especially ready to use violent means to confront the regime's military forces in days of protest.[1] When I asked a former leader in Lo Hermida about the difference between the MDP and other parties on the left, she eloquently explained that "[MJL and FPMR militants] were with the people and from the people, the other parties were not like that" (Interview, February 23, 2013). These grassroots empowering policies represented a sharp contrast from the more managerial leadership that moderate parties on the left simultaneously exercised in Nuevo Amanecer and most other *poblaciones.*

---

[1] Liberated territories also included *poblaciones* such as Villa Francia, La Legua, José María Caro, La Victoria, Yungay, and La Pincoya (Schneider 1995; Peña 2007; Pérez 2013; Molina and Molina 2015; Bruey 2018).

Second, party militants relegitimized disruptive and sometimes violent collective action tactics. In a context of increasing political frenzy before the military coup, political institutions often understood disruptive action as a valid type of protest. In the 1960s and early 1970s, for example, both the Christian Democrats and the MIR organized land seizures together with *pobladores* in order to challenge the state's ineffective social housing policies. In the 1980s, radical militants managed to validate contentious collective action among *población* dwellers once again. They did so by giving people the opportunity to confront the state and to express their visceral frustrations with social exclusion, poverty, and the violence of the dictatorship. "The kids [we recruited] were troubled by poverty. ... They could barely buy food, they couldn't buy cigarettes," Alvaro explained when describing the reasons why youths joined the resistance against the dictatorship (Interview July 30, 2017; see also Johnson 1985; Tironi 1990). The new activists in *poblaciones* were able to reduce the risk of confronting state security forces by joining an organization in which they could interact, coordinate with, and learn from experienced militants (Bruey 2018, 203).

In addition, the secrecy, exclusivity, and political engagement of militant organizations presented an appealing image to people in *poblaciones* – even to those who were not affiliated with the parties, and especially to the youth. Party militants framed their disruptive activism as an epic endeavor. They also presented themselves as representing a noble cause: After all, they were pursuing *población* dwellers' interest at great risk. As a dweller and former young activist in Lo Hermida explained to me (Interview, February 23, 2013):

In 1987, the *Lautaro* [MJL] marched across the *población*. There were about 30 people with shaved heads, all marching with their faces covered and a rifle in their hands. It was so impressive, so powerful! We went crazy for it! We were around 17 years old, and we said "Now is the time!" Then one of the militants shot into the air with their machinegun and yelled a political statement, and then they disappeared. After that we wanted more: "Where are they, where did they go? We want to see them again," me and my friends said to each other.

Third, radical party militants in *poblaciones* continued using the same collective action frames of the 1960s and 1970s. In the words of one of my interviewees, "in the 1980s, people [in Lo Hermida] kept on using the same methods and concepts of the 1970s" (Interview, January 25, 2013). Before the coup, parties and movements on the left used frames that exalted the empowerment of the urban poor and their right to reclaim the resources from which capitalism had dispossessed them, including urban land and state services. The left's socialist project of society included returning those resources to the working classes and the historically underprivileged. It also understood the Chilean elite and (what they saw as) imperialist wealthy countries as the core adversary to the left's goals.

The new regime, after 1973, violently repressed this post-Marxist rhetoric and made these frames much less appealing for moderate political actors on the left. These notions survived among MDP militants, however. These militants rhetorically swapped out their main antagonist – replacing the elite with Pinochet and his security forces – thus motivating collective action. Other than this, however, collective action frames remained largely untouched throughout the dictatorship. In the 1980s, therefore, militants used those same frames to socialize *población* dwellers. During the national protests in Lo Hermida, for example, party militants used and validated notions such as *poder popular*, *autogestión*, and *recuperación* in their interaction with local dwellers. Referring to a well-known event of *recuperación*, in which Communist militants stole chickens from a grocery distribution truck to deliver the food among local dwellers in the neighborhood, a leader in Lo Hermida (a former activist in the 1980s) told me: "that *recuperación* motivated us [the youths in the *población*], it made us feel like we also could fight and beat the dictatorship" (Interview, February 23, 2013). Similarly, a lady who joined the *Jota* as a teenager in Lo Hermida during the 1980s emphatically said, "I was very young, but they [Communist militants] explained to me what *poder popular* was" (Interview, January 17, 2013).

By retrieving these symbols of prior mobilization, radical activists created conditions for neighborhoods such as Lo Hermida to avoid the demobilizing fate that most *poblaciones* experienced after the democratic transition. This is not to say that the militants themselves necessarily remained active in these neighborhoods. Rather, their political socialization built a neighborhood culture of mobilization, in which "place" intimately connects the present with the past. In other words, militants' political socialization made past experiences in the neighborhood a highly legitimate source of symbols to create alternative explanations for the occurrences of the present. In doing so, militants created conditions whereby the urban poor in Lo Hermida were able to defy established societal narratives about their political potential.

## 4.3 REMEMBERING THROUGH TACTICS OF ACTION

In late February 2013, a couple of neighborhood organizations in Lo Hermida coordinated an initiative to promote community cohesion and political reflection among neighbors. The activity was particularly focused on children. A set of games were installed on one of the community streets. The games were designed for kids to interact with their families and activists in a public environment. There were table tennis and racing competitions, as well as a face painting workshop. A plastic swimming pool invited children to escape the summer heat. After this leisure time, tea was served to welcome neighbors of all ages to a discussion on current matters.

The event began at lunchtime. An industrial cooking pot atop a wood fire contained simmering rice and vegetables, welcoming organizers and the first families approaching the site. "Look, we have a community kitchen!", an activist who had been preparing the meal since earlier in the day excitedly announced to those arriving (Field Notes, March 1, 2013). Implementing a community kitchen seemed anachronistic to me, the sort of activity I associated with years gone by. As a local leader had explained to me earlier that year, "it was around 1992 that community kitchens [alleviating] hunger disappeared from Lo Hermida ... afterwards, community kitchens sort of honor the previous ones" (Interview, January 30, 2013b). Through most of the twentieth century, community kitchens were a survival tactic to feed the poorest families in *poblaciones* who could not afford daily meals. The ingredients were usually donated by the Catholic Church or NGOs. Community kitchens became politically salient in the dictatorship, when they were also used symbolically to denounce the military government's regressive economic policies (Hardy 1986b). The confinement brought by the COVID-19 pandemic's quarantines resembled the 1980s in *poblaciones* as it resulted in acute widespread unemployment, and a lack of food and medicine for countless families. The many community kitchens that emerged for a few months during 2020 in Chile's urban margins as a consequence of that exceptional context sought to alleviate hunger in those areas.

In regular circumstances, however, their role today is different. These days, the ingredients for community kitchens are usually donated by a few of its organizers. People do not attend them as a means for survival. Rather, they have a symbolic appeal that comes from their resemblance to scenes of the past. Community kitchens help people keep their sense of historical continuity alive because they confirm that collective actions in Lo Hermida are part of a long-standing tradition of struggle. Besides their memory-building role, community kitchens invite neighbors to share food in public spaces. In this way, they also work as opportunities to challenge local dwellers' increasing preference for private, depoliticized social interactions.

Remarkably, while it is true that *población* activists have implemented some novel forms of collective action in the past decade – including alternative *funas* (informal public denunciations), rap gigs, and gender diversity workshops – their repertoire of contention has remained largely unchanged in the past 50 years. *Pobladores* still coordinate initiatives such as *arpilleras*, the yearly anniversary and *peñas*, critical pedagogy workshops, children's camps, and critical discussions about film screenings. In addition, activists that engage in disruptive acts of protest have continued using tactics such as marches, urban land seizures, roadblocks, fire barricades, and confrontations with the police using Molotov cocktails and stones.

The notion of self-management has also survived as a tactic that cuts across the different forms of action in this repertoire. This concept refers to people's ability to govern themselves in a politically and economically decentralized organization. Its current use in Lo Hermida is another demonstration of activists' tight connection between past and present. The simulated mini-societies[2] that the MIR coordinated in *tomas* during the early 1970s advanced the ideal of self-management (Castells 1983). Later, the MDP's actions in underprivileged neighborhoods during the dictatorship pointed to the same ideal of excluding state control in self-determined urban communities. *Población* activists continue to use this concept in their organizing. Yet, while the notion used to indicate autonomy in all aspects of community life, activists today use it mainly to describe a mobilizing tactic. They speak of self-management to mean the financing of mobilization without external support. Besides its memory-building role, the tactic is also used with practical considerations. First, it reassures activists of their freedom to decide on the goal and scope of their collective action. It is, therefore, a way of sustaining local organizing while also excluding politicians and state agents from their initiatives. Second, it keeps Lo Hermida's SMC active and dynamic by promoting the simultaneous implementation of numerous initiatives in the neighborhood. To self-finance their mobilization, local organizations need to coordinate crowdfunding events. Many of the community parties, gigs, soccer tournaments, and hotdog stalls in the neighborhood are not stand-alone initiatives; they are organized with the goal of collecting enough resources to fund larger events, which require bigger pots of money. Self-management, therefore, keeps the many organizations in Lo

---

[2] See Chapter 1 for details on the structures and organizations that MIR militants promoted in the urban informal settlements that they led.

Hermida active and gives a vibrant atmosphere to the neighborhood. These organizing tactics persist in Lo Hermida because local activists use them to sustain and strengthen a sense of historical continuity among neighborhood dwellers.

## 4.4 MEMORY-BUILDING AND RELATIONAL SETTINGS

Neighborhood activists' sense of historical continuity has a relational dimension. As my interviews and observations suggest, the past provides lessons about other social actors that shape Lo Hermida activists' current representations of those actors as well as the interactions with them. In their stories of the past, local activists in Lo Hermida rarely portray institutional agents as allies. When they do so, it is because they speak of them as supporters of *población* autonomous social mobilization. External agents may be categorized as allies when they have opened opportunities for activists in the urban margins or when they have demonstrated closeness and authentic empathy with underprivileged people's dignity. Given their hierarchical, formal structures, and countrywide operations, local activists also often think of revolutionary organizations, such as the MIR, FPMR or MJL, as institutions. Hence, in my interviews and conversations, these organizations were sometimes compared to other institutional political agents, such as political parties and politically engaged Catholic priests. These radical organizations are, however, regularly admired and praised among *población* activists. Across ages, community organizers in Lo Hermida hold these radical organizations' commitment to grassroots struggles in high regard.

Additionally, on particular historical occasions, other institutional agents are also understood as allies of *pobladores*. Activists remember the Catholic Church as one of their key supporters during the dictatorship. They also maintain the position that some politicians contributed to their cause during specific periods of time. Salvador Allende is possibly the most important among them. Other Christian Democrat, Communist, and Socialist politicians who helped the urban poor to oppose the dictatorship are also perceived as historical allies. All of these actors advanced in one way or another the socialist project that remains a fundamental element of *pobladores'* identity today. Their authentic empathy with underprivileged people's living conditions and their clear efforts to support the autonomous mobilization of the poor are key to their special place in *pobladores'* memory.

Since the democratic transition, *población* activists in Lo Hermida think of the overwhelming majority of institutional political agents as opponents. The origin of this historical distrust comes from the splintering of the left during Chile's democratization process in the 1980s. The MDP, together with other social groups on the left, had high expectations for a new democratic regime. Many influential grassroots leaders in mobilized communities such as Lo Hermida were among them. The new democracy they envisioned would dismantle the neoliberal state developed by the authoritarian regime and tip the balance of power toward the left. As I suggest in Chapter 2, this plan would require defeating the dictatorship by force. In contrast, the AD participated in coordinating a democratic transition in line with the dictatorship's laws.

This division occurred against the backdrop of mounting national protests in the 1980s. Mobilizations discredited the dictatorship's international image and undermined its domestic governability. For many local activists aligned with radical factions of the left, the AD instrumentalized grassroots collective action in order to leverage their negotiations with the military government. "We were cannon fodder (*tontos útiles*); we fought and risked our lives for the cause, and when it was convenient for them [AD politicians], they arranged everything in their interest," indicated a current leader who was an active participant in the national protests against the dictatorship (Interview, February 23, 2013).

Despite returning electoral democracy to the country in 1989, the AD's move consolidated the political position of the right-wing elite and the military. The dictatorship's binding laws gave privileges to the economic elite, protected the military, and limited democratic participation after 1990. Laws privatizing the educational, healthcare, and housing markets were also put in place to ensure the continuity of the dictatorship's economic model.

In all, the radical sections of the left see the democratic transition as a striking political defeat, which is especially pertinent to those in *poblaciones* who lacked the cultural and social resources to take advantage of the country's economic growth in the 1990s. "The No Campaign's success meant a defeat for us, for my project and for all those who were more radical in their thought" explained a local leader who experienced the democratic transition in Lo Hermida (Interview, January 25, 2013). This sentiment of defeat, which is shared by radical leftist activists that experienced the dictatorship, can also be found among some of the youths at the *población*.

While some nuances can be found in how local activists remember political institutions, they persistently and decisively portray the role of state security forces as enemies of the community. This hostile representation of security forces occurs against the backdrop of numerous anecdotes of violence unfairly perpetrated by the police and the military over the years. The first of those stories occurred in the early years of the community's development, when Lo Hermida was still a *toma* in the outskirts of the city. Labeled as a *masacre* (massacre) by local dwellers and activists, the killing of the *población* leader René Saravia in a police raid in 1972 struck the local community. Early in August of that year, the police entered the fourth zone in the *población* searching for a leftist leader from the 16 July National Liberation Front. The police violently broke into the leader's house to find only his family. Given the aggressive treatment suffered by the leader's wife and child, neighbors drove the policemen out of the *población* by shouting insults and throwing stones at their cars. Local activists set up barricades in nearby roads to prevent police cars from entering the *población* afterwards. On the following evening, the police retaliated by breaking into the *población* and aggressively raiding many of the houses. They bullied and beat some residents, and even fired their guns to scare those reacting in opposition. That night, 22-year-old René Saravia was shot dead. Eleven residents were injured and another 160 were arrested (Punto Final 1972).

This event is especially memorable because it brought President Salvador Allende to the *población*. The *massacre* had, indeed, deepened a key divide within the left in those years. One side of that divide was represented by the MIR and other radical organizations, which believed that only mass mobilization would achieve social change. The other side included a group of radical but more moderate activists who emphasized the state's involvement in building a socialist society. The revolutionary block within the left, thus, interpreted this attack by the police in Lo Hermida as a violent provocation of the "reformist left" (MIR 1972). Allende, who was experiencing a deep crisis of governability, decided to visit Lo Hermida himself and discuss the episode with community leaders as a measure to unite the left behind him. He also fired the head of his investigations police force, and publicly promised to compensate victims and hold perpetrators accountable.

While local residents recognized and valued Allende's gestures, both archival documents and local activists' stories of the past indicate that they remained defiant toward most political and security authorities. In a public letter that *pobladores* wrote about their version of the event, published by the MIR on August 8, 1972, they accuse police authorities of "beating and repressing them," and of "betraying the will of the people"

(MIR 2000, 2950). My interviews also indicate a certain skepticism toward the role of political authorities in the event. "I was very young, but I will never forget it, because Allende came to Lo Hermida," a leader in one of Lo Hermida's neighborhood councils told me when referring to this incident. With a tone that combined incredulity and pride, he added "[Allende] came to sort of say 'I am sorry' to us, to the people ... but our leaders back then told him all [of the demands] we had!" (Interview, January 23, 2013).

Stories of the dictatorship are similarly riddled with incidents of police and military brutality. The abusive treatment with which Pinochet's military treated local residents in the many raids it conducted in the *población* is often remembered in stories about the past. Activists speak of *población* residents and community leaders who were beaten, persecuted, or killed by the police in those same years. Countless murals alluding to police and military repression across the *población* also indicate how important past abusive experiences remain for local dwellers' collective memory.

Since the democratic transition, the cases of police brutality have inarguably decreased in *poblaciones*. Yet my interviews and observations indicate that local dwellers continue to experience police stigmatization, humiliations, and excesses of violence in their neighborhood. Furthermore, numerous stories in my interviews and conversations describe how the police continue to repeatedly clash with *población* protesters, using tear gas, water cannons, and arrests to deactivate demonstrations in the neighborhood and surroundings.

Local activists represent these past interactions between community members and external social agents through a myriad of other expressions of collective identity, such as in group discussions, banners, graffiti, and songs. As these representations make clear, they set the precedent for the current relationships that residents have with political institutions and other external social actors. Relational settings further promote the direct connection between collective action of the past and the present in Lo Hermida. Furthermore, they indicate that most relationships of power imbalance are highly threatening for *pobladores*. Past interactions with authorities, for instance, performatively locate community members in vulnerable positions. In Section 4.5, I explain how agentic memory translates this sense of historical vulnerability into a position of agency in the present.

## 4.5 SUBVERSION AND AGENCY

After attending a meeting in the center of Santiago, I headed for Lo Hermida. A group of local organizations were coordinating an event to commemorate the death of 16-year-old Manuel Gutiérrez, a young *pobla-dor* who was shot and killed by the police in August 2011 during a demonstration next to the neighborhood. The event included shows by folk music bands and rappers, as well as a presentation on police brutality by a Mapuche leader. Activists also organized a food market and a small fair in which local organizations from different parts of the city showed their work and engaged in networking. As part of my fieldwork, I was due to attend and help implement the event.

As I crossed the Americo Vespucio highway to reach the *población*, I noticed a few posters and banners that local organizers had installed on the walking bridge I was using. The first poster explained the death of Manuel and the impunity enjoyed by the police. It also included a picture of a large clenched fist, which had been installed as a memorial in the square where the event was held soon after Manuel's death. The other posters made references to state terrorism during the dictatorship. They included images of police and military repression, as well as portraits of people disappeared by the state in those years. The banners insulted the police and the state, and called for an end to police oppression.

Through these posters and banners, local residents in Lo Hermida perform a narrative that connects past and present events to explain their current social reality (see Straubhaar 2015; Lotem 2016). This action is possible because, through memory-building strategies, collectives have developed relational lessons about other social actors (Somers 1994). The posters in my story not only draw parallels between the dictatorship's unaccountable and oppressive state security forces with those of today, but also demonstrate the community's subversive reaction to injustice. Activists in *poblaciones* also use the past to explain their social life through telling stories to each other, painting murals referring to the past, or building memorials. Key to my analysis, however, is the position that communities adopt in front of others during their manifestations of memory-building. Agentic memory is the collective use of the past to promote a position of unconditional political belonging among community members (Shotter 1993).

In my fieldwork in Lo Hermida, I explored how these narratives are transmitted among local dwellers, and I especially focused on those people involved in the neighborhood's SMC. Local activists and residents develop memory-building in the initiatives they organize, their conversations during informal gatherings before and after meetings, and the memorials and murals in the neighborhood. My analysis indicates that local activists create a sense of historical continuity as a platform through which to subvert oppressive events. In doing so, they performatively situate themselves in a position of agency. In their communications and initiatives, activists usually begin by recounting oppressive events that at some point in the past affected neighborhood dwellers, or the urban poor at large. While in my interviews and observations all activists in Lo Hermida refer to events that occurred in the 1970s or 1980s to highlight oppressive matters of the past, young organizers draw on more recent episodes from the past 10-20 years more frequently than their older peers. Although these representations usually allude to specific events, local activists tend to rhetorically connect them with a broader history in which the state regularly inflicts abuse and violence on underprivileged people. These narratives not only outline a diagnosis of oppression, but are, in fact, active performances of denunciation that activists use to amplify their claims (White 1999; Barton 2018). In other words, activists highlight specific deeds or events, thus bringing attention to unfair scenes of the past in their interactions with other SMC members or with people from outside their community. This initial rhetorical tactic is followed by, or connected to, events of successful collective struggle that overcome oppression, and thus subvert injustice and frustration. Amplification also plays a role in this case (see Figure 4.1). Activists frequently glorify the actions of particular heroic leaders or groups that were able to mobilize and advance community empowerment in the past. The ability of the community as a whole to stand up to challenges and injustice is also often praised.

The stories about the San Carlos canal flooding exemplify how this tactic works. It is a well-known event among Lo Hermida's activists, as I observed through interviews and spending time in the community. Reportedly, the winter of 1982 was particularly rainy. By the end of the month, a storm that lasted for a week led to the overflow of Santiago's main rivers, flooding several areas around the city (Díaz 2013). Large portions of Santiago were paralyzed as the flooding affected thousands of people and several of the main roads were waterlogged (El Mercurio 1982). Lo Hermida was one of the numerous *poblaciones* that was flooded on that occasion. People were brought to shelters, and many lost their belongings.

I first heard this story after a meeting in a local organization. One of the oldest leaders narrated the event to younger participants while he shared a cigarette with them. To my surprise, however, he referred to the flooding as an event of political oppression. He recalled the flooding as a targeted attempt by authorities to destroy the neighborhood (Field notes,

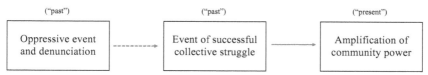

FIGURE 4.1 Subversion through memory-building.

January 4, 2013). Over time, I realized that this particular version of the story is shared by many local dwellers and the large majority of activists. By claiming that the military intentionally bombed the canal to harm Lo Hermida's inhabitants, activists amplify symbols of injustice as well as the importance that the community had in the fight against the dictatorship.

Local activists indicate that the community reacted to rise up against this injustice. In other words, instead of weakening local dwellers, the oppression actually made them stronger. First, the flooding made people's misery more publicly visible. This fact united neighbors because it highlighted the precarious living conditions that they all experienced, as well as authorities' responsibility. "We realized that we were all the same, we went through a change, and we also felt it was unfair," explained a local organizer, referring to people's initial reaction after the flooding (Interview, January 25, 2013).

Second, new organizations emerged, and those that already existed became stronger and better connected. As one of my informants indicated, "many organizations appeared and we all participated" (Interview, February 23, 2013). Community kitchens, for example, multiplied and received the support of many more participants. Additionally, kids who had previously acquired experience as community organizers in children's camps rose as new leaders to help work during the crisis.

"That's when the Coordinadora was created," the older leader told younger activists while still sharing their cigarette (Field notes, January 4, 2013). He continued by proudly explaining that a few days after the flooding, in 1982, local dwellers created the Coordinadora de Organizaciones Sociales de Lo Hermida (Coalition of Lo Hermida's Social Organizations). This association coordinated around 40 locally based organizations – including human rights groups, youth Catholic collectives, community kitchens, and *arpilleras* – seeking to unite in their struggle against the dictatorship. The Coordinadora, the leader explained, boosted Lo Hermida's mobilizing potential in the anti-dictatorial national protests that emerged in 1983.

Simultaneously, the pivotal role of external political agents, such as the Catholic Church, NGOs, political parties, and radical political groups on the left is largely minimized in local narratives of the flooding within Lo Hermida's SMC. As mentioned earlier, external institutions and organizations provided essential economic and human resources to aid local residents affected by the flooding and help them mobilize against the dictatorship. By downplaying their work, neighborhood narratives of the past emphasize the community's power to autonomously challenge injustice and overcome oppression. In this way, stories of the past create the image of a victorious and empowered local community.

Activists in Lo Hermida also use the neighborhood itself as a medium to advance agentic memory. Narratives associate different parts of the neighborhood – including buildings, squares, and streets – with symbols of the past (scenes, events, characters, or tactics). In this way, areas of the neighborhood acquire a symbolic value that serves memory-building. The agentic power of this mechanism comes from these symbols' role in their production and reproduction of narratives of the past. For example, the case of the Martyrs' Square shows the role that activists in Lo Hermida give to these neighborhood symbols as a platform for subverting historical oppression. In other words, by attaching symbols of the past to places in the neighborhood, local activists incorporate them in their memory-building tactics. Therefore, activists are able to employ those neighborhood symbols as sources of agency.

In the mid-1990s, neighborhood organizations decided to christen one of the neighborhood squares with the name: Martyrs' Square. With that name, they paid homage to the people who struggled to defend their rights and were murdered by the dictatorship. This particular place, however, also makes reference to the place where Fredy Palma, a 16-year-old local dweller, was shot and killed by the military during a protest in the 1980s. Local organizations, hence, attach symbols from the past to the square in their neighborhood. The square functions not only as a community reminder of political oppression, but also as a platform for collective action. Over the years, the Martyrs' Square has become the most popular meeting place for local organizers and the starting point of many marches in the neighborhood. Furthermore, *población* residents use the square to defend their dignity and their control over their neighborhood. In 2010, for example, activists stopped a municipality refurbishing plan that was meant to replace the square with a concrete memorial plaza without requesting the approval of the community. As a local leader living near the square explained to me (Interview, February 23, 2013):

They [workers sent by the municipality] were cutting the trees; and we all came to the square on the same day ... and occupied the square. We told them [the workers]: if the people [project managers] from the municipality are not here in 15 minutes we'll [build a barricade and] block the road. Half an hour later, the municipality people [agents] were here talking to us.

The refurbishments to the square were eventually carried out by the municipality, but in close consultation with the local community. Since 2012, the square also features a sculpture made of stone that pays tribute to people from the district who were detained and disappeared by the Pinochet regime. The memorial displays the names of 34 people killed below a sculpture representing a woman, a man, and a child. In addition, local organizations painted a dozen, six-foot tall murals on the walls around the square to represent the MIR militants who were also assassinated by the dictatorship. The active and organized appropriation of the Martyrs' Square advances the same narratives of memory-building of many other collective initiatives in Lo Hermida: It demonstrates the local community's ongoing ability to stand up to oppression.

## 4.6 CONCLUSION

This is the first of three chapters in which I address how civil society development in some urban communities departed from the general trend of demobilization in Chile's urban margins since the democratic transition. The chapter continued my comparative endeavor by focusing on the case of Lo Hermida, a neighborhood in which mobilizational citizenship successfully developed and survives to the present day.

More specifically, the chapter analyzed the historical origin and current manifestations of agentic memory. Activists' engagement in agentic memory is a critical first step in their development of mobilizational citizenship and allows them to resist exclusionary, demobilizing processes in the urban margins. As I demonstrated, such a step requires for activists' use of memory-building to generate a sense of historical continuity and promote community empowerment.

The dictatorship violently disrupted community-building in *poblaciones* and managed to disconnect local collective endeavors from the socialist project of society that had hitherto inspired mobilization in the urban margins. Based on my ethnography in Nuevo Amanecer, in previous chapters I showed how the dictatorship produced a sense of historical discontinuity among dwellers in most *poblaciones*, which diminished those communities' mobilizing potential. In coordinating the 1980s anti-dictatorial national protests in the urban margins, moderate political party activists from the AD produced a managerial leadership, which did not manage to politically socialize residents and legitimized people's detachment between present and past. These communities experienced a wave of exclusionary and demobilizing measures in the democratic transition and later, in the post-transition. Their inability to resort to memory-building to build an alternative citizenship made it impossible for them to stand up to and resist those measures.

In contrast, while they coordinated anti-dictatorial protests in the 1980s, radical militants created subversive leaderships in Lo Hermida. They belonged to the PC, MIR, FPMR, MJL, and some Socialist factions. Following Communist methods in their interactions with grassroots communities, those militants sought to recruit urban dwellers and trained them on political tactics and ideology. Research conducted on leftist mobilization during the dictatorship (Pérez 2013; Arancibia 2015) as well as in the *poblaciones* La Pincoya (Molina and Molina 2015), La Victoria (Briceño 2017), La Legua, and Villa Francia (Pérez 2013; Bruey 2018) indicates that several other communities went through similar political experiences. These radical political groups on the left transmitted a political culture that made memory-building actions a central part of people's repertoire of contention, thus reverting community discontinuity and allowing the development of agentic memory. As my framework indicates, this move is key in the emergence of mobilizational citizenship. The survival of untouched collective action frames and tactics since the 1980s, as well as the persistent reference to past community events in *poblaciones*, attests to local activists' ability to sustain a sense of historical continuity.

The chapter also showed how memory-building can be used to shape relational settings and develop a collective position of agency. I drew on interviews and observations to explain how activists in Lo Hermida challenge stigmatizing and oppressive narratives of the past to empower themselves in their current interactions. In addition, I outlined how, through agentic memory, local activists imagine a political community that goes beyond their immediate social reality. The community extends in time, including symbols, scenes, and characters of the past. Also drawing on my fieldwork in Lo Hermida, Chapter 5 will delve into the symbols and dynamics of interaction sustaining the neighborhood's mobilizing identity.

# 5

# We, the Informal Urban Dwellers

In this chapter, I will continue to focus on the case of Lo Hermida, and in doing so, will deepen my comparative analysis. In previous chapters, I discussed the critical role of agentic memory in the development of mobilizational citizenship. I explained how radical political groups that coordinated protests against the dictatorship in the 1980s socialized local activists in specific communities of Chile's urban margins. They transmitted a political culture to urban dwellers that shapes how collective identity currently motivates mobilization in those communities. This culture updated the legitimacy of the socialist political project of society pursued by various groups on the left before the military coup in 1973. It also made a sense of continuity available to activists by using memory-building to promote mobilization in their community.

I build on these findings to examine the tactics through which collective identity promotes mobilization and citizenship in Chilean *poblaciones*. As my framework in Chapter 1 describes, groups of people use cultural attributes to self-define in particular ways and differentiate from others. As they use these shared attributes to interpret the social reality surrounding them, they create a collective identity (Castells 2010). Identities, in other words, involve sets of shared, self-defining symbols that allow people to make sense of their world. People create communities by expanding their collection of shared symbols in order to set boundaries that differentiate them from others and build particular systems of social legitimacy. My interest here is in the mechanisms of identity-building via which people motivate each other to mobilize. I have called those mechanisms "mobilizing identity." In this chapter, I provide a holistic explanation of how *población* activists promote collective action through identity strategies of belonging and boundary-building.

I argue that *población* activists implicitly outline two different systems of legitimacy in their interactions and tactics of mobilization: the informal and the formal. In other words, these activists implicitly create two distinct spheres that differ in their norms of interaction, ideals, and values. They understand underprivileged people's activism as dominant within the informal sphere. The formal, on the other hand, represents the realm of experience dominated by the elite, institutions, and legal procedures. Local activists in Lo Hermida promote political consciousness and positive assertions of their community based on this distinction. Through these tactics they resist stigmatization and achieve cohesion among participants.

I also argue that the conflicted interaction between these two realms strongly shapes mobilization in *poblaciones*. As external forces threaten the development of informal community-building in the neighborhood, activists react with indignation and their collective action becomes a defensive endeavor. My analysis indicates that the identity symbols of *pobladores*, *lucha*, and *represión* allow local activists to use mobilization as an action of community-building.

This chapter unfolds in three steps. First, I examine activists' differentiation tactics by distinguishing the informal from the formal. Second, I explain how activists use this distinction to develop political consciousness and positive assertions. Third, I discuss how activists use boundary-making to identify antagonists among other social actors. Activists' tactical use of the notion of repression increases the urgency of mobilization and connects their actions with those carried out by radical leftist activists resisting the dictatorship's oppression in the 1980s. Identity symbols connect activists with a political community that extends in time and space, beyond their current neighborhood. In this way, collective identity becomes a catalyst for mobilization and citizenship.

## 5.2 THE INFORMAL

After a few weeks of living in Lo Hermida, I started attending meetings and collaborating with a group of activists conducting an urban land reappropriation at a square in the neighborhood. The square was located in a run-down and neglected section of a park that extends toward the south for several blocks. While the municipality had recently refurbished much of the park, this square had remained untouched. After a meeting in which local activists discussed a rumor suggesting that the municipality intended to transform the square into a profitable spot to be used for commercial purposes, they decided to exert community control over the place. They hence created a new local organization devoted to protecting the square from the private corporate projects seeking to cannibalize their neighborhood. The organization that emerged from this repossession met and worked regularly in the square. The activists involved in this organization described their actions through the notion of *recuperación*. They began by creating an informal monument of a raised fist in the middle of the square; for them, it symbolizes community power and memorializes Manuel Gutierrez, a young *población* activist killed by the police in a protest in 2011.

During most of the summer of 2013, I worked with them in the square. We built and maintained a community orchard and a roof with a few seats. We also built a small play park for children and regularly organized community initiatives that were held there. One day, while I shoveled dirt in the orchard, several of the youths around me suddenly started whistling loudly. Their whistles became a repetitive rhythm, similar to that of the whistling of farmers that herd cattle. As I raised my head, I realized that activists were reacting to a police van that had just passed through the street next to us and had stopped at a traffic light a couple of blocks away. The whistling was an act of defiance against state security forces. The performance was meant to demean policemen by whistling at them, as one would with a flock of passive, domesticated farm animals that follow orders. Although I had heard this sort of whistling before, the cohesion, readiness, and resentment behind this action surprised me.

This experience showed me the powerful effect that collective identity boundaries can have in activating contentious action in people. Through identity boundaries, communities advance relational definitions of who they are in opposition to others. They performatively express who they are by qualifying other social actors. Simultaneously, community members validate symbols that promote in-group identification and cohesion. In this way, collective belonging tactics emerge alongside identity boundary-making. By portraying policemen as submissive animals, activists, by contrast, were describing *themselves* as humane, morally and socially conscious agents. Through their actions, they show each other the legitimacy of these latter traits.

As I show in this chapter, however, boundary- and belonging-making need to go beyond differentiation and cohesion tactics to effectively mobilize people. Boundary-making is effective in mobilizing when it activates collective indignation in response to actors that protestors portray as threatening antagonists (Gamson 1995; Snow 2001). Mobilization is, in this context, a move toward protection and self-determination. In other words, in the face of a threatening enemy – in this case, the police – activists are emotionally compelled to act together defensively. On the other hand, "belonging" has mobilizing potential when activists place the responsibility of their grievances outside of them, in a wider social, political, and economic system. Through mobilizing belonging, activists reject the self-accusatory dynamics of stigmatization and legitimize amplifying, self-defining symbols. As I show in this chapter, activists often use amplification to enhance the mobilizing potential of belonging- and boundary-making. Snow et al. (1986, 469) define amplification as the "clarification and invigoration of an interpretive frame that bears on a particular issue, problem, or set of events." Activists, in other words, invigorate, exalt, idealize, or elevate collective identity symbols that they deem effective in motivating mobilization among current and potential participants (Snow et al. 1986; Benford and Snow 2000).

Key components of boundary-making among *población* activists became apparent during an informal conversation I had with one activist after a *peña*. After touching on several topics, my exchange with the young activist turned to my fieldwork's goals, and my role as a researcher in the community. I carefully explained to him that the aim of my research was to explore collective action in current *poblaciones*. In order to do that, I said, I was participating in and contributing to local organizations, observing people's interactions, and conducting interviews. He commented, however, that what he perceived as my highly structured and systematic study would be unable to properly address and understand Lo Hermida's organizations. I would only be able to understand people's community life, he insisted, if I experienced "the street" or, in his words, "*la calle*." People in Chile's urban margins spend a considerable amount of their time in the neighborhood in public spaces, such as streets or squares. Initially, I thought that he was stating something fairly obvious to me in the development of my fieldwork; I thought he was saying I needed to spend more time observing public encounters to improve the accuracy of my study. What I eventually deciphered, however, was that his advice pointed more to the *quality* than to the quantity of my engagement in community life. In the months that followed, I became more involved in local informal networks and realized that *la calle* doesn't only refer to the physical location of "the street". Rather, it refers to a specific type of *experience*, these diverse scenes and spontaneous encounters that occur in public spaces of the *población*. It is during those interactions that people create meaningful bonds and acquire attitudes that they would not develop in private spaces or in wealthier areas of the city. The concept of *la calle*, therefore, highlights a collective experience that complements formal systems of socialization for local dwellers.

The notion of "*chora*" or "*choro*"[1] is a term with similar meaning. It is also often used by local dwellers to describe a locally accepted experience that goes beyond formal systems and services. The adjective of *chora* or *choro*, however, describes somebody whose behavior replaces institutionally validated systems of redress or justice. It refers to the attitudinal and behavioral code by which *población* residents defy others, or demand something from them, which includes both other people and authorities. It is usually an energic, relatively aggressive behavior that demonstrates the ability to defend yourself, even at a high cost. Spitting on the floor, for example, demonstrates a *chora* or *choro* attitude among youths; it is a nonverbal type of defiance between groups within the neighborhood. "When you speak at the *pobla*[2] you move your hands, like flapping with them. That's to be *choro*, when you go [as an activist] to the municipality, people find that [behavior] strange and it scares them sometimes; it's just things from the *población*!" described a local activist when explaining what it means to be *chora* or *choro* in the neighborhood (Interview, February 28, 2013).

Among *población* activists, *la calle* and *chora* or *choro,* together with a set of other locally validated symbols, legitimize practices of neighborhood community-building by amplifying informality. These symbols outline a congruent and idealized space of social action that I label "the informal." Created via a land invasion and developed through grassroots mobilizing, the *población* community is informal in its very origin. For neighborhood activists, the world of grassroots organizing is the core expression of the informal because in their eyes it authentically represents the needs and dignity of the urban margins. Political dynamics of memory-building coexist with a subculture of marginality in the informal. In other words, the informal includes notions and practices anchored in the community's political history. That is the case of *recuperación*, which is an idea widely used among activists defending Chile's socialist project of society in the 1960s and 1970s. The notion refers to the actions by

[1] *Chora* is feminine and *choro* masculine.
[2] "*Pobla*" is short for "*población*."

which poor people reclaim resources that they were unfairly deprived of by capitalism. As I explain in Chapter 2, radical leftist groups and parties brought this concept of *recuperación* back to *poblaciones* in the 1980s, when they coordinated and trained local activists who were organizing protests against the dictatorship. Simultaneously, the informal incorporates more recent and nonpolitical practices, such as those encapsulated by the notions of *la calle* and *chora* or *choro*. These ideas have developed over time and are the result of a culture of marginality in Chile's excluded urban communities.

Local activists also heavily rely on informal networks of trust and legitimacy. For example, I learned that several of them used their neighborhood connections to make inquiries about who I was before agreeing to meet or talk with me. This move was only partially to assess whether I posed a threat – which was largely unnecessary since they could corroborate my information online. Rather, it was mainly a way of validating their encounter with me within their neighborhood network.

By opposing this space of the informal to a broader, formal world, activists rhetorically and behaviorally outline two distinct realms of legitimacy. Implicit in activists' interactions, the formal refers to a system that regularly excludes and invalidates *población* residents. It encompasses structured and systematic procedures, legal codes, and traditional methods of citizen participation.

The formal becomes apparent, for example, through the recurrent notion of "institutions." *Población* activists often speak about institutions to indicate a set of distant, alien entities designed to undermine them. Similarly, through the recurrent use of words like "them" and "others," activists refer to external social actors who benefit from the formal, hegemonic social order. When characterizing *población* life, a local leader, for example, told me: "Life is different here. The *others* have cars and go around the city in their car, but we, the poor, have to go like sardines on the bus" (Interview, February 22, 2013). These actors include upper class and wealthier people, the bourgeoisie, the rich, academics, artists who avoid political matters, drug dealers, the police, and the military.

The formal also emerges as disqualifying references of social actors that passively abide by institutional rules. These rules, activists suggest, were created by the rich and designed for their own benefit. Therefore, they ignore the historical struggles of the poor, as well as their current concerns. Pointing to the exclusionary quality of these laws, a local activist, for instance, told me: "We have no voice in the model created by the dictatorship and the Concertación" (Interview, February 23, 2013).

Through the notions of "capitalism" and "neoliberalism," local activists and other residents who support their cause also make references to what they consider "the formal." With these words, they point to the social and cultural implications of the many market-oriented policies through which Chilean governments have sustained high levels of inequality and a lack of social protection for the past four decades. "[People] don't want to know about each other anymore ... because this neoliberal system makes them enclosed in their own lives, it makes them individualistic" (Interview, January 25, 2013), a local resident told me, trying to explain the challenges of widening participation in the neighborhood. The formal is understood as a dehumanizing force that promotes isolation, greed, and competitiveness. It also promotes people's sense of uprootedness, because it disconnects communities from their ethnic and historical origins. In contrast, in the informal realm local activists find a space of security and confidence in which they develop mobilizing belonging. In what follows, I delve into the tactics and symbols by which they are able to accomplish this belonging.

## 5.3 MOBILIZING BELONGING

In the time I worked with the organization reappropriating the square in Lo Hermida, activists coordinated several initiatives to collaborate with other local organizations, expand activism to other areas of the neighborhood, and reach potential adherents within the community. While activities included people from all ages, they were particularly tailored to interact with children and adolescents from the nearby houses. These children were often asked to support the events by helping with logistics and organization. For example, they helped by inviting people in the area, delivering pamphlets to neighbors, and preparing the materials for the activity.

One of these events involved inviting neighbors for an afternoon tea at a square. The event included interactive games with children, live music, and a discussion group. Drug dealers had increasing presence in that part of the neighborhood and local activists wanted to assert the importance of community control over the area. A few days before the activity, some children joined us to help make banners to advertise the event. As I used spray paint to write on a banner, a kid placed a large piece of paper on the floor next to me and squatted with a pencil in his hand to draw the contours of letters that he would later paint. After a few minutes of silent work, he stood up and asked a grammatical question to the group. "Is *organización* (organization) spelled with a 'c' or an 's'"? he asked. As I raised my head to deliver an answer, one of the most influential leaders in the group quickly and assertively replied: "it doesn't matter ... write it however you want!" (Field notes, March 1, 2013). Nobody else intervened, so I continued working on my banner.

With his confident remark, the leader was sending a clear message to the child and the rest of the participants: Formally acquired knowledge (in this particular case, school grammar training) is not required to participate in *población* organizations. In a context in which access to quality education is scarce, the leader was promoting a welcoming environment for *pobladores*, an environment in which belonging does not depend on the formal, traditional standards of incorporation that most *pobladores* cannot meet.

During my fieldwork in Lo Hermida, I witnessed several other scenes in which activists symbolically created a space of confidence and safety for fellow participants. In this way, the informal works as a platform on which local organizers create dignity and cohesion. Furthermore, through political consciousness and positive assertions of the community, belonging activates mobilization.

### 5.3.1 Political Consciousness

In this symbolic space that the informal provides, local activists advance mobilizing belonging. This tactic sources identity symbols from the past. In other words, activists use the sense of agency and historical continuity that agentic memory provides them to sustain an oppositional identification process and outline an alternative political community.

Local activists in Lo Hermida and other similar marginalized neighborhoods self-identify as "*pobladores.*" As I explain in earlier chapters, the term *pobladores* refers to the highly politicized communities that dwell in the urban margins. During much of the twentieth century, *pobladores* stood together with workers and peasants as one of the core political, revolutionary agents of the socialist project of society advanced by the Chilean left. Through disruptive urban land invasions and strong political connections, the *movimiento de pobladores* shaped Chilean cities, created innovative initiatives of local community development, and resisted the dictatorship. Through the notion of *pobladores*, neighborhood activists evoke the spirit of all of this movement's events, scenes, and characters.

Their use of this symbol, however, has a nuance that needs to be highlighted. Most local activists currently recognize that mobilization in the urban margins weakened dramatically after the democratic transition. It is also evident to them that mobilization has suffered substantial qualitative changes, which I describe throughout this book. For most of them, therefore, the *movimiento de pobladores* does not exist today in the same way that it did during most of the twentieth century. Therefore, when describing themselves as *pobladores*, local activists are not necessarily referring to the movement (the *movimiento de pobladores*). Instead, they are showcasing their belonging to a community that developed through the many struggles of Chile's urban poor. In other words, using this symbol allows local activists to connect their experience of marginalization and collective action with the practices by which many other urban dwellers in the past also resisted oppression in the urban margins. In self-defining as *pobladores*, they hence outline what might be described as an example of Anderson's (1991) "imagined community." That is to say that, as *pobladores*, activists establish a connection with a large group of urban dwellers and activists that extends in time and space, most of whom are unknown to them. This connection includes all of those fellow members throughout history and across the urban margins that have contributed to building *poblaciones*, both in terms of identity and infrastructure. "This is a place that we, *pobladores*, have built with our own hands . . . the old and the new [urban dwellers], all of us, are important in this [community endeavor]," an activist in his 20s explained to me, echoing what I heard in several other interviews and observations (Interview, February 26, 2013).

Local activists develop political consciousness by combining this identity category of *pobladores* with their distinction between the informal and the formal. As builders of an alternative community that questions and resists formal, traditional institutions, *pobladores* are the core agents of the informal. In their eyes, the formal – institutions, laws, and the elite – is unable to protect or represent *pobladores*. The formal is a highly unfair social order in which they do not have access to the means for personal and collective development. According to my interviews and conversations, activists feel that they have access to low-quality education, a poor health system, and overcrowded public transportation. The formal also exposes them to social marginality and discrimination. As I describe in the framework earlier in this book (Chapter 1), political consciousness also allows *pobladores* to reject self-accusatory attributions. Instead, they place the responsibility of their grievances on Chile's exclusionary and

unfair society. "[Participating in local organizing] is about people understanding that there is a history behind their lives, that they are not poor
for no reason and that this is an unequal society" (Interview, January 29,
2013), a resident and activist told me, explaining the importance of
political consciousness for *población* activism.

Political consciousness advances mobilizing belonging because it promotes cohesion among local activists. Furthermore, the symbol of
*poblador* is in itself empowering because it encapsulates a historically
anchored, territorially defined, and highly politicized actor. In fact, local
activists describe themselves as politically aware agents, who are ready to
stand up to injustice. Reacting to my questions about their *población*,
local activists regularly described it as a rebellious and politically
conscious community: "[Lo Hermida] is a place with informed people,
where people know what's fair; we won't get any pig in a poke!" an
activist, for example, told me (Interview, March 14, 2013b). Another one
described what it means to her to be a *pobladora*, saying: "hostile, tough,
and assertive ... I don't buy anyone's lies. Because I am from Lo
Hermida, I don't believe the humble ones, nor the arrogant ones"[3]
(Interview, February 20, 2013). These accounts are in line with the
slogans written on walls of the *población,* or shouted out loud as calls
for action during local events: "*Lo Hermida, presente, activa y comba-
tiente!*" (Lo Hermida is present, active and militant!) (Medio a Medio
2013; Frente Popular Revolucionario 2019).

Because of their association with national legal codes and formal
procedures, the notions "citizen" and "citizenship" are in direct contra-
diction to the definition of *pobladores* in the mind of local activists. The
traditional idea of citizenship that highlights written rules of national
incorporation and political participation is one of the key frameworks
of the formal.

"What do you think of new youth movements, like the Revolución
Democrática?" I asked three activists in their 20s and 30s while we walked
through the neighborhood after attending a meeting in one of Lo
Hermida's neighborhood councils. Revolución Democrática had emerged
as a political movement headed by former university student leaders, most
of whom belonged to student unions in elite Chilean universities. Since the
movement's beginning in 2012, several of its organizers had publicly

---

[3] The woman here was using very localized slang. Her exact words in Spanish were: "chora,
parada ... porque soy de aquí de Lo Hermida no le compro a nadie las mulas, ni a los
pocos ni a los choros."

declared their intention of creating a political party. My question was part of a longer conversation about political parties, and sought to understand their impressions about new movements that, despite representing a new left in the country, had little presence in working-class neighborhoods.

One of the activists replied promptly and dismissively: "that's *citizen* participation!" (Field notes, February 17, 2013). His assertiveness indicated to me that I was touching on a topic that sparked negative sentiments among activists. I decided to avoid pursuing that line of questioning any further. As I confirmed in many other interviews and observations, the notion of "participation" enjoys validation within *población* organizations, but citizenship-based frames are avoided and rejected. The quote that I provide at the onset of Chapter 1 is another supporting example. It describes an exchange I had with a local leader in which I asked her about how she would define citizenship. Her reply: "citizenship is for the *cuicos*, it's not for us . . . we are not citizens, we are *pobladores*!" During the interview, she eventually elaborated on her answer and explained to me that other *población* activists and leaders would laugh at her if she described them as "citizens" in one of their meetings (Interview, February 23, 2013). This fact shows how identifying as *pobladores* also allows local activists to historicize identity and claim rights, while at the same time avoiding controversial citizenship-based frames.

Another symbol that is key to *población* activists' production of belonging is that of "*lucha*". In conversations and meetings, local activists repeatedly use the notion of *lucha* to describe both the efforts undertaken by the impoverished families who built the neighborhood, and the initiatives of mobilization that have contributed to create their community. This symbol acts as an endorsement that legitimizes activists' tactics within their local SMC, which is why they tend to apply it to a wide range of actions. "This is a place of *lucha*, with a lot of personal and community history. The *lucha* here is multi-faceted; my particular struggle was in the field of football," Mr. Rigoberto, a coach who organizes soccer matches with children, told me (Interview, March 1, 2013). Activists in Lo Hermida generally qualify as *lucha* actions that defy injustice and entrenched institutions. This framing act includes initiatives promoting community cohesion as well as more confrontational types of protest, such as public demonstrations, rallies, and roadblocks.

### 5.3.2 Against Stigma

As it happens in many other countries, the mainstream media and local authorities tend to publicly portray the Chilean urban margins as areas filled with criminality and social deprivation (Cornejo 2012; Ruiz-Tagle 2017). In a widely broadcasted documentary on Chilean television in 2012, one of the country's leading journalists spends time in an underprivileged neighborhood to unveil "*in situ* the fear of conflicted *poblaciones*, the power of gangs, and the shootings." He describes "monstrous ghettos," in which people's chronic exposure to violence turns life into "nightmare" (TVN 2012). Another show in 2016 referred to *poblaciones* as Red Zones: "neighborhoods that resemble jails without walls ... where TV cameras are not admitted; this is the neglected Chile, the backyard of our arrogant country" (Chilevisión 2016). Although sensationalist, these shows feed the prevalent stigmatizations that equate *población* dwellers with criminals. As a local resident in Lo Hermida told me, "for the cops, and for many people, we are all perpetrators here in the *población*" (Interview, February 22, 2013).

Local activists understand the importance that resisting these stigmatizing notions of *poblaciones* has in order to encourage dignity and public engagement among neighborhood residents. Hence, they regularly amplify positive community traits. This is not to say that local activists only praise their neighborhood or the urban margins. They are very critical of the many challenges of neighborhood organizing and *población* life. Yet, aware of how descriptions of the neighborhood performatively shape their community, activists use available opportunities to extol the local behaviors, attitudes, and values that reinforce the virtues of the informal. This tactic makes collective identity and community-building more attractive both within and outside Lo Hermida's SMC. I cluster some of the symbols by which activists amplify informal community-building in four dimensions: autonomy, informal family bonds, solidarity networks, and the *popular*.

### 5.3.2.1 Autonomy

A large banner at the Andean Music Festival organized in Lo Hermida in late 2012 stated, "The people march together, without parties"[4] (Interview, January 25, 2013). This slogan can easily be likened to another, famous one: "The people united will never be defeated."[5] Despite their different content, the two slogans sound similar in Spanish. Despite their similar structure and phonetics, however, these slogans became salient in different contexts. The latter has been frequently used by leftist activists

---

[4] In the original Spanish, "*El pueblo marcha unido, sin partido.*"
[5] In the original Spanish, "*El pueblo unido, jamás será vencido.*"

over the past six decades, often in collaboration with political parties and other supporting institutions. In contrast, the former has only been used in the current decade, and demonstrates the legitimacy that excluding political parties enjoys among social organizers in contemporary Chile. Rejecting political parties as well as other political institutions is, in fact, common among *población* activists.

Evidence suggests that the disconnection between protestors and political parties has progressively increased in Chile since 1990 (Somma and Bargsted 2015). Yet this gap between grassroots and institutional politics has developed more quickly and intensely in the urban margins. Because of its particularly scarce access to resources, underprivileged organizing often experiences the conflict between accepting institutional support together with a relative level of co-optation and the need for substantial autonomy (Piven and Cloward 1977). Furthermore, institutional interventions in the urban margins generally focus on service provision and contribute to stigmatizing people, thus depoliticizing communities. Therefore, political parties are not trusted by politicized poor urban residents. Activists' rejection of political parties in *poblaciones* is also influenced by their ongoing sourcing of symbols from the political identity that radical leftist groups transmitted to local leaders in the 1980s.

Lessons learned in the past have confirmed underprivileged dwellers' institutional distrust on several occasions. A fundamental source of institutional distrust is the democratic transition, which most local organizers read as a defeat and betrayal. Many of the most politicized local leaders in *poblaciones* sided with the radical factions of the left during Chile's democratization process. Their struggle against the military involved assuming high personal costs in the pursuit of fundamental ideals. Yet, the events that unfolded degraded their efforts. The right-wing and the military, they suggest, preserved political power after the transition, while the moderate left abandoned most of its claims for the empowerment of the poor, redistribution, and social justice. According to *pobladores'* diagnosis, in fact, the Concertación coalition implemented an increasingly elitist project that actually preserved most of Pinochet's market-oriented policies.

Although the PC remained a close ally to leftist *población* organizing in the early 1990s, its progressive alignment with policies of the Concertación created increasing conflicts with neighborhood leaders. "The [Communist] Party lost its ideology with the return of democracy … the PC started making agreements with the Concertación and began deactivating demonstrations," describes a local leader who belonged to a Communist cell in the neighborhood in the 1980s (Interview, January 4, 2013). Disappointed with the party's policies, this leader quit its ranks in the late 1990s to devote his energies to grassroots mobilizing.

Collaborating with institutional agents regularly brings discredit to local organizers within the *población*. Despite their frequent interaction with local government officials, the several moderate neighborhood council members, for example, emphatically claimed to be independent from political parties and state control in my interviews. I confirmed local organizers' rejection of political influence in my interviews with municipal council members and local government agents. While most of them report that connecting with organizers in Lo Hermida is a challenge, many politicians on the left describe having experienced intense distrust from and conflicts with *población* activists. My fieldwork indicates that the autonomy of Lo Hermida's SMC is a key trait that motivates and legitimizes collective action among activists. In contrast, organizations in Nuevo Amanecer and other *poblaciones* strongly depend on networks of political loyalty that shape their collective action. As I argue in Chapter 3, in Chile's highly exclusionary political structure, this acquiescent disposition to external influence exposes communities to the disempowering effects of stigmatization.

The autonomy that *población* organizations in Lo Hermida seek in their interactions with authorities is particularly evident if we compare it with how local organizers interact with political institutions in Nuevo Amanecer. As in similar neighborhoods, organizers in Nuevo Amanecer regularly engage in active collaborations with local politicians or government officials. Their organizations also often seek to model themselves after government institutions. Local leaders frame their work as a "service" that they provide to the community and their organizational roles are formally defined. They have an organized management system that follows a regular schedule with strict authorization rules for the use of their *sede*. Their *sede* also imitates government buildings with a clean aesthetic that avoids political expressions. Conversely, some *sedes* in Lo Hermida welcome the informality of local organizing and allow graffiti and mosaics produced by local artists on their walls.

### 5.3.2.2 Informal Family Bonds

When I asked activists about their experience in Lo Hermida, one of them replied: "I feel that the *población* is like my family. Lo Hermida is a sort of bigger family than my own family" (Interview, March 13, 2013a). This woman was echoing other local activists. In their conversations, meetings, and collective actions, I found that activists repeatedly highlight the

importance of trustworthy, close connections that resemble family interactions in the neighborhood. "This is a great place, because people know
each other, people help each other, you walk in the streets and you say
hello to people" (Group Interview, February 26, 2013), an activist
emphasized when I asked him to describe Lo Hermida. By having their
neighborhood as their most frequent mobilizing site, local activists create
networks of collaboration and trust with each other and other residents.

This practice of amplifying the community's closeness is rooted in the
neighborhood's composition. It is the case for many residents that their
extended families in fact live in Lo Hermida, or at least close by in the
district of Peñalolén. Since many families have lived in the neighborhood
since its inception, they have a history of shared experiences and know
each other well. As an organizer in his 50s told me, "back then [in the
land takeover, in 1970], I came with my father to settle in a plot nearby;
then my father called his brother, and my mother called one of her
brothers and a sister. They all settled here with their families"
(Interview, February 19, 2013). These informal family bonds allow activists to extend calls to action to other local dwellers who are likely to
recognize how their close interactions have grown from the community's
historical struggle.

For example, a set of housing committees in the neighborhood have
mobilized using this tactic. They gather families applying for the state's
social housing subsidy who refuse to be displaced further away from the
center of the city. They are coordinated by the MPL. In the challenge of
seeking new families in the neighborhood to join their protests, these
housing committee activists have been successful in referring to how much
of an asset the close network is for *población* residents. A recent committee member who had joined these mobilizations after attending a few
meetings with MPL activists told me: "[in those meetings] I realized that
I want to get my house here and not in some other district far away,
because this is where I grew up, where I know the people and where my
mother struggled to raise seven children" (Interview, March 4, 2013).

The social closeness used by activists in Lo Hermida to describe their
neighborhood promotes a positive emotional connection with their community. Local activists speak of Lo Hermida with enthusiasm and dignity.
"This [neighborhood] is my place ... I am in love with Lo Hermida!"
(Group Interview, March 11, 2013). This is also often the case for
residents who do not participate in local organizations. Both in Nuevo
Amanecer and other demobilized neighborhoods in Chile's urban
margins where I conducted interviews, people's descriptions of their

community are substantially different. Although security and socio-demographic factors in most of these areas are akin to those found in Lo Hermida, local residents tend to highlight criminality, social alienation, and social fragmentation when referring to their neighborhood. The words of affection and pride with which people describe Lo Hermida are seldom uttered by local residents who live in demobilized neighborhoods.

### 5.3.2.3 Solidarity Networks

"We have solidarity, this is how it is here. Once I remember that a child didn't have shoes to wear, and people who saw this moved quickly and got new shoes for him, and they were good, new shoes!" (Group Interview, February 26, 2013). As these words from a local activist highlight, *población* organizers also advance mobilizing belonging by amplifying people's humane, solidarity-oriented interactions in their community. This tactic challenges stigmatizing conceptions of the urban poor that depict them as lacking civility, representing them as fundamentally anomic and antisocial.

While local activists and other residents often recognize that a mentality of individualism and competitiveness has taken over many people in the *población*, they amplify solidarity as being part of the community's DNA. Conversations and interviews indicate that besides a mobilization tactic, the urban land invasion through which *pobladores* created Lo Hermida was a founding event of collective survival and solidarity, in which people built community by committing to helping each other. For them, this historical memory serves as evidence of a community that is solidaristic in its origin. A local resident and soccer club organizer in the *población*, for instance, echoed others when he described: "we were a *toma*; [therefore] people here are used to helping each other and organizing" (Interview, January 30, 2013). Activists also use this sense of community solidarity to explain opportunities in which local organizations have coordinated their actions to mobilize together. This notion of solidarity is so strong that according to many activists, burglars in the neighborhood tend to prefer other areas of the city to carry out their crimes in order to protect their own community.

Despite their distrust toward institutions, the higher class, and individuals of the elite, activists also amplify the community's inclusivity. They often describe their community as a mobilization hub that welcomes activists and people from outside the neighborhood who are ready to contribute to their cause. In addition, *pobladores'* lifestyles are often portrayed as simple and humble among activists. This emphasis adds to their amplification of local solidarity. "Many here are poor, but they're clean, they are simple people . . . [Lo Hermida has] a provincial air; people say hello to each other, like in the countryside, you know?' (Interview, March 13, 2013b), a local resident and activist indicated when describing his community to me in an interview. He went on to explain that many of the families that invaded Lo Hermida's lands in 1970 had migrated from the countryside to the city. The provincial ethos they brought to the neighborhood made them honest and humble people. Hence, presumably, they are less concerned with personal benefits and more likely to help each other.

### 5.3.2.4 The Popular

The notion of the *popular* (the popular) articulated collective action and community-building in Chile's urban margins during the 1980s (Oxhorn 1995), and it currently survives among the symbols by which *población* activists amplify the informal. As jazz and hip-hop emerged as the voice of the marginalized, the *popular* refers to the cultural and artistic expressions of the lower classes. It stands in opposition to the mainstream cultural expressions of the higher class. In local activists' view, "fine art" has historically portrayed the experience and visions of the elite. In contrast, the political value of the *popular* stems from its ability to reflect poor people's lifestyle, reality, and claims. Furthermore, activists see the *popular* as evidence of the poor's ability to develop their own traditions, beauty, and art outside privileged social circles.

Local activists refer to the neighborhood as a center for *popular* art, and organizations understand it as part of their *lucha*. "Lo Hermida is a cultural hub. ... We have had the best puppet masters, guitar players, folklore groups, batucada groups, circus groups, people doing theatre, even guys doing rap or dancing" a local leader explained to me (Interview, January 14, 2013). Numerous neighborhood organizations develop art and present their work in local events, *peñas,* and protests.

In the past couple of decades, a group of hip-hop artists has grown increasingly cohesive in Lo Hermida. They describe their actions as *lucha* and express the *popular* through graffiti painting, tattooing, and rapping. Under the banner of *Rap Autónomo Poblacional* (Autonomous Neighborhood Rap, RAP) several of them organize gigs, fundraising events, and commemorations. This group frames its work as part of their community's *lucha* in their performances, meetings, and informal conversations. Their increasing cohesion has allowed them to expand their network of activism with organizers across the urban margins and with Mapuche organizations in the South of Chile.

The different traditions and parties in the neighborhood are also part of the *popular*. Local street markets, or *ferias*, are one of these traditions. They are set up two or three times a week, depending on the season, and sell all sorts of goods for only a proportion of their average market value. Local activists proudly talk about these street markets, stating, for example, that "they [street markets] make life here independent from the large corporations" (Interview, January 30. 2013b) and "in street markets neighbors sell to neighbors... we help each other" (Interview, March 11, 2013a). The neighborhood's development of the *popular* also includes neighborhood parties, or *peñas*, and the yearly anniversary, the commemoration of the disappeared by the dictatorship, and the commemoration for Manuel Gutierrez's killing.

These dimensions amplify the informal through collective behavior and rhetorical tactics. They contribute to mobilization by boosting positive assertions of the community. In other words, activists use these dimensions to show off their community's attractiveness and dignity. This strategy rejects stigmatization. Therefore, it increases identification with the *población*, which in turn promotes organizers' cohesion and makes others more likely to join local organizations.

## 5.4 REPRESSION

During my first few weeks in Lo Hermida, I devoted my time to getting to know the neighborhood as well as possible. I met many people and got acquainted with the different areas of the neighborhood. I wanted to understand where mobilization occurred, the history of the different places, and the boundaries of the neighborhood, as well as its more dangerous areas. With that goal in mind, I asked some of the informants I was meeting to show me around the neighborhood. One of them, a young leader in his late twenties, took the task particularly seriously and decided to show me the spots he considered most important. As we walked toward El Valle Avenue, a street that hosts many protests in the *población*, he began describing some of the conflicts that local organizations have had with authorities. He spoke of "*represión*" (repression) when describing the interactions with the police and politicians. Suddenly, we reached a square in which several exercise machines had been installed by the municipality. He pointed to the machines and told me "this is the repression I'm talking about." Despite my follow-up questions, I was unable to properly understand this link he was making between the exercise machines and their oppressive interaction with the police.

Through my interviews and observations, over time, I would come to understand that the idea of repression organizes boundary-making because it describes the interaction between the informal and the formal. Therefore, it is at the center of *pobladores*' mobilizing identity. Activists described state participatory funding schemes and urban regeneration programs as repressive. They also spoke of repression when describing public schools, the health system, and voting. Facing what they call "repression" symbolically makes *pobladores* participants in the same *lucha* (struggle) that radical leaders fought in the 1980s against the dictatorship. Their descriptions of repression include state discrimination and coercion, as well as police violence, on some occasions. Furthermore, the spectacular levels of police and military brutality in the 2019 protests made repression particularly present and concrete. Undeniably, however, the repression they currently experience has changed and no longer involves the sheer physical violence it did during the dictatorship. As activists explained to me, repression today is covert; it is disguised as policies and social interactions that appear to foster inclusion and freedom. Instead, these policies create manipulation and political exclusion in *poblaciones*. Their struggle is, therefore, strongly cultural and community-based.

I have outlined the implicit distinction that *población* activists make between two realms of legitimacy, the informal and the formal. The informal promotes *población* dwellers' belonging because it provides appealing contents that facilitate identification processes. The informal symbolically provides the sense of protection and community that formal institutions have regularly denied *pobladores*. Yet, the relationship between the informal and the formal is conceived by local organizers as an ongoing conflict. Their symbols and interactions indicate that the formal is constantly seeking to formalize and destroy the informal. Activists call this formalizing power, "repression." My analysis, therefore, indicates that mobilization is further enhanced by local activists' defensive reaction toward what they read as repressive institutions.

The notion of repression has a high emotional and political impact within the Chilean left. It inevitably recalls the human rights violations perpetrated by Pinochet's dictatorship. By speaking about repression, neighborhood activists imply that organizations currently experience a level of oppression similar to the atrocities perpetrated by the dictatorship. In fact, most activists that I spoke with suggest that Chile is currently a "dictatorship," in which dissention is severely punished. As an activist in his late 20s told me, "there was [in the *población*] a powerful feeling of injustice, especially during the dictatorship, because of how [the military] persecuted, repressed, and killed Chile's best guys; and that is a feeling that we keep on having today" (Interview, February 15, 2013b). Similarly, a neighborhood leader in his 50s explained to me "the repression that we experienced during the dictatorship never lowered; now it's more disguised, but it never changed" (Interview, January 4, 2013).

The manner in which activists equate experiences of the past with the present moment is particularly powerful when it comes to speaking of repression. Both while I conducted my interviews, and when I later analyzed my fieldwork material, I realized that activists often communicate by superposing past events of dictatorial repression with more recent oppressive events. Several times, I found myself shocked by stories in which my informants described scenes of brutal state violence in the neighborhood. These stories were explained as though they were recent events that required immediate reaction. Yet, when I followed up, I often found that those stories in fact referred to human rights violations that had taken place during the dictatorship. I encountered this dynamic repeatedly in the fieldwork I conducted from 2012 through 2017. Either intentionally or unintentionally, local activists presented past events of state brutality as recent facts, taking place in modern Chile. For instance, after listening to a group of activists reflecting on the violence with which the police confronted protestors in current *poblaciones*, I asked them about additional examples of state abuse. One of them said, "do you remember the kid they killed in a protest in Vespucio? His name was Pedro Mariqueo." I later confirmed, however, that Pedro Mariqueo was a young local resident and member of the Christian Left Party, who was killed by the police during a protest on May 1, 1984 (Field notes, December 27, 2012).

### 5.4.1 Antagonists

Neighborhood activists frame those social actors that actively participate in formalizing the informal as antagonists who exercise repression. These are, for instance, the central and local governments, the police, and political parties, the educational system, academia, and even some NGOs. Activists encapsulate these actors under the umbrella term, "institutions." Despite not directly conducting formalization processes, other social actors are understood as enemies because they benefit from and promote repression. For activists, the upper class and "the rich" are part of this category because they corruptly shape the legal framework that organizes the formal. According to activists, hard drugs were introduced in the urban margins by state authorities with the goal of deactivating poor people's political potential, and therefore for them, drug dealers also play a collaborating role in this repressive system, and should be understood as another enemy. For those more radical activists, neighborhood organizers who avoid challenging institutions and passively comply with authorities, also fit this category.

Political parties and the police have a special role among antagonists because they epitomize the wide array of repressive tactics. Instead of supporting mobilization, political parties are understood to repress by instrumentalizing, controlling, and manipulating local organizations. Belonging to political parties is, therefore, strictly and emphatically discouraged among *población* activists. In response to my questions about party membership among local activists, a leader in Lo Hermida in his late 20s explained:

> [If an activist declared their party membership] they would probably be kicked out [of the organization]! People in organizations at the *población* don't trust them [party members] and have resentment towards them … When somebody from an organization belongs to a party, that person ultimately ends up paying attention to party commands and not to what they should construct with the organization. (Interview, January 30, 2013a)

The exclusion that local activists experience in their neighborhood's SMC when they publicly engage in electoral politics is epitomized by the conflict between *población* organizations and the MPL. Initially, the MPL was a local organization coordinating a group of families who were living as *allegados* in Lo Hermida and other areas of Peñalolén. These families belonged to housing committees and were applying to the state's social housing subsidy. The MPL assisted those families to reject the state's most common provision of houses in the urban outskirts and demand that their new houses were located within the same district. Although once deeply involved in Lo Hermida's network of neighborhood organizing, the MPL lost much of its support among local activists when it became involved in electoral politics. This organization's conflicts with *población* leaders began after the MPL started running for municipal council elections. The MPL was repeatedly accused of instrumentalizing local residents when its activists tried to use local events for electoral campaigning. Frictions mounted further when the MPL joined the Equality Party (PI), in 2009. This relationship eventually collapsed when a group of local activists organized the destruction of the campaign banners that the PI had installed in the district for the 2012 municipal election. Several heated discussions between activists after that incident ended up disconnecting MPL leaders from most of the initiatives implemented at the *población.*

Local activists see the police force as a more violent repressive agent. It is, in fact, a target of great anger and fear, that sparks emotional and indignant reactions from local activists and other residents. In conversations and interviews, policemen are often represented as submissive actors within an authoritarian and hierarchical structure, who are brainwashed to obstruct poor people's collective action to the benefit of politicians and the upper class. Activists interpret the police's presence in the neighborhood as a repressive action that oversteps community boundaries. As I walked through the neighborhood with a group of local organizers, for instance, some of them referred to a police car parked in the neighborhood, saying, "they [policemen] must be buying drugs [here in the neighborhood]". My later inquiries were unable to substantiate this accusation (Field notes, March 10, 2013). The many actions of police brutality against protestors in late 2019, confirmed activists' negative emotions of fear and distrust toward state security forces.

Local activists' resentment toward the police and other authorities is partially a response to their chronic exposure to state abuse. Since the neighborhood's inception, local residents' interactions with authorities have been tense. Local organizers accuse recurrent manipulation by government officials. They also describe experiencing ongoing disrespect, discrimination, and violence in daily encounters with the police. In my fieldwork in different *poblaciones,* I myself have faced the unjustified, authoritative, and aggressive treatment of policemen. Several of the activists I interviewed also report having suffered intimidation, arrests, and beatings by policemen, whose goal was to discourage protests. The police are quick at retaliating when activists challenge their authority. Activists' distrust for state security forces is epitomized by their ongoing conflict with a local police station, which was built in the neighborhood in 2009. As I describe in Chapter 2, for months in late 2019 *población* residents and activists engaged in unprecedented daily violent confrontations with policemen in that station. Although sparked by the police's response to an attempted land seizure and in the context of country-wide disruptive mobilizations, those confrontations resulted from years of growing distrust and resentment.

The killing of local resident Manuel Gutierrez at the hands of a policeman from that station in 2011 built indignation among local activists. Additionally, my interviews suggest, policemen have repeatedly demonstrated discrimination toward *población* organizing. On several occasions, for instance, the police emphatically quelled *pobladores'* mobilizations and appeared more conciliatory when dealing with student protests in better-off areas of the district. The station has also directly contacted *población* leaders and made attempts to monitor their collective action in the neighborhood. Policemen from that station at some point even infiltrated organizations in Lo Hermida to seek evidence about those activists participating in contentious collective action (Ciper Chile 2020). Describing activists' resulting distrust and anger toward the police, a young organizer in his 20s told me:

There is a lot of hatred [toward the police], and it goes beyond what one would want. I mean, they [protestors] kill a policeman and you get happy! You tend to forget that those guys [policemen] are also human beings, who have families, too. That feeling [of resentment] comes from us being always under the boot [oppressed by the police]; they have always fucked us, they repress us, that's why we have hoarded hatred. ... They killed a kid [Manuel Gutiérrez] last year near here, and the policeman who did it is free, he didn't even go to trial! (Interview, February 15, 2013)

Through these emotional reactions of indignation, boundary-making motivates mobilization. Yet, while it is true that this anger triggers cohesion and action, for mobilization to occur people need to learn to legitimize contentious action as a valid reaction to what they read as external threats. In other words, anger over police oppression will not in itself mobilize neighborhood activists. In fact, many residents in Lo Hermida who *did not* participate in collective action also described their anger with the police and other authorities in my interviews. A mobilizing identity requires local activists to learn that reacting to repression through *lucha* provides a social reward and a sense of political incorporation. I address the political socialization processes by which this occurs in Chapter 6.

## 5.5 CONCLUSION

In this chapter, I have focused on the case of Lo Hermida; a community that despite social and political exclusion has managed to sustain grassroots mobilization over the past five decades. Through this case study, I examined how collective identity advances mobilizational citizenship in Chile's urban margins. I showed how neighborhood activists share identity symbols, such as *"pobladores," "lucha,"* and *"repression,"* to connect their collective endeavor with a long-standing community of political fighters in Chile's underprivileged urban areas. Collective identity, therefore, allows activists to imagine a community that extends in time and space; a community that provides them with a system of legitimacy that resists the norms of validation through which formal institutions stigmatize and exclude them.

This strategic construction of collective identity cannot be found in neighborhoods that demobilized after Chile's democratic transition in 1990. To explain how this process of demobilization occurred and survives, I addressed the case of Nuevo Amanecer in detail in Chapter 3. Despite its similarities with Lo Hermida, Nuevo Amanecer is a case that represents many other neighborhoods in the urban margins because the dictatorship, as well as ulterior political dynamics, promoted its community's sense of historical discontinuity. As I address in detail in previous chapters, these developments undermine the ability for urban dwellers in Nuevo Amanecer to share cohesive symbols and transmit collective identity in local processes of political socialization.

Chapter 6 further highlights the contrast between these two communities. It looks at the micro-mobilizing dynamics of *población* activism to explain how local organizers use mobilizing identity as political capital. I show how instead of monopolizing leadership skills and resources, as community leaders do in demobilized neighborhoods, activists in Lo Hermida and other mobilized urban communities have developed tactics to decentralize protagonism, leadership, and community-building.

# 6

# Protagonism and Community-Building

## 6.1 INTRODUCTION

"*¡Juegue!*" (play!). With just this word, one of Lo Hermida's leaders enthusiastically replied to my idea of strengthening connections between neighborhood organizations across Latin America's Southern Cone (Field notes, December 16, 2012). While in its formal meaning the word *juegue* is a command for somebody else to play something, it is informally widely used in Chile to encourage another person to carry out the necessary actions leading to any given result. This leader was, in other words, telling me to take the initiative and autonomously build networks abroad on behalf of the organization. I would later understand that this sort of interaction fed mobilizational citizenship by decentralizing protagonism.

In this chapter, I examine how these micro-mobilizing dynamics – in other words, face-to-face interactions that fuel mobilization – decentralize protagonism among *población* activists. I show the role that socialization occurring in different kinds of encounters has in both sustaining collective action over time and building an alternative form of political incorporation. I use Gamson's threefold typology of micro-mobilizing acts to explore the grassroots dynamics leading to this outcome (see Chapter 1). Decentralized protagonism results from *población* activists' tendency to transmit political capital. It is using a mobilizing identity as political capital in order to socialize other activists and community members that has allowed collective action to survive in the urban margins. In contrast, in neighborhoods that suffered post-dictatorial depoliticization, where acquiescent collective action prevails, local leaders tend to be highly concerned with monopolizing political capital. The enduring collective action that results from mobilizational citizenship allowed Lo Hermida activists to develop the required mobilizing capabilities to engage in the large-scale protests that erupted in 2019.

I begin this chapter by showing *población* activists' commitment to transmitting mobilizing identity in the form of political capital. I explain that political socialization is often imparted by older activists who seek to transmit mobilizing symbols to younger and more inexperienced *población* activists. This socialization occurs through role modeling and in encounters of activism. As bearers of mobilizing identity, activists perform protagonism and deepen its decentralization. In the following section of this chapter, I examine how activists embody and promote decentralized protagonism further, both individually and collectively. As in the previous chapter, I pay particular attention to my fieldwork experience participating in an organization occupying a local square in Lo Hermida in the summer of 2012–2013 to flesh out my comparative analysis. I show that decentralizing protagonism spreads leadership among activists. This dynamic promotes the reemergence of leaders willing to facilitate mobilization and makes activists legitimate community-builders. Finally, I provide examples to demonstrate the progressive buildup of mobilizing capabilities in Lo Hermida in recent decades and explain how those capabilities have interacted with activists' decentralized protagonism.

## 6.2 TRANSMITTING MOBILIZING IDENTITY

As McIntosh and Youniss (2010, 23) suggest, key to developing public political engagement is the "doing within a political context." In other words, we grow to be politically active citizens as we become procedurally involved in a community in which we learn about habits and identity. A 26-year-old activist in Lo Hermida echoed these theoretical notions when I asked him how he began participating in local organizations:

My story within [Lo Hermida] organizations begins before I was born [with the *pobladores*' long-standing struggle] ... but what marked me and made me become part of organizations here is very simple: when I was a child, during long weekends, my [grown-up] neighbors would block my street, gather money (*hacían una vaca*), organize a football match [on the street] for us children, and give us ice creams and biscuits. They did so for no reason, only to celebrate the fact that we were kids, nothing else. On weekdays the streets had cars [and we couldn't play there], but on those weekends the cars were fucked, and that's it! They did the same for Christmas, and it was even cooler! One of my neighbors would dress up like Santa, you know? I think that's when I got my interest in community life (*me picó el bichito de lo que es vivir en comunidad*). (Interview, December 3, 2020)

Later in the interview he highlights that this early community experience gave him the disposition to become increasingly publicly engaged in his neighborhood. Describing his interactions with other local activists and leaders, he explained "Later, as a teenager [other organizers] told me that I was good at coordinating others, structuring meetings, and taking notes, so I felt I wanted to contribute, give organizational tools to others" (Interview, December 3, 2020). Henceforth, Lo Hermida's SMC welcomed a new activist.

Collective action in *poblaciones* involves a relatively diverse mix of organizations and activists. This mobilization is only partially made of stable neighborhood organizations. The largest portion of collective action is produced by short-term organizations, and it stems from the dynamic implementation of initiatives by groups that appear or change depending on their necessity. Underlying this organization is a twofold leadership structure.

On the one hand, specific individuals act as leaders. They inspire and coordinate others' mobilization by concentrating more networks, knowledge, and access to resources. Crucially, these leaders are able to build strong grassroots legitimacy. Much as Bénit-Gbaffou and Katsaura (2014) have highlighted for the South African case, these leaders manage to develop political capital within local micro-mobilizing dynamics. As Rolando, a young local activist in Lo Hermida, described, these leaders use their access to resources and networks to facilitate the implementation of initiatives in different areas of the neighborhood:

[I]n every area here, you find someone who is representative, and you can count on that person to help you or open doors for you if you want to organize something there... this allows us to maintain what we are doing, for example, we decided to keep on doing the *pascuas populares*.[1] (Interview, February 26, 2013)

On the other hand, leaders tend to transfer mobilizational identity symbols, making political capital accessible to other local activists and community members. The resulting dissemination of political capital allows active residents to acquire a sense of protagonism. The decentralized acquisition of protagonism is a platform for activists who are willing to build leadership skills further in the neighborhood. Protagonism, together with leaders' assistance, motivates and validates isolated groups

---

[1] *Pascuas populares* (popular Christmas) are events organized by local activists at the Victor Jara square every December to celebrate Christmas together with the neighborhood's homeless.

of activists to implement initiatives of collective action. Ultimately, these mechanisms promote the emergence of new *población* leaders, which is essential for the survival of collective action over time.

This emphasis on transmitting mobilizational identity symbols in *poblaciones* such as Lo Hermida is conscious and explicitly recognized by local activists. Both leaders and activists spoke to me about their deliberate intention of sharing mobilizing identity symbols. While the specific strategies of socialization are less clear for *población* activists, they include tailoring events of identity transmission to be appealing to younger neighborhood residents, often children. This transmission complements previous political socialization processes that youths and children experience through other meaningful relationships (usually with parents, siblings, or other family members) that may also expose young community members to mobilizing identity symbols (Cornejo et al. 2020). Local leaders, however, contribute to confirming those symbols at the public level, thus promoting unity and mobilization in neighborhood organizations. Additionally, activists' continual interaction with *población* children expands their networks of acquaintance to those children's family members and other residents, which contributes to developing the local SMC's mobilizing capabilities further.

Those *población* leaders that others consider more capable of collective identity transmission (because of their past experiences and knowledge) enjoy higher local legitimacy. As I argued in earlier chapters, this mobilizing identity has its roots in political socialization processes of the 1980s. Among Lo Hermida activists, I noticed how those leaders with the ability to demonstrate knowledge and applied experience about strategies used in the 1980s were particularly admired. They are bestowed with a high moral standing among SMC members. Gonzalo, a 27-year-old local activist, confirmed this dynamic by telling me:

[I]t's about identity, it's an identity that *emerges* from the old [residents], I think that's one of the most important things here, the identity of the older [people], of the workers, of those who participated in social struggle (*dieron la pelea*). The [socialist] revolution became a reality for us at that time, it was not a dream or a utopia here [when current old residents were younger and more active in the local SMC], both with intellect and with arms. (Interview, February 15, 2013)

As we know from Effron and Miller's (2012) work, attributions of high moral reputation are powerful sources of legitimacy. A leader's legitimacy is boosted among local dwellers and activists when they narrate anecdotes and display knowledge resulting from their involvement in anti-dictatorial protests during the 1980s. Referring to her admiration for one of those older leaders, for example, an activist in her early 20s explained to me: "She [the older leader] was *there* [in the anti-dictatorial protests], you know? she fought against the *milicos* (military), I don't know if she was from the *Frente* (FPMR) or if she knows people from the MIR; but the woman knows!" (Group Interview, February 13, 2013).

How does this mobilizing identity transmission occur? My observations and interviews suggest that *población* activists obtain mobilizing identity symbols in two broad ways: through role modeling and in encounters of activism.

### 6.2.1 Role Modeling

The learning process by which somebody acquires the attitudes, values, and behaviors of another person through the emulation of her role and actions is what I call role modeling. Role models provide exemplary and desirable traits to others who learn from them. Based on admiration, role modeling is a privileged platform for the transmission of mobilizing identity symbols. My observations suggest that local organizations coordinate activities that promote this sort of interaction among residents.

In Lo Hermida, as well as in other mobilized *poblaciones*, activists tend to organize initiatives aimed at attracting children and young people. Coordinated events include setting up entertainment activities and games for children in open *población* spaces. Organization members, for example, might install a table tennis table and an inflatable swimming pool, or organize a stilt and face-painting workshop, as well as other fun activities. Children are invited to spend an afternoon of entertainment together with activists. Events like this occur on a square or at the intersection of two roads that organizers block to keep cars away. Organization members set up banners a couple of days in advance around the area promoting the event. As the event starts, activists use a speaker to attract people's attention in the neighborhood while simultaneously knocking on the doors of houses in the surrounding area to invite children. They provide snacks and coordinate games, typically fun competitions. Usually, activists also plan activities for collective reflection, for example, through a simple allegorical film.[2] A discussion about the film is meant to boost critical thinking and political consciousness in children.

---

[2] The Bolivian short film *Abuela Grillo* (Cricket Grandmother) is, for example, highly popular in workshops on *población* activism. The plot symbolically represents the conflict between the capitalist commodification of natural resources and the needs of local

Similarly, *colonias urbanas* invite children to fun activities monitored by local activists that occur a few days each week during the summer holiday. They are planned and advertised well in advance, and are held at the neighborhood council's building. Another sort of activity tailored for children by local organizations involves art workshops. Usually taking place in squares, these workshops provide children with the opportunity to learn a craft or play a musical instrument. In art workshops, young activists teach *población* children how to play the guitar, paint graffiti, or make stencils, among other activities. Parents, especially those of younger children, regularly orbit these activities and interact with local activists. According to my fieldwork, those interactions create or sustain bonds of acquaintance and relative trust between local activists and neighbors who do not belong to Lo Hermida's SMC. Eventually, in 2019, those links made local organizers' calls to engage in protests more persuasive.

These events aim to politically train young people and children in the *población* by exposing them to public interactions, critical debates, and material that advances political awareness. Yet, according to my observations, this strategy's effectiveness is rather indirect. In other words, while the events promoted children's interaction and closeness with the local SMC, they hardly provide them with new cognitive skills and ideological viewpoints. First, I saw that instances of collective reflection do not occur at every event. Second, social issues tend to be formulated univocally by the organizers, giving little space for children to discuss issues critically. Third, children are usually less willing to spend time thinking and discussing than expected. What I did notice, however, is that these events are effective in building bonds between children and other active residents – usually young *población* activists. These bonds serve as access for children into the local community. During these events, I too built relationships with the children. After participating in a couple of activities, I learned a few of the children's names; they would later call and wave to me as I walked around the neighborhood. Through this type of interaction, children began admiring young activists and, ultimately, saw them as role models. In the time I spent in the *población*, several children started rapping and learned a few breakdance steps, following the example of several activists who were hip-hop artists. This role modeling also motivated children to attend and

communities. The film tells the story of an indigenous old woman who walks around rural Bolivia bringing rain and fertility to farmers. She is eventually captured by capitalist forces represented by characters dressed in suits who exploit the grandmother and make profits from the water she makes provoking drought in the Bolivian countryside.

participate enthusiastically in subsequent events organized by activists. Relationships of role modeling provide trustworthy interactions in which rap songs, conversations, discussions, and even lessons that young activists give to children in improvised conversations can effectively transmit mobilizing identity symbols.

Similar intergenerational relationships are established in local soccer clubs. Traditionally, Lo Hermida has been divided into several *villas*, each comprising a few blocks and represented by a soccer club. A soccer club includes several teams, each covering an age range, and some of the clubs also have female teams. Despite all sorts of differences, neighbors (especially men) of all ages unite over soccer clubs. Training sessions occur a few times a week, and championship matches are played during the weekend, bringing families together. Adult community members act as coaches for young residents' teams. In turn, the young residents train children's teams. Often, when coaches are committed to their work, they create close bonds with their teams. When young activists train children's teams, they often become role models and transmit their mobilizing identity to the younger generations. Aware of the strong political value of soccer clubs in Lo Hermida, some local activists take coordinating positions within the clubs and the local league.

Many other activities provide children with opportunities to bond with neighborhood activists, namely, neighborhood council events, rap or folklore music gigs, commemorations, and *peñas*. Even random encounters in the neighborhood may serve as meaningful interactions of political socialization. Children in the *población* spend much of their time in the streets, hence meeting them spontaneously is rather easy. Oftentimes, young activists invite children to their meetings and other activism initiatives. While children get the opportunity to collaborate in the implementation of activities, young leaders teach them the basics of activism. Children play around activists while they discuss future plans, prepare their activities, or work in a crowdfunding event. Consequently, intergenerational relationships develop naturally.

### 6.2.2 Encounters of Activism

In meetings, discussions, informal conversations, and other encounters of activism, the older leaders transmit mobilizing identity symbols to younger activists. They do so by taking the lead in key situations, such as reframing opportunities, promoting a particular repertoire of collective action, and narrating anecdotes.

While most *población* activists have already assimilated a mobilizing identity, the oldest leaders take charge of reinterpretation processes that use mobilizing symbols to reframe reality as unfair. They do this by being especially emphatic and using their high legitimacy to strengthen mobilizing symbols. In some strategic situations, I observed how the older leaders created discursive connections between present events and past cases of injustice. They, therefore, strengthened the mobilizing power of the reframing process.

In a conversation I witnessed in January 2013, for example, activists in Lo Hermida reflected on how the police crack down on protests. In this case, older leaders repeatedly reminded younger ones that oppressive and violent policemen had assassinated innocent young men, such as Pedro Mariqueo and Manuel Gutiérrez, only a few years before. Furthermore, older leaders also made connections equating the current regime with the dictatorship. In reframing oppressive situations, they repeatedly declared, "This is a dictatorship!" (Field notes, January 8, 2013). Through these declarations community leaders reframe the group's collective experience, implicitly portray police forces as "repressive," and extend activists' experience of oppression through time to connect past and present. In this way, decentralizing protagonism activates agentic memory and mobilizing boundaries, thus feeding back the social and psychological dynamics underlying mobilizational citizenship (see Chapters 4 and 5 for further details).

In meetings and planning discussions, older leaders incorporate mobilizing symbols to keep the local collective identity alive. For example, when one of our meetings was almost over and most decisions had been made to organize an activity with neighbors at a square, one of the older leaders suggested hosting a community kitchen at the event to feed everyone during lunchtime. A strong symbol of *población* mobilization from the past, the community kitchen was a way of incorporating the local collective identity in the event. Including a community kitchen was therefore an act of identity certification. The others agreed enthusiastically.

The square occupation I participated in with other local activists had in fact originated through a similar dynamic. Its inception can be traced to a group of youths, new to local activism, who decided to create a critical pedagogy school for *población* residents. Their project aimed to provide political socialization to local children. Soon, the group grew and included some more experienced young activists in their 20s who were better connected with the SMC's local networks of mobilization. During one of their meetings, one of the more experienced attendants suggested running their project by some of the oldest leaders. He specifically mentioned a former Communist activist who had participated in disruptive protests against the dictatorship in the 1980s. "Telling [older leaders] is a good idea because they know more [about tactics and identity] and they know more people here" (Field notes, March 17, 2013), explained that same young activist when I later asked him about his suggestion in the meeting. By seeking older leaders' approval, these young activists, in fact, obtained access to additional resources – such as building tools and construction materials – and neighborhood networks. Crucially, I would later realize, older leaders were also a source of identity certification. Eventually, the group would incorporate an older local leader in its meetings, who pushed them to recruit new participants, branch out their project to other local organizations, and organize a *recuperación* with the goal of repossessing the land they needed in order to install the school in the neighborhood. The organization invested a great deal of effort into occupying the square, as I already described in Chapter 5. This example unveils the conflicts that local organizers may engage in when learning local identity symbols. By using the *recuperación* as a platform for their critical pedagogy project, local young dwellers were combining notions and tactics anchored in the Left's socialist project of society with new initiatives of activism. The interactions and lessons that they acquired in this process would gradually make them new protagonists of local community-building.

Older leaders also use anecdotes about the past to transmit mobilizing identity symbols. On the one hand, anecdotes confirm older leaders' privileged position of knowledge about past *población* activism, thus boosting admiration from other members and fostering less experienced participants' assimilation of mobilizing identity symbols. On the other hand, anecdotes promote a sense of belonging to a community that extends in time. In many cases, local organization members stayed after meetings. I spent several evenings listening to anecdotes that members shared among themselves. Sometimes, members told stories about daily life, such as parties, sports, or job issues. Many of these sessions involved the exchange of stories about collective action experiences, such as events or conflicts within other local organizations in which those activists participated simultaneously. In these situations, leaders (especially the oldest ones) were eloquent in telling charming stories of activism. At various opportunities, the oldest leader in the repossessed square spoke about the adventures of the FPMR during the 1980s. He spoke about how concealed and militarized the FPMR's organizational structure was, even for militants within the movement. The *Frente* coordinated missions that were secret even to those conducting them. He said that on many occasions, FPMR members were asked to carry out actions – taking a package from point A to B, for example – without knowing the consequences of doing so. At other times, the leader spoke of heroic confrontations with the military during the 1980s. Younger members listened to these stories with admiration (Field notes, February 2, 2013). These stories not only confirmed the leader's legitimacy, but also fostered current activists' identification with former leaders organizing antidictatorial protests in the 1980s. In assimilating identity and participating in local contentious collective action, *población* dwellers foster a sense of incorporation within a broader imagined community. The abstract community underlying this process is comprised of neighborhood activists and heroic militants who have participated in local dwellers' struggles at the urban margins since the first decades of the nineteenth century. As current urban dwellers in Lo Hermida will never meet most of those *población* activists from the past and other neighborhoods, an act of imagination that connects them is required. The resulting sense of community extends in time to reach past, present, and future.

Activists diffuse collective identity symbols through role modeling dynamics and these encounters of micro-mobilization. In doing so, they bring identity to urban dwellers across ages and from different areas of the neighborhood. Crucially, the identity being transmitted locally validates and motivates collective action. The survival of mobilizational citizenship depends on these and other potential mechanisms that may be devised in other contexts able to effectively diffuse mobilizing identity symbols. The next section explains how, by transmitting mobilizing identity in the form of political capital, activists promote the decentralization of protagonism.

### 6.3 DECENTRALIZING PROTAGONISM AND LEADERSHIP BUILDING

The neighborhoods in which I focus my analysis – Lo Hermida and Nuevo Amanecer – present a sharp contrast between their leadership structures. Organizations in Nuevo Amanecer, as well as in other demobilized *poblaciones*, show a rather hierarchical structure. In most state-recognized *población* organizations – such as neighborhood councils, local development councils, and housing committees – leaders have formal roles. Most of these organizations have obtained legal personality, which is an institutional recognition that allows neighborhood organizations to engage in municipal bureaucratic procedures and access state benefits. Getting legal personality implies a set of requirements that, albeit simple, involve engaging in legal procedures. Local organizers need to create norms and a formal structure within the organization, and provide personal details at a municipal registry indicating their stable position and responsibilities. In this context, some members will be hierarchically situated above others within the same organization. According to Chile's law on Civil Participation (Law 20,500), for instance, each neighborhood council should have a democratically elected board of hierarchically distinguished members, which includes a president, a secretary, and a treasurer. Additional positions are also elected depending on the council's statutes, and a number of other, none-lected community members regularly collaborate in organizing the council's activities. Having obtained the highest number of votes in the community, the neighborhood council's president will be hierarchically superior to all other community members. The president will concentrate access to networks and relevant information.

Leadership structures in most other state-recognized neighborhood organizations are also strictly hierarchical and, as the case of Nuevo Amanecer demonstrates, their leaders often act as brokers between local political authorities and neighborhood residents. This dynamic is most noticeable in neighborhood development committees, organizations designed for the implementation of specific, short-term local development projects. Often, these development projects are subsidized housing improvements. Obtaining those subsidies requires several households in the neighborhood to carry out a collective application to state benefits. Development committees coordinate this application and eventually participate in supervising the works. Requiring fewer members than other types of local organizations (neighborhood committees, e.g.) to become legally recognized, development committees usually concentrate power on one diligent and well-connected local leader. All other members act only as beneficiaries of the development project to be implemented. Consequently, they tend to be loyal and quite obedient to their leader. These followers have low or no decision power in the organization. These organizational traits are beneficial for local leaders acting as brokers in networks of clientelism.

As I observed during my time in Nuevo Amanecer, youth-dominated organizations with a more informal set of internal roles, like La Casita Periférica, also shared this hierarchical structure. A leader acting as head of the organization in La Casita Periférica had oversight over most decisions. That structure was explicitly recognized by all members. "We use that [hierarchical leadership] here ... we agreed that he would be the head ... like a *Lonco* ... if they [authorities or other neighborhood leaders] want to talk to us, they know that they can call him," stated one of the organization's members (Interview, November 11, 2014). In contrast, while some active residents in Lo Hermida informally choose leaders – because they are more committed, experienced, better connected, or knowledgeable – they tend to support a horizontal leadership structure explicitly and emphatically.

In my time in Nuevo Amanecer, I also approached a local organization coordinating a street band. This group functions as a well-trained band that performs in different local events, both in Nuevo Amanecer and in other *poblaciones*. The band acts mainly as a batucada, but it incorporates other instruments besides drums, such as trumpets, a saxophone, a guiro, and a maraca. I had connected with one of the band's members, who invited me to their activities. I attended some of their practice sessions and accompanied them while they played in Nuevo Amanecer and in other *poblaciones*. During my research, the group had caught my attention because it seemed to be more informally coordinated and horizontally structured than other local organizations. Yet, as I began approaching other band members, I realized that the organization also centralized decision-making among a few specific leaders. After some conversations with one of the band members at the events, I asked him whether I could meet him for a more structured interview. "I need to ask Juan first," he said, explaining that he needed authorization from the band leader to agree on discussing organizational matters with me (Field notes, November 10, 2014).

In sharp contrast, face-to-face interactions among Lo Hermida activists are substantially more horizontal. Rather than using coercive, hierarchical leadership structures, Lo Hermida activists intentionally seek to decentralize protagonism and spread leadership. At the micro-mobilization level, identity provides feelings of power, pride, and effective agency, thus making Lo Hermida activists understand themselves as *protagonist* social agents. Decentralized protagonism prevents a disproportionate concentration of political capital in specific leaders by distributing it across organization members. By making it easier for individuals to attain leadership positions, decentralizing protagonism fosters the emergence of new leaders. This dynamic makes mobilizational identity more sustainable, largely explaining its survival over time.

The desire to build leadership among activists generally stems from their sense of protagonism. In interviews, activists explained to me how participating in organizations empowered them, making them feel that they could have a role in community-building. When the organization in which Rolando was working disbanded, for example, he decided to restore *pascuas populares*. This celebration was organized every year in the early years of the *población*. He decided to reactivate the celebration at a square near his house called Victor Jara. "I felt like I had something to contribute to the place ... I felt like I could have an impact in other people's life, like I could impact them with my actions," Rolando told me (Interview, February 26, 2013). By doing this, Rolando restored a local tradition in accordance with mobilizing identity and was able to put into practice the sense of protagonism he had developed in his previous organizational experience within Lo Hermida. He therefore exercised his locally legitimized unconditional position as a community builder. Eventually, other organizations supported his initiative by spreading the word in the neighborhood, helping him in the organization of the event, and providing him with additional resources. Consequently, *pascuas populares* became once again part of the yearly events organized by Lo Hermida's SMC. Now, other local activists regard Rolando as a leader who facilitates initiatives for other residents and activists in their square.

Analyzed through Gamson's (1992) framework of micro-mobilization acts, Lo Hermida's decentralization of protagonism becomes more evident. Micro-mobilization acts motivate collective action in activists' face-to-face interactions within local organizations. Three types of micro-mobilization acts can be identified: *organizing acts*, which promote active residents' cohesive engagement in collective action; *reframing acts*, which reinterpret an event as unfair; and *divesting acts*, which energetically break off interactions with or foster distance from authorities (see Chapter 1 for further details).

### 6.3.1 *Organizing Acts*

After a meeting at the occupied square in which I carried out my participant observation, a young leader talked about his childhood. He shared stories of playing for a neighborhood soccer team as a kid. He explained how he got to know other neighbors well in training sessions and competing in championship matches. He also coached younger neighborhood residents for a couple of years. In his story, this activist talked about how he developed close relationships of trust and solidarity with other neighbors. As he spoke, other young activists listening to the story interrupted him with enthusiastic remarks that highlighted how rewarding it had been for them to play for neighborhood soccer teams during their childhood and adolescence. Like former housemates who recall the good old times of living together, they named older neighbors who acted as coaches for several years and imparted their wisdom in long training sessions. They remembered funny anecdotes on the soccer field that included particularly skillful players and long-standing rivalries between teams. They also recalled violent disputes between local gangs who supported different teams. Intrigued about this interaction, I suddenly asked them about the significance of those stories. "Why is this important to you?" I inquired. One of the young activists replied: "Because it's the same that we do here [in the organization]: making community" (Field notes, February 7, 2013). The rest emphatically nodded in agreement.

As I analyzed my field notes and connected several events in which Lo Hermida activists strengthened their unity, I realized that their organizing acts contribute to decentralize protagonism. Interactions like the one I present above have a collective impact for activists because they not only foster cohesion by highlighting people's shared experience, they also symbolically situate activism within the realm of citizenship-building. In other words, their interactions performatively demonstrate that the work carried out at that organization belongs to the local community-building tradition. In fact, community-making interactions of this sort are common among local organizers. By sharing these stories, activists were collectively defining themselves as valid protagonists of community construction. In other similar dynamics, activists repeatedly portrayed themselves as active legitimate builders of *poblaciones*' historical community struggle.

This tactic of decentralizing protagonism also occurs at the individual level. In fact, organizers are emphatic in giving each individual responsibility and autonomy, which they experience both in their personal lives and within the organization. Knowing her to be one of the few local dwellers with access to higher education, I asked an activist in her 20s why she had decided not to submit the final documents to obtain her undergraduate degree. "I don't need a university to tell me what I know and what I don't know!" she replied. She explained that after passing all her university courses, paying her graduation fee, and attending the ceremony was plausible enough for her, but she did not need an institution's diploma to certify the skills she had acquired throughout the past years. Socially and professionally validating her abilities was her own task, and not an institution's, she argued (Field notes, February 17, 2013). Sitting on the grass at a square in Lo Hermida, another activist I was interviewing echoed this sense of self-determination by telling me "[neighborhood activism] is about being *autogestionado* (self-managed) ... each of us should be *autogestionado* in life and in organizations" (Interview, March 16, 2013). In different ways, these activists were performing the local mobilizing identity in their individual decisions. Students of collective action and mobilization have already described the same dynamic for other movements in which activists implement collective identity in their intimate decisions on aesthetics, relationships, or consumption (Calhoun 1994; Laraña, Johnston, and Gusfield 1994; Taylor and Whittier 1998; Bertuzzi 2020).

This emphasis on individual autonomy is also evident in how organizations exercise control on their members. In fact, explicitly demanding attendance and active participation when members failed to do so was rare within organizations. Activists (even the older leaders) asked for others' commitment only timidly and indirectly by alluding to their frustrations at having to coordinate actions with unresponsive participants. Instead of using coercive methods, local leaders and activists sought to motivate others by demonstrating empathy. Thus, on the rare occasions activists gave excuses to the group over missing meetings, others always appeared understanding. But what seemed more effective in encouraging participants' responsiveness was giving them individual autonomy. This tactic boosted activists' personal accountability and empowerment.

Activists stimulate each other's autonomous engagement in two ways. On the one hand, leaders explicitly encourage other activists to adopt a more autonomous position. On the other hand, activists themselves praise and assert individual self-determination. When I was relatively new to the square occupation, I spent time getting acquainted with the place and the different activists involved in the organization. My work began by collaborating in the building of a community orchard. During those first days, I accompanied a leader to collect some materials in his car. The organization often used this car to carry working materials around the neighborhood. By this point, I had noticed a great deal of distrust coming from some of the activists in the occupation, and had decided to build my networks carefully. Thus, I was still hesitant to make my own decisions and reticent to assume any proactive role. The leader in the car, however, surprised me when he explicitly encouraged me to take the initiative by using his car without anyone's permission in the future. He told me "You should start taking this car on your own, you could have gone to pick up these things by yourself without telling me" (Field notes, January 26, 2013). With this sentence, the leader was setting up a very clear code of conduct: As a new activist I was expected to contribute in a highly proactive manner. Similarly, all other activists are encouraged to develop a strong sense of protagonism within neighborhood organizations.

In other situations, participants highlighted individual autonomy as a desirable attribute. During a meeting at the square, for example, somebody asked about an activist who had missed two meetings in a row. Energetically, another member uttered a quick sentence to establish the importance of self-responsibility: "This is her issue, she knows what she is doing" (Field notes, March 1, 2013). Other activists approved this statement by nodding or avoiding further comments. One activist confirmed this defense over individual self-determination by telling me "I think everyone should be responsible for him or herself, be responsible for your own life ... I can't find another way in which you can be the owner of your own actions and be autonomous" (Interview, February 21, 2013).

Local organizations also use the identity symbol of the *popular* to develop autonomy through artistic expressions that often complement their mobilization (see Chapter 5). Hearing the sounds of drums, guitars or flutes while walking around Lo Hermida on any given evening is very likely. Although an uncommon practice in most of the urban margins, groups of residents meet in neighborhood squares of Lo Hermida to implement workshops in which they rehearse, teach, and learn musical instruments or different types of performances. Local activists understand these artistic expressions of the *popular* as a form of resistance against hegemonic, elite culture. They see this type of art as one that can build unity and political consciousness among underprivileged groups. Importantly, the acquisition and development of artistic skills in the *población* is an autonomous endeavor. In workshops and other similar initiatives, local dwellers teach each other, train, or learn a skill on their own. Similarly, the growing number of young rappers, who also understand their music as an expression of the *popular*, proudly praise *autoformación* (self-training) in their work.

### 6.3.2 Divesting and Reframing Acts

Activists' interpretation of social events as unfair can have a strong mobilizing power. The sentiments of anger and indignation that they experience from those reframing acts propel them to action. Academic work has shown how these emotions can develop very quickly, as a collective outburst. As Goodwin, Jasper, and Polletta (2001, 8) write when describing the emotions that reframing may spark within movements, "suspicion, hostility, anger, and other emotions may arise even before blame is allocated through more cognitive processes." Consequently, divesting acts, in which activists break off interactions with authorities, more often occur only after a reframing act and once those activists have had the opportunity to point to specific culprits. In *poblaciones* like Lo Hermida, however, these micro-mobilizing acts occur under a long-standing mobilizing identity, which has already outlined a relatively durable and limited set of antagonists in advance. I consequently found that divesting and reframing acts not only complement each other in *poblaciones*, but they frequently work in tandem. In other words, once local activists reframe an event as "repression," many times they almost automatically attribute blame to a few political institutions, such as the police, the municipality, or political parties. In this section, I explain how these micro-mobilization dynamics function within Lo Hermida's organizations to spread protagonism among *población* activists.

Unlike in Lo Hermida, divesting acts in Nuevo Amanecer are rare and reframing opportunities do not often lead to frames of injustice. In fact, during my time in Nuevo Amanecer, I never observed a confrontation with authorities. In November 2014, for example, a few young residents organized a meeting in Nuevo Amanecer. They aimed to inform neighbors about delays in finishing the construction on a new community-building, managed by the municipality. The leading architect and a project administrator came to the meeting, representing the company in charge of the project. A few organizations also attended the meeting, which included members of La Casita Periférica. During the meeting, the architect expressed concern saying, "[T]here is an issue in which we need your help." The building site had been robbed a few times, he explained, and their work was delayed as a result. "They [the thieves] must be from here ... maybe you know who they are," the architect said. He asked residents for help by guarding the site. Uncritically, organization leaders took this issue very seriously. Local organizers emphatically showed their disapproval of what they understood as ill-intentioned neighbors who robbed the company. "Those motherfuckers! We will beat them up if we see them in here [in the building site]!" yelled one of the leaders furiously. After some discussion and a few questions, the local community organizers agreed to guard the building site (Field notes, November 15, 2014). In their reaction, however, neighborhood organizers failed to consider that it was either the police or the company's responsibility to protect the site. These face-to-face interactions did not acknowledge the role of grassroots organizations in holding institutions accountable, thus detaching the organizers from the neighborhood's historical legacy of contentious politics.

In fact, on several occasions I witnessed how Nuevo Amanecer's local organizers reacted compliantly during events in which policemen treated them with defiance and disdain, which were perhaps significant opportunities to develop indignation through injustice frames. On a sunny afternoon of late October, in 2014, I joined a group of young organizers in painting a large banner on an isolated road on the southern side of Nuevo Amanecer, an area adjoining a narrow canal and where traffic flow was lower than in other parts of the neighborhood (Field notes, October 31, 2014). The banner was meant to decorate the background of the stage for the upcoming neighborhood anniversary on November 1. It resembled one created in 1970 to celebrate the neighborhood's inception. Using white, black, and red colors, the banner showed Che Guevara's iconic face together with a small representation of a house, which was meant to symbolize urban dwellers' struggle over housing in those years. The group strung the banner in the shade, on the pavement, between two parked cars, and began working on it. They took explicit measures not to block the road, which was wide enough to allow cars to pass comfortably next to the banner. After about 45 minutes of drawing and painting, three policemen on motorcycles and in a car approached. They stopped suddenly next to us, as if conducting an operation to prevent the escape of those under investigation.

Speaking loudly and using contemptuous commands, the policemen carried out a stop and search in which they requested our identity cards, asked us to empty our pockets, and searched a bag we had. While doing so they asked pointed questions and passed remarks on the banner we were making (Field notes, October 31, 2014).

"Who is he?" the policeman asked referring to Che Guevara's iconic face in the banner.

"Che Guevara" a couple of residents replied.

"And who is he? I don't know him!" demanded the policeman in a mocking tone, while smiling at his two companions.

Eventually, the policemen left; the young *población* residents I was with hardly reacted to the situation (Field notes, October 31, 2014). What would have probably been reframed as repression and triggered strong sentiments of indignation in Lo Hermida was in Nuevo Amanecer received peacefully. The processes of identity boundary making by which Lo Hermida activists carry out reframing and divesting acts were absent in Nuevo Amanecer.

My fieldwork provides contrasting anecdotes to depict the sharp differences between organizations in these two communities. As I participated in building the community orchard in Lo Hermida's occupied square, a couple of activists brought attention to a rumor coming from the municipality. Allegedly, the municipal council had agreed to evict the organization occupying the square to allow planned infrastructural works on that site. These works were ready to begin, and municipal authorities needed to clear the square as soon as possible, the rumor suggested. Consequently, the municipal council would send a government representative to discuss the decision with the occupying organization leaders. The organization had invested time, effort, and resources in that square repossession. In fact, together with local activists, I had participated in building an orchard and a roof to protect ourselves from the sun during meetings and events. Activists had also created a playing area for children with colorful seats and simple games. The potential eviction threatened to destroy months of work, which frustrated and angered the participants at the square.

After a few minutes, the rumor had informally spread among participants and some of them seemed restless and outraged. They had quickly reframed the potential eviction as repression unfairly inflicted on the organization by politicians within the municipality. Activists called a gathering under the roof we had installed and agreed to refuse any possible contact with municipal agents. This divesting act had a particularly tense and violent tone. In fact, a couple of activists exclaimed insults and defiant remarks against the authorities and said that they would fight the police if necessary to defend the square (Field notes, February 23, 2013). As this situation unfolded, a more conciliatory approach crossed my mind. Finding out the veracity of the rumors was fundamental for any decision, I thought. Furthermore, it occurred to me that we would be heard if we attended a public audience at the municipal council and demanded the withdrawal of their project on the grounds of the value that the square had for the local community. Yet, as Gamson (1992, 72) rightly points out, in divesting acts such as this any "disruption has the character of moral transgression." In other words, my dissonant tactic was likely to be read as a moral threat, thus sparking activists' anger toward me.

I witnessed how reframing acts occurred with relative frequency within local organizations in Lo Hermida. When activists reframe an event as repressive, they are making an urgent call to action, which is, in turn, highly empowering. Reframed as repressive, an event automatically portrays local activists' actions as a matter of humanitarian concern, in which their righteous deeds are being unfairly quelled. This tactic automatically rejects any condition imposed by authorities to regulate local participation and, instead, creates a self-validated, unconditional authorization for collective action. As participants engage in reframing acts, they are procedurally socialized into the local mobilizing identity, thus contributing to spreading the legitimacy of their collective endeavor. Consequently, through these reframing acts, activists reject becoming passive victims of stigmatization, acquire collective identity, and decentralize a sense of protagonism within the organization. As activists' protagonism is a reaction to their experience of stigmatization and exclusion, it regularly implies a passionate defense of identity and dignity. Additionally, it often involves disruptive or violent performances tailored to reflect their strong emotions of anger and urgency.

As Han (2012) suggests in her ethnographic account of protests in another of Santiago's mobilized *poblaciones*, the neighborhood La Pincoya, local activists sometimes actively engage in events that seem to be staged performances of defiance and oppression. They then exploit these events as opportunities to recreate their reframing and divesting acts. The performative aspect of these tactics is fundamental to decentralize protagonism. In January 2013, I participated in a march organized by a group of Lo Hermida organizations to support the Mapuche land liberation movement. Activists had coordinated the rally after extending their frame of repression to include recent violent raids conducted by the police within indigenous communities in the south of Chile. A couple of hundred protestors met at Lo Hermida's Martyr's Square and walked west, blocking much of the traffic through Grecia Avenue. As expected, the police rushed to the site to disperse the protest and clear the avenue. With large speakers, the police commanded that the march must end. Instead of leaving, activists reacted in defiance. They built a human chain to prevent policemen from breaking up the protest. Very soon, the march transformed into a direct violent confrontation with policemen, who were trying to either disperse or arrest the uncompliant protestors. As the police deployed a water cannon and tear gas, most activists sought refuge in the narrow roads of the surrounding *población*. Meanwhile, I had slowly walked out of the road to stand on the sidewalk, a couple of dozen meters away from the struggle underway. Together with several other bystanders and neighbors, I was able to observe the unfolding events very closely. The performance I witnessed resembled the confrontations between *población* activists and the police during the 1980s. "Bastard cops! This was pure repression!" uttered one of the activists angrily as some of them regrouped after the protest in a road nearby (Field notes, January 12, 2013).

Key to understanding this event is that the rally organizers gave no previous notice of any public protest to the intendency or regional governor, as Chile's legislation requires. Had activists taken the precaution of obtaining permission from the authorities in advance, maybe the march would have occurred with no exceptional incidents. The universal goals of a march – public expression and safety – would presumably have been furthered by this. However, the goals of this march were different. Besides showing support for Mapuche claims, it was staged as an act of defiance toward the formal procedures designed to force civil society to permanently validate their public actions in front of the authorities. Furthermore, while most activists in the march may not have been aware of it, the norms regulating the police's actions were created by the dictatorship in 1983 and remain in place within Chile's legislation despite their anti-democratic quality (Lovera 2018). Activists were, in other words, defying an anti-protest mindset that has endured within the state for the past four decades. Either consciously or unconsciously, therefore, this march echoed many other events in which activists performatively situated themselves in a historical *pobladores* movement, one that stood up against the dictatorship's repression and to many other events of injustice in the twentieth century. In turn, this performative function of the march gave each activist a sense of protagonism and allowed the endurance of mobilizational citizenship.

Importantly, however, while most reframing acts evolve into divesting acts within *población* organizations, not all of them do. Exceptionally, the opportunities and resources offered by institutions seem tactically convenient to local organizers, which compels their pragmatic avoidance of divestment. For instance, an increasing number of community leaders within *poblaciones* have coordinated applications for state participatory funds in the past decade, despite simultaneously reframing the application process as repressive authorities' conditions for civil society's access to public resources. Similarly, in their arduous quest for accessing public housing and despite adhering to Lo Hermida's mobilizing identity, housing committees have no alternative but to regularly engage in relatively harmonious exchanges with authorities. By grouping several of these committees, the MPL has managed to combine institutional means with autonomous protests that advocate for policy change with some success. More and more groups of radical young activists have been using the notion of "*recuperación*" to get control of neighborhood councils in the area, a position that inevitably exposes them to compromising with the municipality in collaborative interactions. They need to therefore avoid divesting acts, even under circumstances they may deem highly frustrating. In this case, the use of mobilizing identity to name or shape tactics still secures activists' sense of protagonism, but it is often slower and requires additional work. It usually results from a group that diverges from locally validated norms. Although collective scrutiny can feel constraining for some local activists, the strong appreciation for autonomous engagement within their SMC usually allows for novel initiatives to emerge, even when they demonstrate some tactical collaboration with authorities.

### 6.4 MOBILIZING CAPABILITIES

The tactics that I describe here decentralize protagonism within local organizations and have resulted in an enduring and highly vibrant SMC in Lo Hermida. This survival of mobilizational citizenship in *poblaciones* since the 1980s allowed the progressive buildup of mobilizing capabilities within the neighborhood's SMC. Despite the disaggregation effect that decentralized protagonism can have in Lo Hermida's SMC, those capabilities have allowed its local organizations to react cohesively to scenarios that were demanding either because they provided unavoidable opportunities or were highly threatening to local activists.

The successful coordinated campaign implemented by most of the organizations in Lo Hermida's SMC in 2011 against a new master plan aimed to gentrify the area and that would threaten the local community is indicative of how the buildup of mobilizing capabilities can spark joint reactive collective action. As I explain in Chapter 2, several SMCs in the Pedro Aguirre Cerda and Lo Espejo districts engaged in a very similar conflict, which also endangered underprivileged communities' survival. The powerful protests of 2019 led to a similar response. This case, however, had an additional quality. Local activists saw the abusive treatment by and brutality of security forces in dealing with protestors as the reification of their so-feared repression. This menace to their community mobilized them. In addition, for the first time Chilean society seemed ready to mobilize at large to effect social change, which was a highly compelling opportunity that local activists did not want to miss. Given how strongly motivating these events seemed to those activists, Lo Hermida's SMC responded cohesively and swiftly to spearhead support for these protests.

Lo Hermida's SMC had developed the mobilizing capabilities that made these concerted actions possible by perfecting their access to funding, widening networks within and beyond the neighborhood, using those networks to share tactical lessons, and increasing the impact of mobilization within and outside their community. The SMC's decentralized protagonism provided these dynamics of capability development with a strong sense of autonomy. It also gave activists the opportunity to participate in those dynamics regardless of their interests, skills, experience, and particular ideological perspective within the Left.

Organizers' persistent implementation of self-management tactics to fund their collective action initiatives has made them skillful fundraisers and event organizers, who do not need the financial support of political institutions or elite allies. "Only with self-management we organize an event here at the *población* in an hour, brother!" exclaimed a young activist in one of my interviews (Group Interview, March 11, 2013). Despite his bravado, however, he was correctly describing his organization's strong skills to organize artistic initiatives in the neighborhood. Activists in Lo Hermida regularly rely on informal networks beyond their neighborhood created through years of activism to access additional resources of mobilization. Large speakers, a stage, and even contacts with famous artists can be obtained for free from fellow activists or friends in other *poblaciones*. As decentralized protagonism produces loose, informal, and trusted bonds among the neighborhood's SMC members, quickly accessing resources through informal means becomes ever more possible for them.

Soccer clubs have been powerful platforms for informal network-building within neighborhoods and across the urban margins for many years. In recent decades, soccer championships have brought club organizers, coaches, and players from within each neighborhood and different *poblaciones* together on many occasions, thus building bonds of trust. As those club members are sometimes activists in their *población*, soccer matches have progressively contributed to a loose network of activism that includes organizations in different mobilized neighborhoods. Aware of this dynamic, young activists have begun using their participation in these neighborhood soccer clubs to advance what they call "social soccer." Beyond being a soccer competition, social soccer tournaments are opportunities to educate children and adolescents in the urban margins about community engagement, solidarity, and social justice. Therefore, they include workshops or tea parties in which organizers and players get to know each other to reflect together on social issues. A couple of soccer clubs within Lo Hermida have spearheaded this social soccer movement.

Hip-hop has also worked as a powerful platform for the network-building of Lo Hermida's SMC in the past few decades. Santiago's rap scene has become increasingly dynamic since its first large festival in 2008, Planeta Rock. The growing number of rappers in Lo Hermida have regularly attended that festival and participated in its organization. Eventually, in 2012, those rappers created their own Peñalolén Hip-Hop Festival. The event brings hip-hop artists to Lo Hermida coming from the urban margins all over the country. Every year, the festival has a social justice theme, such as the human rights of immigrants or indigenous demands over land rights. Since its inception, this festival has been a hub for *población* activists associated with the world of rap and street art. According to my interviews, this event allowed Lo Hermida activists to extend their collaborative networks with local organizers in many neighborhoods and especially in the *poblaciones* La Victoria, José María Caro, and Villa O'Higgins. Additionally, rappers in the *población* Parinacota sought to emulate this festival. They imported from Lo Hermida not only the event's structure, but also its self-management funding tactic. To boost their political impact, rappers in Lo Hermida and other *poblaciones* created the Hip-Hop Activist Network (RHA). The network sought to promote social awareness and give political training to youths across the urban margins while they learned hip-hop related skills, such as break-dancing or graffiti.

Through the MPL and FENAPO, Lo Hermida's housing committees have also participated in expanding networks beyond their *población* boundaries, and many other local organizations have done a similar job. Across these networks, Lo Hermida activists both exchanged lessons with other mobilized *poblaciones* and exported mobilizational citizenship to other, less mobilized neighborhoods. My interviews indicate that decentralizing protagonism is common practice within many local organizations across the urban margins. Activists in *poblaciones*, consequently, tend to regularly agree on the fundamental importance of autonomy and the need to exclude traditional political party tactics from their work. Simultaneously, self-management as a tactic to fund local initiatives and develop autonomous collective action has been slowly spreading across the urban margins, beyond the traditionally mobilized *poblaciones*.

Furthermore, network-building has allowed Lo Hermida's SMC to increase its impact by interacting with Chile's growing wave of contentious politics of the last few decades. For example, a few Lo Hermida activists belonged to the *No+AFP* movement's assembly in 2016. As the movement's assembly incorporated organizations from different *poblaciones*, it acquired the ability to reach those neighborhoods with calls to action. A small coalition of organizations within Lo Hermida channeled these exchanges with the movement and spread the information within the neighborhood's SMC. Local organizations used their decentralized protagonism to react to these calls freely, depending on their interest and availability.

The events I describe here are examples of the many actions by which Lo Hermida activists have built the necessary capabilities to trigger joint action. Furthermore, they demonstrate that by promoting enduring collective action, mobilizational citizenship can progressively create the strong collective identity, social ties, and access to resources that communities need to support large-scale protest and broader democratizing processes.

## 6.5 CONCLUSION

By examining dynamics of micro-mobilization, I have explained how *población* activists disseminate a sense of protagonism in their local organizations by transmitting a mobilizing identity in the form of political capital. This decentralization of protagonism advances mobilizational citizenship because, on the one hand, it promotes the emergence of new local leaders among young activists, which is crucial to sustaining mobilization. On the other hand, it allows activists to build an alternative sense of political incorporation in their collective action.

A twofold approach to leadership underlies the creation of protagonism. Activists not only think of leadership as bestowed by a specific person, but they also understand it as a set of cultural and interpersonal skills that every activist can acquire. At the core of this leadership is a sense of protagonism that legitimizes activists as unconditional agents of community-building, both individually and collectively. Role modeling is one of the channels by which leading activists politically socialize children and young people in mobilized *poblaciones*. Socialization also occurs around initiatives of collective action, for example, in situations where activists reframe reality as unfair, on occasions in which leaders promote a particular type of collective action repertoire, and through leaders' anecdotes of successful mobilization.

*Población* activists embrace and perform the decentralization of this protagonism in different ways. Unlike in demobilized SMCs at the urban margins, where leadership tends to be hierarchical, in mobilized *poblaciones* activists' organizations emphasize informal, horizontal networks.

Organizing acts of micro-mobilization support this structure. In conversations during meetings or after initiatives of collective action, activists share a sense of cohesiveness that validates each other's work as a contribution to local community-building. Additionally, they promote a sense of decentralized protagonism at the individual level. Focusing on their intrinsic motivation, activists encourage each other's proactivity and responsibility in their mobilization.

Reframing and divesting acts refer to activists' reinterpretation of reality as unfair and to their ceasing of interactions with authorities. These two types of micro-mobilization encounters boost *población* activists' sense of empowerment and validate their role as defenders of community and dignity. The dynamics developed in these acts, therefore, also advance a decentralized sense of protagonism.

Together with mobilizing identity symbols, these dynamics of micro-mobilization constitute tools that activists learn and performatively deploy to collectively activate mobilization. The disposition of activists to socialize others to disperse political capital sharply differs from my observations in *poblaciones* where mobilization died out over the past 30 years. In other words, the transmission of political capital (especially across generations) among activists and community members should be understood as a key factor for the survival of mobilizational citizenship in *poblaciones*. In contrast, local leaders' insistence on accumulating and monopolizing political capital at the local level is a central factor for the demobilization of the urban margins in post-dictatorial urban Chile.

As mobilizational citizenship promoted the survival of collective action at the urban margins over time, it allowed local activists to progressively develop the needed mobilizing capabilities to effectively support the large-scale protests that began in October 2019. This chapter has provided empirical examples to depict how these dynamics developed in Lo Hermida and interacted with activists' decentralized protagonism in recent decades. Through their prior sustained mobilization, activists improved their access to resources, built networks of trust, used those networks to share tactical lessons, and interacted with other movements to expand their impact beyond the neighborhood.

# Conclusion

In a world in which civil society actors and their defiance of the institutional status quo are more prominent than ever, the scholarship on social movements has not provided enough insight into the mobilization of highly excluded groups. This book has developed a novel framework that explains how collective action survives over time in the urban margins under highly unfavorable conditions. It involved researching how urban contentious politics and local organizing can endure with minimal influence from elite actors or political opportunities. In these situations, collective action persists because it provides activists and other community members with an alternative sense of political incorporation that challenges the entrenched, unequal citizenship structure organizing people's lives in the urban margins. In this process, neighborhood activists preserve and renovate their repertoires of contention, collective identities, and leadership positions. I call the concept synthesizing these dynamics "mobilizational citizenship." It involves the dynamic interaction between four mechanisms: agentic memory, mobilizational belonging, mobilizational boundaries, and decentralized protagonism. The book also shows that mobilizational citizenship can provide neighborhood activists with the knowledge, resources, and networks to actively engage in broader processes of social change.

To substantiate this theoretical argument, the book has delivered an empirical exploration of Chile's underprivileged urban communities, also called *poblaciones*. It has explained why some of those marginalized neighborhoods have maintained social mobilization for the past 30 years, while most of them demobilized during Chile's democratic transition in the early 1990s. It used a paired comparison between two urban communities in the neighborhoods of Lo Hermida and Nuevo Amanecer, both in Santiago. These communities share very similar origins, socio-economic traits, ideological underpinnings, and histories of mobilization in the years before the military coup d'état in 1973 and during the dictatorship. Their economic and broad political conditions have also been similar since Chile's return to democracy. However, these neighborhoods' social movement communities describe diverging developments of public engagement after the democratic transition. While Nuevo Amanecer demobilized and its organizations created compliant relationships with authorities, Lo Hermida continued to mobilize to defy unjust, exclusionary institutions.

My analysis traces this difference to the 1980s, when these two communities engaged in protesting the dictatorship. Political groups working underground came to *poblaciones* in those years to coordinate country-wide mobilizations. They included political parties and well-organized militant movements on the left. Depending on their ideological and methodological perspectives, these political groups brought about differing kinds of leaderships in the neighborhoods. The more moderate political parties produced a managerial type of leadership that was able to coordinate and control collective action across many organizations in the country. These party activists constructed loyalty networks in the urban margins with young local leaders that became instrumental in future political campaigns. Furthermore, their actions perpetuated a sense of historical discontinuity created by the dictatorship in *poblaciones*. Radical groups, in contrast, produced subversive leadership structures oriented to train and recruit urban dwellers in their revolutionary struggle against the military regime. Through tactics of political socialization, these groups updated socialist ideals and symbols of the past in neighborhoods of the urban margins, thus promoting a notion of community development that endured over time. This sense of historical continuity made retrieving symbols of the past a recurrent resource to validate and promote collective action among *población* activists. These activists can, therefore, instrumentalize symbols of the past in their interactions to promote feelings of empowerment in local organizations. Furthermore, by connecting current neighborhood activism with a larger community of *pobladores* that extends in time and space, their actions of memory-building create an imagined community, similar to the one famously described by Anderson (1991). The tactics of memory-building by which activists advance a sense of agency in their organizations and with other supporters constitute the first theoretical step of the mobilizational citizenship framework, and I call it agentic memory.

Collective dynamics of mobilizing belonging and mobilizing boundaries can develop as a result. They provide shared symbols and values that legitimize collective action among local community dwellers. Through mobilizing belonging, activists take ownership of collective traits that promote contentious politics. They also engage in mobilizing boundary-making to differentiate their group from other social and political actors, some of which may be understood as antagonists. In their narratives and interactions, activists in *poblaciones* outline an informal realm of legitimacy and confidence. This informal realm includes tactics of *población* activism, locally validated codes of marginality, and networks of trust. Protecting this informal dimension is what often motivates collective action in Chile's urban margins.

The story of these neighborhoods is also about political capital. The book shows how activists in mobilized urban communities treat collective identity as political capital. In other words, activists understand their symbols and codes of legitimacy as highly mobilizing. Acquiring those symbols means developing leadership in the *población*. Through socialization tactics, activists transmit identity symbols and manage to spread political capital. This decentralization of protagonism makes activists valid agents of community-building, both at the individual and collective levels. As younger *población* dwellers acquire political capital, they create new initiatives of collective action and replace older leaders who stop mobilizing. In this way, mobilizational citizenship secures the continuous renewal of leadership and tactics in some neighborhoods of the urban margins. It also provides local dwellers with the opportunity to engage in an alternative political incorporation, an experience historically denied by formal institutional mechanisms of national belonging.

The unprecedented protests of 2019 in Chile demonstrated the powerful democratizing impact of mobilizational citizenship. Decades of sustained collective action resulting from mobilizational citizenship provided neighborhoods like Lo Hermida with readily available knowledge, tactics, and resources for disruptive mobilization. Activists in these communities also had trustworthy networks of collaboration within and outside their neighborhoods that could be quickly activated to grow collective action. Therefore, they were capable of actively supporting the large-scale protests that evolved in the weeks after mid-October that year.

Reaching these conclusions has involved my regular involvement in *población* grassroots politics. I went to Lo Hermida in late 2012, when

I started my doctoral fieldwork. Initially, I spent over five months meeting local dwellers and activists, participating in organizations, and conducting interviews in the neighborhood. I did the same, later, in Nuevo Amanecer. Earning people's trust was, at first, very slow and frustrating. I was often not told when organizers changed the place or time of meetings, and individual activists who had agreed to meet with me stood me up many times. My comments or suggestions were often ignored or dismissed in meetings, especially by the more radical organizers, who were more culturally distant from me and had a stronger background of marginality. The fact that I engaged in local initiatives humbly, was careful in respecting local relational dynamics, and lived in the neighborhoods in which I conducted my research helped validate my work among the activists. I came back to these neighborhoods to continue collaborating with local organizations regularly in the following six years, which grew my networks and legitimacy in these areas. The contacts I built allowed me later to reach critical informants to explore the engagement of *población* organizers in the 2019 protests.

## THE CONCEPT

The notion of mobilizational citizenship emerges in the intersection between critical citizenship studies and social movement theory. A growing number of critical approaches to citizenship are moving beyond mainstream, liberal definitions of the concept. Liberal theories, critics claim, conceive a passive citizen, and are unable to account for the new political subjectivities emerging in today's public realm (Lister 2003; Purcell 2003; Isin 2009; Attoh 2011; McLaughlin, Phillimore, and Richardson 2011; Lazar 2013). Following the work of authors such as Hannah Arendt and Henry Lefebvre, those critical views understand "the citizen" not as a given condition, but as the result of collective practices of identity-building and rights-claiming. New political subjectivities, they argue, emerge as the result of globalization effects, urbanization, and interconnectedness (Isin 2000; Sassen 2008). Their theoretical and empirical analyses also address the varied ways in which collectives create political incorporation beyond the framework of the nation-state (Holston 1999; Isin 2002; O'Byrne 2003; Sassen 2008; McNevin 2011; Lazar 2013; Swerts 2017; Hildebrandt et al. 2019). In studying these forms of politicization, this research has paid attention to a range of collective endeavors, from cultural groups to organized protests. Among them, Holston (2008) and Lazar (2008) have studied urban Brazil and Bolivia to deliver insights into the potential of neighborhood organizing to politicize the urban poor and challenge exclusionary regimes of citizenship. Their work demonstrates the success of local-level mobilization when the Latin American urban underprivileged are able to strategically take advantage of institutional resources. This research has been successful in empirically substantiating its conceptual claims through the study of cases that address "new types of political actors, which may have been submerged, invisible or without voice" (Sassen 2005, 89).

This book has built on these theorizations to develop a framework that analytically explains the emergence of citizenship and its interaction with sustainable mobilization in Chile's urban margins. The mobilizational citizenship framework brings a new lens to the study of citizenship because it addresses the specific mechanisms and tactics by which underprivileged, excluded urban dwellers activate collective identity to promote mobilization and social change.

The concept of mobilizational citizenship is also a contribution to the literature on social movements. Dominant, long-standing theoretical traditions in this field have outlined the importance of political opportunities. Activists will pay strict attention, the theory predicts, to changes in the structure of public political arrangements that may create favorable moments of influence for the movement. The strategic use of resources has also been theorized as critical for movements. The efficiency with which activists manage the different types of mobilizing resources will influence their success (Oberschall 1973; Piven and Cloward 1977; Cable, Walsh, and Warland 1988). Elite allies that may open opportunities and provide external resources are therefore key to a movement's goals. In this context, collective identity shapes groups' willingness to implement certain tactics (Tarrow 2011). Deeming them unfit for their values, activists may reject some types of protest. Furthermore, identity-building will allow organizing and contentious politics to remain active over time and prompt the creation of social movement communities (Buechler 1990).

Mobilizational citizenship adds another layer to this analysis. It brings political socialization and citizenship into the theoretical equation. In contexts of strong marginalization, movements may find ways to circumvent elite allies who seem unwilling to deliver activists' needed autonomy. Activists will keep mobilization afloat despite having very little access to resources and political opportunities. The mobilizational citizenship framework shows how, in those contexts, mobilization can be motivated by people's quest for community-building and local legitimacy. In other words, the framework explains how building alternative political incorporation can fuel collective action. This collective action will be shaped as a social movement community that puts contentious politics into practice through local organizing, community development, and occasional protests. Activists' diffusion of political capital within local networks is fundamental to sustaining this collective action and citizenship in communities at the urban margins. As these dynamics endure over time, they will promote youth engagement in local organizations. They will also build strong cross-generational ties among local organizers and expand activists' networks to other communities in the urban margins and movements. Although diverse and relatively loose, these ties can provide activists with needed resources for collective endeavors. Furthermore, mobilizational citizenship dynamics can consolidate successful organizational arrangements and legitimized mobilization tactics in the urban margins. In cases in which collective action frames and shared emotions of indignation prompt large-scale collective action, this buildup of mobilizing capabilities in underprivileged urban communities will allow their activists to react quickly in support of broader protests advancing deeper democracy. They will be able to use their knowledge, access to resources, and tactics to activate mobilization both through their established networks and in an autonomous, decentralized manner.

Furthermore, the framework in this book explains the demobilization of the urban underprivileged, which is a matter often overlooked by academics. Government policies have discouraged mobilization in the urban margins on many occasions and in different parts of the world. Market-oriented policies have led to urban sprawl, segregation, and poverty concentration in many of the main cities we know, which erode urban communities. Simultaneously, governments make direct efforts to prevent the mobilization of excluded groups. Officials put pressure on mobilized excluded actors, provide them with concessions that diminish their social change goals, make direct efforts to split their ranks, and give institutional positions or resources to more moderate leaders (Piven and Cloward 1977; Haines 1984; Wolff 2007). Institutional agents also regularly exercise repression over their challengers (Davenport 2015).

This book provided a rereading of these mechanisms. It showed how what these policies accomplish is limiting and controlling people's access to political capital within their communities in the urban margins. In other words, states and other political institutions strategize to diminish the resources by which grassroots urban dwellers legitimize local, autonomous leadership and collective action tactics. Political institutions will then seek to manage the few mobilizing resources in those urban communities, thus intervening in the local dynamics of political legitimacy.

The mobilizational citizenship framework takes into account the role of community leaders in these local political processes of demobilization. Local leaders often contribute to these institutional demobilizing effects by engaging in networks of political loyalty and clientelism. To feed these networks with political legitimacy, local leaders learn tactics of political capital hoarding. They become ready at all times to take advantage of local collective events to amass validation, both from politicians and from specific groups in the community. Previous research on collective action highlights the hierarchical aspect of clientelism. It describes brokers' need to accumulate legitimacy as a pressure that they experience "from below" (citizens) and "from above" (one or more patrons), simultaneously (Tarlau 2013; Bénit-Gbaffou and Katsaura 2014; Lapegna 2016). This "dual pressure" – in Lapegna's (2016) terms – may increase to levels that make mobilization unsustainable, and in most cases it is the result of too much pressure coming from powerful patrons. My emphasis on political capital, however, presents brokers as agents able to partially decide over and benefit from demobilizing local political dynamics. As the book demonstrates, these dynamics are structurally and historically anchored, and allow for a clear contrast with cases in which mobilization is able to survive. In cases in which political loyalties and clientelism prevail, local leaders are concerned with accumulating political capital, which in turn prevents them from transmitting it to other community members. This tactic often alienates other community members who would benefit from local leaders with a socializing mission – which is especially the case in adolescents thirsting for collective identity symbols and group values. Ultimately, the resulting local political dynamics prevent community members from developing mobilizational citizenship.

In this way, the framework creates a contrast between communities that demonstrate the conditions to successfully diffuse political capital and others where local and national developments have led to sustained political capital hoarding.

## SCOPE OF THE RESEARCH

Despite appearances, Chile has developed a highly closed political structure that systematically excludes civil society from public decisions. As I argue in Chapters 2 and 3, this phenomenon is particularly intense and paradoxical in the urban margins, where political parties promote exclusionary mechanisms of political incorporation. The study of *población* mobilization is, therefore, the study of collective action surmounting highly

disadvantageous conditions. This persistent fencing off of political institutions stands in contrast with the more variable and flexible developments
described by other Latin American countries and democracies across the
world (Álvarez 2017; Silva and Rossi 2018). Yet, despite the particularities
of the Chilean case, the mobilizational citizenship framework should allow
the study of emerging political subjectivities that lead to the sustainable
mobilization of excluded urban communities in other political contexts.

First, the framework's components have been active in other
neighborhood-based mobilizations in Latin America's urban margins, as
well as in other movements in various parts of the world. In El Alto,
Bolivia, which is probably Latin America's most prominent example of
activism in the urban margins, activists have long developed a mobilizing
identity. They display agentic memory when using their experience of
solidarity, political unrest, and state violence to connect their current
struggles with those of the past. The October 2003 protests – also called
the Gas War – in which neighborhood communities in El Alto organized
roadblocks, resisted strong military repression and managed to oust
president Gonzalo Sánchez de Lozada, are a historical landmark that
activists use to performatively demonstrate the effectiveness of past
collective action and promote a position of agency among current local
organizers (Arbona 2008; Achtenberg 2009). Despite their differences,
the approximately 550 neighborhoods in El Alto display a collective
identity with coexisting traditions of resistance, which include symbols
belonging to indigenous, class, union, neighborhood, and progressive
mestizo identities. Reportedly, similar tactics of mobilizing identity-
building have been used by local urban organizations across the world
(Crenson 1983; Martin 2003; Chuang 2005; Donner 2011; Bravo 2013;
Blank 2016; Zulver 2017).

Second, when used to analyze whether activists are capable of instrumentalizing collective identity to diffuse its symbols in the form of
political capital, the framework adds a subtle but important distinction,
often neglected by other studies. It shows how a shift in people's conception of citizenship may discredit institutionally recognized local organizations to replace them with new, alternative forms of collective action,
which use more informal leadership structures and motivate youth
engagement. To return to El Alto, for example, this analytical tool would
show the diverging development of mobilizational citizenship between its
neighborhoods. Reports indicate that some neighborhood communities
have learned political socialization tactics to diffuse their collective identity across generations (Arbona 2008; Lazar 2008). This tactic spreads

political capital and promotes the creation of new, younger leaders within local communities, which is what I call decentralizing protagonism.

However, some neighborhood communities exhibit a different development of civic participation. In these neighborhoods, older local leaders' engagement in networks of clientelism and partisan loyalties has promoted dynamics of political capital hoarding within neighborhood councils. This dynamic has resulted in increasing local distrust toward the autonomy of neighborhood councils and the relative deactivation of contentious politics (Lazar 2008). Furthermore, these organizations have alienated the youth and do not provide them with political training, ultimately marginalizing them. As Merkle (2003, 210) writes in his research on El Alto organizations, "young people, in some cases, are welcome to join the assemblies, but their voice is barely taken into account." In this context, young people decided to advance mobilizational citizenship through the creation of "critical youth groups," which are alternative, informal organizations that reject institutional and partisan politics, promote horizontal leadership structures, and seek self-organization and autonomy (Merkle 2003). A similar process of legitimacy erosion was suffered by the established territorial organizations of the settlement Villa El Salvador, a stronghold of leftist urban mobilization in Lima, Peru. There, too, the self-managed communities (or CUAVES, which are similar to neighborhood councils in El Alto) saw the spread of strong partisan political loyalties that undermined their ability to promote autonomous mobilization, thus prompting the emergence of new local organizations (Hordijk 2005).

The mobilizational citizenship framework could also shed light on the Piquetero movement, in Argentina's urban margins. This movement had its peak in 2002, when it mounted over 2,000 roadblocks in several protests. Its actions progressively declined after 2003 because a broad section of its activists was ready to negotiate concessions with Kirchner's government. However, a group of radical organizations remained active and were increasingly marginalized. They continued operating at the local level, within different urban communities. They now run soup kitchens and a self-managed educational system for underprivileged urban dwellers. They also sustain a range of local organizations that emphatically defend political autonomy and advance local community development, thus rejecting collaboration with the government, political parties, and trade unions. Analyzing this phenomenon through the mobilizational citizenship framework would explain why and how these organizations remain active in the urban margins.

The framework could also travel beyond the urban margins and Latin America to investigate movements with territorial community development, strong collective identity, and distributed leadership structures, such as Black Lives Matter (Jackson 2021), the White Power Movement (Belew 2018), or Extinction Rebellion (Fotaki and Foroughi 2021).

Expanding this research to test this framework in other communities is necessary. While it is true that qualitative approaches do not intend to be representative, adding other case studies would allow for the strategic testing of its dynamics. A first step could be testing how communities develop mobilizational citizenship in other similar neighborhoods, but with different particularities. That is, for example, the case of *poblaciones* that were created after the democratic transition in 1990. Such case studies would allow examining how agentic memory is constructed in such disadvantaged scenarios.

I would also like to bring mobilizational citizenship to the study of different Latin American urban contexts. Argentina, Uruguay, and Brazil provide interesting cases because despite their authoritarian legacies, the openness in their political processes differs from the Chilean case. Despite its similarities with Chile in its centralized administration structure and presidential political system, Uruguay possesses a more open political culture that allows for stronger collaboration in policy design between grassroots movements and political parties. Argentina and Brazil, with their federal administrative systems, also offer political processes that are more open to the influence of underprivileged urban movements. Understanding how mobilizational citizenship develops in those cases would contribute to strengthening the explanatory power of the framework. Additionally, this framework could be tested in societies that have a different history, for example Latin American countries that have not experienced dictatorial regimes in their recent past, such as Mexico and Colombia. Southern European countries that have developed clientelism and urban marginality may also provide useful case studies of mobilizational citizenship.

This book explored how communities in the urban margins can develop sustainable mobilization and engage in broad processes of social change despite experiencing highly disadvantageous conditions. Despite focusing on two case studies in Santiago, Chile, this book's lessons should enlighten empowering and democratizing processes in the urban peripheries of Latin America and other regions of the world.

# Appendix 1 Complementary Tables

TABLE A.1.1 *Comparative summary of case studies, Nuevo Amanecer and Lo Hermida.*

| | | Neighborhoods | |
|---|---|---|---|
| | | Nuevo Amanecer | Lo Hermida |
| **Similarities** | District | La Florida | Peñalolén |
| | | • Social priority classification.* | |
| | | • Level of inequality (Agostini 2010, 243). | |
| | | • Structure of residential wealth accumulation (Hidalgo 2004a, 39; Ortiz and Escolano 2013). | |
| | Neighborhood | • Located in Santiago's Eastern zone. | |
| | | • Relatively central (not peripheral). | |
| | | • High initial mobilization (1970–1973). | |
| | | • Dictatorial repression (1973–1990). | |
| | | • The name of the neighborhood, *villas/campamentos* or roads were changed by the dictatorship (Nueva La Habana became Nuevo Amanecer). | |
| | | • Developed resistance against the dictatorship. | |
| | | • Spatial configuration. | |
| | | • Similar socioeconomic levels (income, poverty, employment structure, education, and consumption). | |
| | | • Urbanized and well connected (large roads and regular public transportation). | |
| | | • Well equipped: good access to services (police station, health center, schools, subsidies, etc.). | |
| | | • Founded in 1970 through land invasions (Nuevo Amanecer included a relocation). | |
| | | • The MIR and other leftist movements coordinated land takeover and other mobilizations (early 1970s). | |
| **Variation** | Type of activism/ organization | • Mostly formal organizations managing state benefits. | • Formal and informal organizations co-exist. |
| | | • Few youth organizations. | • High youth involvement. |
| | | • Little intergenerational exchange. | • High intergenerational exchange. |
| | | • Strong connection with political parties. | • Highly critical of/rejection of political parties. |
| | | | • Autonomy highly valued. |

206

| Contentious initiatives (last 30 years) | • Spontaneous invasion of recently built social housing in 2005 (Renna 2011, 60).<br>• Local organizations reacted with fear to the protests in 2019. Organizers only joined disruptive protests once they had spread and seemed socially validated. | • Leaders involved in Chile's two largest land invasions after 1990: Esperanza Andina (1992) and Toma de Peñalolén (1998).<br>• Organizations led campaign to reject new district gentrification plan (2011).<br>• Organizations rejected top-down plan and convinced municipality to include them in the design of Martyr's Square (2011).<br>• Highly contentious Movement of Dwellers in Struggle (MPL) emerged from LH (Castillo Couve 2014).<br>• Local neighborhood council managed by critical young residents who reject party politics.<br>• Prompt and strong support of protests in 2019 (Rasse 2019). Activists also participated in creating broad inter-territorial coalitions to create disruptive urban mobilizations. |

*Source:* created by the author.

* The Chilean Ministry of Social Development (Ministerio de Desarrollo Social 2014) ranks Santiago's districts by a social priority index, which includes data on income, health, and education. Both selected districts rank as 'medium priority' in that ranking, receiving similar scores.

TABLE A.1.2 *Individual income quintiles in Chile.*

| | US dollars | | Chilean pesos | |
| Quintiles* | Lower limit | Upper limit | Lower limit | Upper limit |
| --- | --- | --- | --- | --- |
| 1 | – | 108.8 | – | 74,969 |
| 2 | 108.9 | 182.21 | 74,970 | 125,558 |
| 3 | 182.22 | 280.23 | 125,559 | 193,104 |
| 4 | 280.24 | 511.89 | 193,105 | 352,743 |
| 5 | 511.9 | – | 352,744 | – |

*Source*: data obtained from Universidad de Chile (2015).
* Quintiles have been defined by the 2011 National Survey on Socio-economic Characterization (CASEN).

TABLE A.1.3 *Individual income quintile distribution in Nuevo Amanecer and Lo Hermida.*

| | Nuevo Amanecer (percent) | Lo Hermida (percent) | | |
| Quintiles | UV 25 | UV 17 | UV 18 | UV 19* |
| --- | --- | --- | --- | --- |
| 1 | 47.8 | 37.4 | 29.40 | 21.90 |
| 2 | 23.2 | 46.10 | 41.90 | 21.90 |
| 3 | 15.9 | 15.50 | 19.60 | 41.40 |
| 4 | 9.9 | 1.10 | 9.20 | 14.80 |
| 5 | 3.2 | 0 | 0 | 0 |

*Source*: The data for Lo Hermida in this table has been obtained from Peñalolén Municipality (2011). The data on Nuevo Amanecer was self-calculated using datasets provided by La Florida Municipality.
*UV refers to *Unidad Vecinal* (Neighborhood Unit).

TABLE A.1.4 *Employment of residents in Nuevo Amanecer and Lo Hermida.*

| Employment | Nuevo Amanecer (percent) | Lo Hermida (percent) |
| --- | --- | --- |
| Unskilled workers | 19.9 | 26.8 |
| Officials, workers, and craftsmen in mechanic arts | 15.5 | 15.7 |
| Service and retail market vendors | 14.2 | 13.7 |
| Ignores | 12.7 | 11.5 |
| Middle-range professionals and technicians | 11.3 | 8.8 |
| Office employees | 9.5 | 7.7 |
| Installations, machinery and assembling workers | 8.4 | 7.0 |
| State executive or legislative powers or public administration | 3.7 | 3.8 |
| Scientific or intellectual professionals | 3.1 | 2.7 |
| Agricultural and fishing qualified workers | 1.2 | 2.0 |
| Armed forces | 0.5 | 0.2 |
| Total employed population | 38.0 | 37.9 |

*Source*: self-calculation using data from Census 2002.

TABLE A.I.5 *Educational levels of residents in Nuevo Amanecer, Lo Hermida and the Metropolitan Region.*

| Educational level | Nuevo Amanecer (percent) | | Lo Hermida (percent) | | Metrop. Region (Urban*) (percent) | |
|---|---|---|---|---|---|---|
| | 2002 | 2017 | 2002 | 2017 | 2002 | 2017 |
| University | 3.7 | 15.2 | 3.2 | 6.9 | 11.8 | 19.2 |
| Technical institute | 4.6 | 8.8 | 3.7 | 5.4 | 7.1 | 7.9 |
| High school | 40.8 | 40.1 | 37.0 | 40.7 | 37.2 | 35.2 |
| Primary education | 37.0 | 24.4 | 42 | 33.1 | 30.8 | 22.6 |
| No formal education | 1.8 | 5.8 | 2.2 | 6.4 | 1.5 | 5.7 |

*Source*: Self-calculation using data from Census 2002 and 2017.
* The analysis has excluded all nonurban areas of the Metropolitan Region.

TABLE A.I.6 *Additional socioeconomic indicators in Nuevo Amanecer, Lo Hermida and the Metropolitan Region.*

| | Nuevo Amanecer (percent) | | Lo Hermida (percent) | | Metrop. Region (Urban)* (percent) | |
|---|---|---|---|---|---|---|
| | 2002 | 2017 | 2002 | 2017 | 2002 | 2017 |
| Precarious homes** | 4.4 | 1.0 | 4.8 | 3.0 | 4.1 | 1.1 |
| Connection to water supply | 96.2 | 99.9 | 96.6 | 99.9 | 92.7 | 96.4 |
| Social housing deficit | – | 10.7 | – | 12.9 | – | 6.9 |
| *Allegados* in overcrowded conditions*** | – | 4.0 | – | 5.0 | – | 2.2 |
| Landline | 68.8 | – | 68.2 | – | 71.8 | – |
| Computer at home | 14.8 | – | 13.2 | – | 28.5 | – |
| Internet connection | 4.6 | – | 4.9 | – | 15.6 | – |
| Vehicle at home | 22.0 | – | 23.7 | – | 39.3 | – |
| Color TV | 92.9 | – | 91.0 | – | 93.3 | – |
| Laundry machine | 82.5 | – | 81.4 | – | 84.5 | – |
| Refrigerator | 87.6 | – | 87.6 | – | 89.9 | – |

*Source*: Self-calculation using data from Census 2002 and 2017.
* The analysis has excluded all nonurban areas of the Metropolitan Region.
** I have called "precarious homes" those cases in which families lived in emergency housing, shacks, tents, or rented a room in collective housing.
***A household is considered overcrowded when each room of its house accommodates 2.5 or more people, and when it keeps ratio of 2.5 or fewer inactive members for each active member.

# Appendix 2  List of Interviews and Field Notes

## LIST OF INTERVIEWS

Interview (2013, January 4). *Fieldwork in Lo Hermida*. Santiago de Chile.

Interview (2013, January 14). *Fieldwork in Lo Hermida*. Santiago de Chile.

Interview (2013, January 17). *Fieldwork in Lo Hermida*. Santiago de Chile.

Interview (2013, January 23). *Fieldwork in Lo Hermida*. Santiago de Chile.

Interview (2013, January 25). *Fieldwork in Lo Hermida*. Santiago de Chile.

Interview (2013, January 29). *Fieldwork in Lo Hermida*. Santiago de Chile.

Interview (2013a, January 30). *Fieldwork in Lo Hermida*. Santiago de Chile.

Interview (2013b, January 30). *Fieldwork in Lo Hermida*. Santiago de Chile.

Interview (2013, January 31). *Fieldwork in Lo Hermida*. Santiago de Chile.

Interview (2013a, February 5). *Fieldwork in Lo Hermida*. Santiago de Chile.

Interview (2013b, February 5). *Fieldwork in Lo Hermida*. Santiago de Chile.

Interview (2013c, February 5). *Fieldwork in Lo Hermida*. Santiago de Chile.

Interview (2013a, February 6). *Fieldwork in Lo Hermida*. Santiago de Chile.

Interview (2013b, February 6). *Fieldwork in Lo Hermida*. Santiago de Chile.

Interview (2013, February 7). *Fieldwork in Lo Hermida*. Santiago de Chile.

Group Interview (2013, February 8). *Fieldwork in Lo Hermida*. Santiago de Chile.

Interview (2013, February 9). *Fieldwork in Lo Hermida*. Santiago de Chile.

Group Interview (2013a, February 13). *Fieldwork in Lo Hermida*. Santiago de Chile.

Group Interview (2013b, February 13). *Fieldwork in Lo Hermida*. Santiago de Chile.

Interview (2013a, February 13). *Fieldwork in Lo Hermida*. Santiago de Chile.

Interview (2013b, February 13). *Fieldwork in Lo Hermida*. Santiago de Chile.

Interview (2013, February 14). *Fieldwork in Lo Hermida*. Santiago de Chile.

Interview (2013a, February 15). *Fieldwork in Lo Hermida*. Santiago de Chile.

Interview (2013b, February 15). *Fieldwork in Lo Hermida*. Santiago de Chile.

Interview (2013, February 16). *Fieldwork in Lo Hermida*. Santiago de Chile.

Interview (2013a, February 19). *Fieldwork in Lo Hermida*. Santiago de Chile.

Interview (2013b, February 19). *Fieldwork in Lo Hermida*. Santiago de Chile.

Interview (2013c, February 19). *Fieldwork in Lo Hermida*. Santiago de Chile.

Interview (2013, February 20). *Fieldwork in Lo Hermida*. Santiago de Chile.

Interview (2013a, February 21). *Fieldwork in Lo Hermida*. Santiago de Chile.

Interview (2013b, February 21). *Fieldwork in Lo Hermida*. Santiago de Chile.

Interview (2013, February 22). *Fieldwork in Lo Hermida*. Santiago de Chile.

Interview (2013, February 23). *Fieldwork in Lo Hermida*. Santiago de Chile.

Group Interview (2013, February 26). *Fieldwork in Lo Hermida*. Santiago de Chile.

Interview (2013, February 26). *Fieldwork in Lo Hermida*. Santiago de Chile.

Interview (2013, February 28). *Fieldwork in Lo Hermida*. Santiago de Chile.

Interview (2013, March 1). *Fieldwork in Lo Hermida*. Santiago de Chile.

Interview (2013a, March 4). *Fieldwork in Lo Hermida*. Santiago de Chile.

Interview (2013b, March 4). *Fieldwork in Lo Hermida*. Santiago de Chile.

Interview (2013, March 5). *Fieldwork in Lo Hermida*. Santiago de Chile.

Group Interview (2013, March 6). *Fieldwork in Lo Hermida*. Santiago de Chile.

Interview (2013a, March 6). *Fieldwork in Lo Hermida*. Santiago de Chile.

Interview (2013b, March 6). *Fieldwork in Lo Hermida*. Santiago de Chile.

Group Interview (2013, March 7). *Fieldwork in Lo Hermida*. Santiago de Chile.

Interview (2013, March 8). *Fieldwork in Lo Hermida*. Santiago de Chile.

Interview (2013a, March 11). *Fieldwork in Lo Hermida*. Santiago de Chile.

Interview (2013b, March 11). *Fieldwork in Lo Hermida*. Santiago de Chile.

Interview (2013, March 12). *Fieldwork in Lo Hermida*. Santiago de Chile.

Interview (2013a, March 13). *Fieldwork in Lo Hermida*. Santiago de Chile.

Interview (2013b, March 13). *Fieldwork in Lo Hermida*. Santiago de Chile.

Interview (2013a, March 14). *Fieldwork in Lo Hermida*. Santiago de Chile.

Interview (2013b, March 14). *Fieldwork in Lo Hermida*. Santiago de Chile.

Interview (2013c, March 14). *Fieldwork in Lo Hermida*. Santiago de Chile.

Interview (2013d, March 14). *Fieldwork in Lo Hermida*. Santiago de Chile.

Interview (2013a, March 16). *Fieldwork in Lo Hermida*. Santiago de Chile.

Interview (2013b, March 16). *Fieldwork in Lo Hermida*. Santiago de Chile.

Interview (2014, December 20). *Fieldwork in Lo Hermida*. Santiago de Chile.

Interview (2017, July 30). *Fieldwork in Lo Hermida*. Santiago de Chile.

Interview (2020, June 7). *Fieldwork in Lo Hermida*. Santiago de Chile.

Interview (2014, September 4). *Fieldwork in Nuevo Amanecer*. Santiago de Chile.

Interview (2014, September 19). *Fieldwork in Nuevo Amanecer*. Santiago de Chile.

Interview (2014, September 22). *Fieldwork in Nuevo Amanecer*. Santiago de Chile.

Interview (2014, September 25). *Fieldwork in Nuevo Amanecer*. Santiago de Chile.

Group Interview (2014, September 26). *Fieldwork in Nuevo Amanecer*. Santiago de Chile.

Interview (2014, September 28). *Fieldwork in Nuevo Amanecer*. Santiago de Chile.

Interview (2014, October 6). *Fieldwork in Nuevo Amanecer*. Santiago de Chile.

Interview (2014, October 7). *Fieldwork in Nuevo Amanecer*. Santiago de Chile.

Interview (2014a, October 9). *Fieldwork in Nuevo Amanecer*. Santiago de Chile.

Interview (2014b, October 9). *Fieldwork in Nuevo Amanecer*. Santiago de Chile.

Interview (2014a, October 13). *Fieldwork in Nuevo Amanecer*. Santiago de Chile.

Interview (2014b, October 13). *Fieldwork in Nuevo Amanecer*. Santiago de Chile.

Interview (2014c, October 13). *Fieldwork in Nuevo Amanecer*. Santiago de Chile.

Interview (2014a, October 16). *Fieldwork in Nuevo Amanecer*. Santiago de Chile.

Interview (2014b, October 16). *Fieldwork in Nuevo Amanecer*. Santiago de Chile.

Interview (2014, October 20). *Fieldwork in Nuevo Amanecer*. Santiago de Chile.

Interview (2014, October 22). *Fieldwork in Nuevo Amanecer*. Santiago de Chile.

Interview (2014a, October 24). *Fieldwork in Nuevo Amanecer*. Santiago de Chile.

Interview (2014b, October 24). *Fieldwork in Nuevo Amanecer*. Santiago de Chile.

Interview (2014a, October 27). *Fieldwork in Nuevo Amanecer*. Santiago de Chile.

Interview (2014b, October 27). *Fieldwork in Nuevo Amanecer*. Santiago de Chile.

Interview (2014a, October 28). *Fieldwork in Nuevo Amanecer*. Santiago de Chile.

Interview (2014b, October 28). *Fieldwork in Nuevo Amanecer*. Santiago de Chile.

Interview (2014a, October 29). *Fieldwork in Nuevo Amanecer*. Santiago de Chile.

Interview (2014b, October 29). *Fieldwork in Nuevo Amanecer*. Santiago de Chile.

Interview (2014, October 30). *Fieldwork in Nuevo Amanecer*. Santiago de Chile.

Interview (2014, November 3). *Fieldwork in Nuevo Amanecer*. Santiago de Chile.

Interview (2014, November 4). *Fieldwork in Nuevo Amanecer*. Santiago de Chile.

Interview (2014, November 7). *Fieldwork in Nuevo Amanecer*. Santiago de Chile.

Interview (2014a, November 11). *Fieldwork in Nuevo Amanecer*. Santiago de Chile.

Interview (2014b, November 11). *Fieldwork in Nuevo Amanecer*. Santiago de Chile.

Interview (2014a, November 15). *Fieldwork in Nuevo Amanecer*. Santiago de Chile.

Interview (2014b, November 15). *Fieldwork in Nuevo Amanecer*. Santiago de Chile.

Group Interview (2014, November 17). *Fieldwork in Nuevo Amanecer*. Santiago de Chile.

Interview (2014, November 17). *Fieldwork in Nuevo Amanecer*. Santiago de Chile.

Group Interview (2014, November 18). *Fieldwork in Nuevo Amanecer*. Santiago de Chile.

Interview (2014, November 18). *Fieldwork in Nuevo Amanecer*. Santiago de Chile.

Interview (2014a, November 27). *Fieldwork in Nuevo Amanecer*. Santiago de Chile.

Interview (2014b, November 27). *Fieldwork in Nuevo Amanecer*. Santiago de Chile.

Interview (2014, November 28). *Fieldwork in Nuevo Amanecer*. Santiago de Chile.

Interview (2014, December 1). *Fieldwork in Nuevo Amanecer*. Santiago de Chile.

Interview (2014, December 2). *Fieldwork in Nuevo Amanecer*. Santiago de Chile.

Interview (2014, December 3). *Fieldwork in Nuevo Amanecer*. Santiago de Chile.

Interview (2014a, December 5). *Fieldwork in Nuevo Amanecer*. Santiago de Chile.

Interview (2014b, December 5). *Fieldwork in Nuevo Amanecer*. Santiago de Chile.

Interview (2014c, December 5). *Fieldwork in Nuevo Amanecer*. Santiago de Chile.

Interview (2014, December 12). *Fieldwork in Nuevo Amanecer*. Santiago de Chile.

Interview (2014a, December 13). *Fieldwork in Nuevo Amanecer*. Santiago de Chile.

Interview (2014b, December 13). *Fieldwork in Nuevo Amanecer*. Santiago de Chile.

Interview (2014, December 29). *Fieldwork in Nuevo Amanecer*. Santiago de Chile.

Interview (2014, December 30). *Fieldwork in Nuevo Amanecer*. Santiago de Chile.

Interview (2017, June 12). *Fieldwork in Lo Hermida*. Santiago de Chile.

Interview (2017, July 30). *Fieldwork in Lo Hermida*. Santiago de Chile.

Interview (2017, October 13). *Fieldwork in Nuevo Amanecer on Policy Implementation*. Santiago de Chile.

Interview (2017, October 16). *Fieldwork in Nuevo Amanecer on Policy Implementation.* Santiago de Chile.

Interview (2017, May 5). *Fieldwork in Nuevo Amanecer.* Santiago de Chile.

Interview (2017, June 5). *Fieldwork in Lo Hermida.* Santiago de Chile.

Interview (2020, June 7). *Fieldwork in Lo Hermida.* Santiago de Chile.

Interview (2020, December 3). *Fieldwork in Lo Hermida.* Santiago de Chile.

Interview (2020, December 4). *Fieldwork in Lo Hermida.* Santiago de Chile.

Interview (2020, December 9). *Fieldwork in Lo Hermida.* Santiago de Chile.

Interview (2020, December 11). *Fieldwork in Lo Hermida.* Santiago de Chile.

Interview (2020, December 14). *Fieldwork in Lo Hermida and Jaime Eyzaguirre.* Santiago de Chile.

Interview (2021, June 16). *Fieldwork in Villa Frei.* Santiago de Chile.

Interview (2021, May 30). *Fieldwork in Nuevo Amanecer.* Santiago de Chile.

Interview (2021, June 26). *Fieldwork in Lo Hermida and Villa Frei.* Santiago de Chile.

Interview (2021, June 14). *Fieldwork in Nuevo Amanecer.* Santiago de Chile.


### LIST OF FIELD NOTES

Field notes (2012a, November 10). *Fieldwork in Lo Hermida.* Santiago de Chile.

Field notes (2012b, November 10). *Fieldwork in Lo Hermida.* Santiago de Chile.

Field notes (2012, November 13). *Fieldwork in Lo Hermida.* Santiago de Chile.

Field notes (2012, November 15). *Fieldwork in Lo Hermida.* Santiago de Chile.

Field notes (2012, November 16). *Fieldwork in Lo Hermida.* Santiago de Chile.

Field notes (2012, November 18). *Fieldwork in Lo Hermida.* Santiago de Chile.

Field notes (2012, November 20). *Fieldwork in Lo Hermida.* Santiago de Chile.

Field notes (2012a, November 23). *Fieldwork in Lo Hermida*. Santiago de Chile.

Field notes (2012b, November 26). *Fieldwork in Lo Hermida*. Santiago de Chile.

Field notes (2012, November 30). *Fieldwork in Lo Hermida*. Santiago de Chile.

Field notes (2012, December 4). *Fieldwork in Lo Hermida*. Santiago de Chile.

Field notes (2012, December 6). *Fieldwork in Lo Hermida*. Santiago de Chile.

Field notes (2012, December 16). *Fieldwork in Lo Hermida*. Santiago de Chile.

Field notes (2012, December 20). *Fieldwork in Lo Hermida*. Santiago de Chile.

Field notes (2012, December 27). *Fieldwork in Lo Hermida*. Santiago de Chile.

Field notes (2013, January 4). *Fieldwork in Lo Hermida*. Santiago de Chile.

Field notes (2013, January 8). *Fieldwork in Lo Hermida*. Santiago de Chile.

Field notes (2013, January 12). *Fieldwork in Lo Hermida*. Santiago de Chile.

Field notes (2013, January 20). *Fieldwork in Lo Hermida*. Santiago de Chile.

Field notes (2013, January 26). *Fieldwork in Lo Hermida*. Santiago de Chile.

Field notes (2013, January 29). *Fieldwork in Lo Hermida*. Santiago de Chile.

Field notes (2013, February 2). *Fieldwork in Lo Hermida*. Santiago de Chile.

Field notes (2013, February 10). *Fieldwork in Lo Hermida*. Santiago de Chile.

Field notes (2013, February 17). *Fieldwork in Lo Hermida*. Santiago de Chile.

Field notes (2013, February 23). *Fieldwork in Lo Hermida*. Santiago de Chile.

Field notes (2013, March 1). *Fieldwork in Lo Hermida*. Santiago de Chile.

Field notes (2013, March 10). *Fieldwork in Lo Hermida*. Santiago de Chile.

Field note (2013, March 17). *Fieldwork in Lo Hermida*. Santiago de Chile.

Field notes (2013, March 23). *Fieldwork in Lo Hermida*. Santiago de Chile.

Field notes (2014, August 16). *Fieldwork in Nuevo Amanecer*. Santiago de Chile.

Field notes (2014, August 18). *Fieldwork in Nuevo Amanecer*. Santiago de Chile.

Field notes (2014, August 24). *Fieldwork in Nuevo Amanecer*. Santiago de Chile.

Field notes (2014, August 27). *Fieldwork in Nuevo Amanecer*. Santiago de Chile.

Field notes (2014, September 1). *Fieldwork in Nuevo Amanecer*. Santiago de Chile.

Field notes (2014, September 5). *Fieldwork in Nuevo Amanecer*. Santiago de Chile.

Field notes (2014, September 6). *Fieldwork in Nuevo Amanecer*. Santiago de Chile.

Field notes (2014, September 7). *Fieldwork in Nuevo Amanecer*. Santiago de Chile.

Field notes (2014, September 10). *Fieldwork in Nuevo Amanecer*. Santiago de Chile.

Field notes (2014, September 17). *Fieldwork in Nuevo Amanecer*. Santiago de Chile.

Field notes (2014, September 25). *Fieldwork in Nuevo Amanecer*. Santiago de Chile.

Field notes (2014, October 22). *Fieldwork in Nuevo Amanecer*. Santiago de Chile.

Field notes (2014, October 24). *Fieldwork in Nuevo Amanecer*. Santiago de Chile.

Field notes (2014, October 27). *Fieldwork in Nuevo Amanecer*. Santiago de Chile.

Field notes (2014, October 31). *Fieldwork in Nuevo Amanecer*. Santiago de Chile.

Field notes (2014, October 8). *Fieldwork in Nuevo Amanecer*. Santiago de Chile.

Field notes (2014, November 2). *Fieldwork in Nuevo Amanecer*. Santiago de Chile.

Field notes (2014, November 4). *Fieldwork in Nuevo Amanecer*. Santiago de Chile.

Field notes (2014, November 9). *Fieldwork in Nuevo Amanecer.* Santiago de Chile.

Field notes (2014, November 10). *Fieldwork in Nuevo Amanecer.* Santiago de Chile.

Field notes (2014, November 11). *Fieldwork in Nuevo Amanecer.* Santiago de Chile.

Field notes (2014, November 15). *Fieldwork in Nuevo Amanecer.* Santiago de Chile.

Field notes (2014, November 24). *Fieldwork in Nuevo Amanecer.* Santiago de Chile.

Field notes (2014, November 27). *Fieldwork in Nuevo Amanecer.* Santiago de Chile.

Field notes (2014, November 30). *Fieldwork in Nuevo Amanecer.* Santiago de Chile.

Field notes (2014, December 4). *Fieldwork in Nuevo Amanecer.* Santiago de Chile.

Field notes (2014, December 5). *Fieldwork in Nuevo Amanecer.* Santiago de Chile.

Field notes (2014, December 9). *Fieldwork in Nuevo Amanecer.* Santiago de Chile.

Field notes (2014, December 11). *Fieldwork in Nuevo Amanecer.* Santiago de Chile.

Field notes (2014, December 12). *Fieldwork in Nuevo Amanecer.* Santiago de Chile.

Field notes (2014, December 14). *Fieldwork in Nuevo Amanecer.* Santiago de Chile.

Field notes (2014, December 15). *Fieldwork in Nuevo Amanecer.* Santiago de Chile.

Field notes (2014, December 18). *Fieldwork in Nuevo Amanecer.* Santiago de Chile.

Field notes (2014, December 22). *Fieldwork in Nuevo Amanecer.* Santiago de Chile.

Field notes (2014, December 23). *Fieldwork in Nuevo Amanecer.* Santiago de Chile.

Field notes (2014, December 29). *Fieldwork in Nuevo Amanecer.* Santiago de Chile.

Field notes (2015, January 5). *Fieldwork in Nuevo Amanecer.* Santiago de Chile.

Field notes (2015, January 6). *Fieldwork in Nuevo Amanecer.* Santiago de Chile.

Field notes (2015, January 8). *Fieldwork in Nuevo Amanecer*. Santiago de Chile.

Field notes (2016, October 13). *Fieldwork in Lo Hermida*. Santiago de Chile.

Field notes (2016, November 4). *Fieldwork in Lo Hermida*. Santiago de Chile.

Field notes (2016, November 12). *Fieldwork in Lo Hermida*. Santiago de Chile.

Field notes (2016, November 25). *Fieldwork in Lo Hermida*. Santiago de Chile.

Field notes (2016, December 15). *Fieldwork in Lo Hermida*. Santiago de Chile.

Field notes (2017, January 13). *Fieldwork in Lo Hermida*. Santiago de Chile.

Field notes (2017, May 6). *Fieldwork in Lo Hermida*. Santiago de Chile.

Field notes (2017, October 16). *Fieldwork in Nuevo Amanecer*. Santiago de Chile.

Field notes (2020, January 16). *Fieldwork in Lo Hermida*. Santiago de Chile.

Field notes (2020, March 10). *Fieldwork in Lo Hermida*. Santiago de Chile.

Field notes (2020, July 14). *Fieldwork in Lo Hermida*. Santiago de Chile.

Field notes (2020, August 13). *Fieldwork in Lo Hermida*. Santiago de Chile.

Field notes (2020, December 15). *Fieldwork in Lo Hermida and Jaime Eyzaguirre*. Santiago de Chile.

Field notes (2021, January 20). *Fieldwork in Lo Hermida*. Santiago de Chile.

Field notes (2021, February 12). *Fieldwork in Lo Hermida*. Santiago de Chile.

Field notes (2021, March 11). *Fieldwork in Lo Hermida*. Santiago de Chile.

Field notes (2021, March 26). *Fieldwork in Lo Hermida*. Santiago de Chile.

Field notes (2021, June 18). *Fieldwork in Lo Hermida*. Santiago de Chile.

# References

Acevedo, Nicolás. 2014. *MAPU-Lautaro*. Santiago de Chile: Escaparate.

Achtenberg, Emily. 2009. "Community Organizing, Rebellion, and the Progressive State: Neighborhood Councils in El Alto, Bolivia." In *Engaging Social Justice: Critical Studies of 21st Century Social Transformation*, edited by David Fasenfest, 275–88. Leiden: Brill.

Agostini, Claudio A. 2010. "Pobreza, Desigualdad y Segregación en la Región Metropolitana." *Estudios Públicos* 117: 219–68. www.estudiospublicos.cl/index.php/cep/article/view/413.

Aillapan, Diego Jesús, and Miguel Ángel Poch-Plá. 2017. "Experiencias, Territorio y Subsistencia: Contexto y Vida de la Niñez Popular en la Población Lo Hermida durante Dictadura 1973–1989." Universidad de Chile. http://repositorio.uchile.cl/bitstream/handle/2250/148425/Experiencias-territorio-y-subsistencia-con texto-y-vida-de-la-ninez-popular-en-la-poblacion-Lo-Hermida-durante-dictadura.pdf?sequence=1&isAllowed=y.

Alldred, Pam, and Nick J. Fox. 2019. "Assembling Citizenship: Sexualities Education, Micropolitics and the Becoming-Citizen." *Sociology* 53 (4): 1–18. https://doi.org/10.1177/0038038518822889.

Almeida, Paul, and Linda Brewster Stearns. 1998. "Political Opportunities and Local Grassroots Environmental Movements: The Case of Minamata." *Social Problems* 45 (1): 37–60. https://doi.org/10.2307/3097142.

Álvarez, Rolando. 2017. "Las Juventudes Comunistas de Chile y el Movimiento Estudiantil Secundario: Un Caso de Radicalización Política de Masas (1983 – 1988)." In *Un Trébol de Cuatro Hojas: Las Juventudes Comunistas de Chile en El Siglo XX*, edited by Rolando Álvarez and Manuel Loyola, 170–217. Santiago de Chile: Ariadna Ediciones.

Anderson, Benedict. 1991. *Imagined Communities: Reflections on the Origins and Spread of Nationalism*. London: Verso.

Angelcos, Nicolás, and Miguel Pérez. 2017. "De la 'Desaparición' a la Reemergencia: Continuidades y Rupturas del Movimiento de Pobladores en Chile." *Latin American Research Review* 52 (1): 94–109. https://doi.org/10.25222/larr.39.

Angell, Alan, and Benny Pollack. 1990. "The Chilean Elections of 1989 and the Politics of the Transition to Democracy." *Bulletin of Latin American Research* 9 (1): 1–23.

Arancibia, Eduardo. 2015. *Las Milicias de la Resistencia Popular, el MIR y la Lucha Social Armada en la Dictadura 1979–1984*. Santiago de Chile: Escaparate.

Arbona, Juan Manuel. 2008. "'Sangre de Minero, Semilla de Guerrillero': Histories and Memories in the Organisation and Struggles of the Santiago II Neighbourhood of El Alto, Bolivia." *Bulletin of Latin American Research* 27 (1): 24–42. https://doi.org/10.1111/j.1470-9856.2007.00255.x.

Arendt, Hannah. 1973. *The Origins of Totalitarianism*. London: Harcourt Brace.

Arriagada, Camilo, Daniela Sepúlveda, Enrique Cartier, and Carlos Gutiérrez. 2004. *Chile, Un Siglo de Políticas en Vivienda y Barrio*. Santiago de Chile: Pehuén Editores.

Attoh, Kafui A. 2011. "What Kind of Right Is the Right to the City?" *Progress in Human Geography* 35 (5): 669–85. https://doi.org/10.1177/0309132510394706.

Auyero, Javier. 2000. "The Logic of Clientelism in Argentina: An Ethnographic Account." *Latin American Research Review* 35 (3): 55–81.

2001. *Poor People's Politics: Peronist Survival Networks and the Legacy of Evita*. Durham and London: Duke University Press.

Badilla, Manuela. 2019. "The Chilean Student Movement: Challenging Public Memories of Pinochet's Dictatorship." *Mobilization* 24 (4): 493–510. https://doi.org/10.17813/1086-671X-24-4-493.

Barton, Ruth. 2018. "'Our Tarkine, Our Future': The Australian Workers Union Use of Narratives Around Place and Community in West and North West Tasmania, Australia." *Antipode* 50 (1): 41–60. https://doi.org/10.1111/anti.12353.

Bastías Saavedra, Manuel. 2013. *Sociedad Civil en Dictadura: Relaciones Transnacionales, Organizaciones y Socialización Política en Chile (1973–1993)*. Santiago de Chile: Ediciones Universidad Alberto Hurtado.

Belew, Kathleen. 2018. *Bring the War Home: The White Power Movement and Paramilitary America*. Cambridge and London: Harvard University Press.

Bellinger, Paul T., and Moisés Arce. 2011. "Protest and Democracy in Latin America's Market Era." *Political Research Quarterly* 64 (3): 688–704. https://doi.org/10.1177/1065912910373557.

Benford, Robert, and David Snow. 2000. "Framing Processes and Social Movements: An Overview and Assessment." *Annual Review of Sociology* 26 (1): 611–39. https://doi.org/10.1146/annurev.soc.26.1.611.

Bénit-Gbaffou, Claire, and Obvious Katsaura. 2014. "Community Leadership and the Construction of Political Legitimacy: Unpacking Bourdieu's 'Political Capital' in Post-Apartheid Johannesburg." *International Journal of Urban and Regional Research* 38 (5): 1807–32. https://doi.org/10.1111/1468-2427.12166.

Bertuzzi, Niccolò. 2020. "The Individualization of Political Activism: A Reflection on Social Movements and Modernization, Starting from the Case of Italian Animal Advocacy." *International Journal of Sociology and Social Policy* 40 (3–4): 282–303. https://doi.org/10.1108/IJSSP-09-2019-0180.

Blank, Martina. 2016. "De-Fetishizing the Analysis of Spatial Movement Strategies: Polymorphy and *Trabajo Territorial* in Argentina." *Political Geography* 50: 1–9. https://doi.org/10.1016/j.polgeo.2015.09.002.

Bonnefoy, Pascale, Claudio Pérez, and Ángel Spotorno. 2008. *Internacionalistas: Chilenos en la Revolución Popular Sandinista*. Santiago de Chile: Editorial Latinoamericana.

Bourdieu, Pierre. 1986. "The Forms of Capital." In *Handbook of Theory and Research for the Sociology of Education*, edited by John Richardson, 241–58. New York: Greenwood Press.

1991. *Language and Symbolic Power*. Cambridge: Polity Press.

Bravo, Nazareno. 2013. "El Barrio como Razón de Ser y Hacer: La Biblioteca Popular Pablito González, del Estigma a la Organización." In *(Re)Inventarse en la Acción Política*, edited by Nazareno Bravo, Mariano Salomone, and Gabriel Liceaga, 19–57. Cuyo, Argentina: Ediunc.

Bravo, Viviana. 2010. *¡Con la Razón y la Fuerza Venceremos! La Rebelión Popular y la Subjetividad Comunista en los '80*. Santiago de Chile: Ariadna Ediciones.

2017. *Piedras, Barricadas y Cacerolas: Las Jornadas Nacionales de Protesta Chile 1983–1986*. Santiago de Chile: Ediciones Universidad Alberto Hurtado.

Briceño, Pablo. 2017. "Waiting for Power: Affection, Ethics and Politics in the Everyday Life of Popular Chile." University of Edinburgh. www.era.lib.ed.ac .uk/handle/1842/29600?show=full.

Bruey, Alison J. 2009. "Neoliberalism and Repression in 'Poblaciones' of Santiago de Chile." *Stockholm Review of Latin American Studies* September (5): 17–28.

2018. *Bread, Justice, and Liberty: Grassroots Activism and Human Rights in Pinochet's Chile*. Madison: University of Wisconsin Press.

Buechler, Steven M. 1990. *Women's Movements in the United States: Woman Suffrage, Equal Rights, and Beyond*. London: Rutgers University Press.

Bystydzienski, Jill, and Steven Schacht. 2001. *Forging Radical Alliances Across Difference: Coalition Politics for the New Millennium*. London: Rowman & Littlefield Publishers.

Cable, Sherry, Edward J. Walsh, and Rex H. Warland. 1988. "Differential Paths to Political Activism: Comparisons of Four Mobilization Processes After the Three Mile Island Accident." *Social Forces* 66 (4): 951–69. https://doi.org/10 .1093/sf/66.4.951.

Caldeira, Teresa. 2000. *City of Walls: Crime, Segregation, and Citizenship in São Paulo*. Berkeley: University of California Press.

Calhoun, Craig. 1994. *Social Theory and the Politics of Identity*. Oxford: Blackwell.

Canel, Eduardo. 1992. "Democratization and the Decline of Urban Social Movements in Uruguay: A Political-Institutional Account." In *The Making of Social Movements in Latin America: Identity, Strategy, and Democracy*, edited by Arturo Escobar and Sonia E. Alvarez, 276–90. Oxford: Westview Press.

Casey, Kimberly L. 2005. "Defining Political Capital: A Reconsideration of Bourdieu's Interconvertibility Theory." St. Louis. https://cpb-us-w2 .wpmucdn.com/about.illinoisstate.edu/dist/e/34/files/2019/09/Casey.pdf.

Castañeda, Ernesto. 2012. "Places of Stigma: Ghettos, Barrios, and Banlieues." In *The Ghetto: Contemporary Global Issues and Controversies*, edited by Ray Hutchison and Bruce D. Haynes, 151–90. Boulder: Westview Press.

Castells, Manuel. 1982. "Squatters and Politics in Latin America: A Comparative Analysis of Urban Social Movements in Chile, Peru and Mexico." In *Towards a Political Economy of Urbanization in Third World Countries*, edited by Helen Safa, 283–304. Delhi: Oxford University Press.

1983. *The City and the Grassroots: A Cross-Cultural Theory of Urban Social Movements*. London: Edward Arnold.

2010. *The Information Age: Economy, Society, and Culture. The Power of Identity*. 2nd ed. Oxford: Wiley-Blackwell. https://doi.org/10.1002/9781444318234.

Castillo Couve, María José. 2014. "Competencias de los Pobladores: Potencial de Innovación para la Política Habitacional Chilena." *Revista INVI* 29 (81): 79–112.

Chilevisión. 2016. *En la Mira: Zonas Rojas*. Chile: Chilevisión. www.chilevision.cl/en-la-mira/capitulo-completo/p/4.

Chuang, Ya-chung. 2005. "Place, Identity, and Social Movements: Shequ and Neighborhood Organizing in Taipei City." *Positions: East Asia Cultures Critique* 13 (2): 379–410. https://doi.org/10.1215/10679847-13-2-379.

Chung, Angie Y. 2001. "The Powers that Bind: A Case Study of Collective Bases of Coalition Building in Post-Civil Unrest Los Angeles." *Urban Affairs Review* 37 (2): 205–26. https://doi.org/10.1177/10780870122185262.

Ciper Chile. 2020. "Carabinero Infiltrado en Lo Hermida fue Descubierto porque Protagonizó Programa de Canal 13 con su Identidad Real" https://www.ciperchile.cl/2020/10/15/carabinero-infiltrado-en-lo-hermida-fue-descubierto-porque-protagonizo-programa-de-canal-13-con-su-identidad-real/.

CNN Chile. 2019. "Fontaine: 'Quien Madrugue Puede Ser Ayudado a través de una Tarifa Más Baja.'" www.youtube.com/watch?v=nFO4zjFniso.

Cofré, Boris. 2007. *Campamento Nueva La Habana: El MIR y el Movimiento de Pobladores, 1970–1973*. Santiago de Chile: Escaparate.

Cohen, Anthony. 1989. *The Symbolic Construction of Community*. London: Routledge.

Coll, Kathleen M. 2010. *Remaking Citizenship: Latina Immigrants and New American Politics*. Stanford: Stanford University Press.

Cooperativa. 2011. "Adimark: Apoyo al Movimiento Estudiantil Subió al 79 por ciento." *Cooperativa.cl*, October 5, 2011. www.cooperativa.cl/noticias/pais/politica/encuestas/adimark-apoyo-al-movimiento-estudiantil-subio-al-79-por-ciento/2011-10-05/121430.html.

Cornejo, Catalina. 2012. "Estigma Territorial como Forma de Violencia Barrial. El Caso del Sector El Castillo." *Revista INVI* 27 (76): 177–200.

Cornejo, Marcela, Carolina Rocha, Diego Castro, Micaela Varela, Jorge Manzi, Roberto González, Gloria Jiménez-Moya, et al. 2020. "The Intergenerational Transmission of Participation in Collective Action: The Role of Conversation and Political Practices in the Family." *British Journal of Social Psychology* 60 (1): 1–21. https://doi.org/10.1111/bjso.12420.

Cortés, Alexis. 2013. "A Struggle Larger than a House: Pobladores and Favelados in Latin American Social Theory." *Latin American Perspectives* 40 (2): 168–84. https://doi.org/10.1177/0094582X12467763.

2014. "El Movimiento de Pobladores Chilenos y la Población La Victoria: Ejemplaridad, Movimientos Sociales y el Derecho a la Ciudad." *EURE* 40 (119): 239–60.

Cortés, Sandra, María-Soledad Martínez-Gutiérrez, and Samanta Anríquez Jiménez. 2021. "Vulneración de Derechos Humanos en las Movilizaciones de Octubre de 2019 en Chile." *Gaceta Sanitaria* xx (February): 2020–22. https://doi.org/10.1016/j.gaceta.2020.12.029.

Craib, Ian. 1998. *Experiencing Identity*. London: SAGE.

Crenson, Matthew A. 1983. *Neighborhood Politics*. London: Harvard University Press.

Cuba, Lee, and David M. Hummon. 1993. "A Place to Call Home: Identification with Dwelling, Community, and Region." *The Sociological Quarterly* 34 (1): 111–31. https://doi.org/10.1111/j.1533-8525.1993.tb00133.x.

Dagger, Richard. 1981. "Metropolis, Memory, and Citizenship." *American Journal of Political Science* 25 (4): 715–37.

Dammert, Lucía. 2004. "Ciudad sin Ciudadanos? Fragmentación, Segregación y Temor en Santiago." *Eure* 30 (91): 87–96. https://doi.org/10.4067/S0250-71612004009100006.

Dammert, Lucía, and Enrique Oviedo. 2004. "Santiago: Delitos y Violencia Urbana en una Ciudad Segregada." In *Santiago en la Globalización: ¿Una Nueva Ciudad?*, edited by Carlos De Matos, María Elena Ducci, Alfredo Rodríguez, and Gloria Yáñez, 273–94. Santiago de Chile: SUR Corporación & IEUT.

Davenport, Christian. 2015. *How Social Movements Die: Repression and Demobilization of the Republic of New Africa*. New York: Cambridge University Press.

Davidson, Alastair. 1997. *From Subject to Citizen: Australian Citizenship in the Twentieth Century. Studies in Global Justice*. Vol. 3. Cambridge: Cambridge University Press. https://doi.org/10.1007/978-1-4020-5662-8_7.

Dávolos, Patricia, Marcela Jabbaz, and Estela Molina. 1987. *Movimiento Villero y Estado (1966–1976)*. Buenos Aires: Centro Editor de América Latina.

Degler, Carl N. 1971. *Neither Black nor White: Slavery and Race Relations in Brazil and the United States*. London: Palgrave Macmillan.

Delamaza, Gonzalo. 1995. *Construcción Democrática, Participación Ciudadana y Políticas Públicas en Chile*. Leiden University. https://openaccess.leidenuniv.nl/bitstream/handle/1887/15360/proefschrift?sequence=1.

Delamaza, Gonzalo, and Carlos Ochsenius. 2006. "Trayectorias, Redes y Poder: Sociedad Civil y Política en la Transición Democrática Chilena." In *La Disputa por la Construcción Democrática en América Latina*, edited by Evelina Dagnino, Alberto J. Olvera, and Aldo Panfici, 450–500. Mexico: Fondo de Cultura Económica.

Díaz, Vanessa. 2013. "Santiago bajo el Agua, Historia Repetida." *Blogs El Mercurio*, May 26, 2013. www.elmercurio.com/blogs/2013/05/26/12079/Santiago-bajo-el-agua-historia-repetida.aspx.

Disi, Rodolfo. 2018. "Sentenced to Debt: Explaining Student Mobilization in Chile." *Latin American Research Review* 53 (3): 448–65. https://doi.org/10.25222/larr.395.

Dolgon, Corey. 2001. "Building Community amid the Ruins: Strategies for Struggle from the Coalition for Justice at Southampton College." In *Forging Radical Alliances across Difference*, edited by Jill Bystydzienski and Steven Schacht, 220–32. London: Rowman and Littlefield Publisher.

Donner, Henrike. 2011. "Locating Activist Spaces: The Neighbourhood as a Source and Site of Urban Activism in 1970s Calcutta." *Cultural Dynamics* 23 (1): 21–40. https://doi.org/10.1177/0921374011403352.

Donoso, Sofia. 2016. "When Social Movements Become a Democratizing Force: The Political Impact of the Student Movement in Chile." *Research in Social Movements, Conflict and Change* 39: 167–96. https://doi.org/10.1108/S0163-786X20160000039008.

Drogus, Carol Ann, and Hannah Stewart-Gambino. 2005. *Activist Faith: Grassroots Women in Democratic Brazil and Chile*. Pennsylvania: Pennsylvania State University Press.

Dubet, François, Eugenio Tironi, Vicente Espinoza, and Eduardo Valenzuela. 2016. *Pobladores: Luchas Sociales y Democracia en Chile*. Santiago de Chile: Ediciones Universidad Alberto Hurtado.

DuBois, Ellen. 1998. *Woman Suffrage and Women's Rights*. New York: New York University Press.

Ducci, María Elena, and Giulietta Fadda. 1993. "Políticas de Desarrollo Urbano y Vivienda en Chile. Interrelaciones y Efectos." In *Chile: 50 Años de Vivienda Social, 1943–1993*, edited by Luis Bravo and Carlos Martínez, 74–111. Valparaiso: Universidad de Valparaiso.

Dyke, Nella Van. 2003. "Crossing Movement Boundaries: Factors That Facilitate Coalition Protest by American College Students, 1930–1990." *Social Problems* 50 (2): 226–50.

Dyke, Nella Van, and Bryan Amos. 2017. "Social Movement Coalitions: Formation, Longevity, and Success." *Sociology Compass* 11 (7): 1–17. https://doi.org/10.1111/soc4.12489.

Effron, Daniel A., and Dale T. Miller. 2012. "How the Moralization of Issues Grants Social Legitimacy to Act on One's Attitudes." *Personality and Social Psychology Bulletin* 38 (5): 690–701. https://doi.org/10.1177/0146167211435982.

El Mercurio. 1982. "Estragos del Temporal: Un Muerto, Inundaciones, Naufragio y Derrumbes." *Section C*, June 27.

Escoffier, Simón. 2017a. "Politicization and Social Mobilization in Twenty-First-Century Chile." In *Global Encyclopedia of Public Administration, Public Policy, and Governance*, edited by Ali Farazmand, 1–6. New York: Springer. https://doi.org/10.1007/978-3-319-31816-5_3330-1.

———. 2017b. "Policy Metaphors and Deep Local Democracy: The Case of the Chilean Neighbourhood Recovery Programme." *Revista Iberoamericana de Estudios Municipales* 8 (15): 35–64. https://doi.org/10.32457/riem.vii5.340.

———. 2018. "Mobilisational Citizenship: Sustainable Collective Action in Underprivileged Urban Chile." *Citizenship Studies* 22 (7): 769–90. https://doi.org/10.1080/13621025.2018.1508412.

Espinoza, Vicente. 1988. *Para una Historia de los Pobres en la Ciudad*. Santiago de Chile: Ediciones SUR. www.memoriachilena.cl/archivos2/pdfs/MC0033320.pdf.

Eyerman, Ron. 2004. "The Past in the Present: Culture and the Transmission of Memory." *Acta Sociologica* 47 (2): 159–69. https://doi.org/10.1177/0001699304043853.

Feagin, Joe R., Paul E. Peterson, and Christopher Jencks. 1991. "The Urban Underclass." *Annual Review of Sociology* 17: 445–66. https://doi.org/10 .2307/2075843.

Figueroa, Yanny. 2003. "Campamento Esperanza Andina." In *Ampliando la Ciudadanía, Promoviendo la Participación: 30 Innovaciones Locales*, edited by Antonieta Surawski and Julia Cubillos, 557–93. Santiago de Chile: LOM. www.innovacionciudadana.cl/portal/imagen/File/30experiencias.pdf.

Finn, Janet L. 2008. "La Victoria: Claiming Memory, History, and Justice in a Santiago Población." *Journal of Community Practice* 13 (3): 9–31. https://doi .org/10.1300/J125v13n03.

Flam, Helena. 2014. "Micromobilization and Emotions." In *The Oxford Handbook of Social Movements*, edited by Donatella Della Porta and Mario Diani, 1–14. Oxford: Oxford University Press. https://doi.org/10 .1093/oxfordhb/9780199678402.013.31.

Flesher, Cristina. 2010. "Collective Identity in Social Movements: Central Concepts and Debates." *Sociology Compass* 4: 393–404. https://doi.org/10 .1111/j.1751-9020.2010.00287.x.

Flinders, Matthew, and Matt Wood. 2015. *Tracing the Political: Depoliticisation, Governance and the State*. Bristol: Policy Press. https://doi.org/10.1332/pol icypress/9781861349071.001.0001.

Fotaki, Marianna, and Hamid Foroughi. 2021. "Extinction Rebellion: Green Activism and the Fantasy of Leaderlessness in a Decentralized Movement." *Leadership* 18 (2): 1–23. https://doi.org/10.1177/17427150211005578.

Foweraker, Joe. 1995. *Theorizing Social Movements. Critical Studies on Latin America*. London: Pluto.

Frente Popular Revolucionario. 2019. "Van a Volver." Facebook. www.facebook .com/FPRNacional/videos/1068243173551763/?t=546.

Gamson, William. 1992. "The Social Psychology of Collective Action." In *Frontiers in Social Movement Theory*, edited by Aldon Morris and Carol Mueller, 53–76. New York: Yale University Press.

1995. "Constructing Social Protest." In *Social Movements and Culture*, edited by Hank Johnston and Bert Klandermans, 85–106. Minneapolis: University of Minnesota Press.

Ganz, Marshall. 2010. "Leading Change: Leadership, Organization, and Social Movements." In *Handbook of Leadership Theory and Practice: A Harvard Business School Centennial Colloquium*, edited by Nitin Nohria and Rakesh Khurana, 527–68. Boston: Harvard Business Press.

2016. "Resources and Resourcefulness: Strategic Capacity in the Unionization of California Agriculture, 1959–1966." *American Journal of Sociology* 105 (4): 1003–62.

Garcés, Mario. 2002. *Tomando Su Sitio: El Movimiento de Pobladores de Santiago, 1957–1970*. Santiago de Chile: LOM.

Garcés, Mario, and Alejandra Valdés. 1999. "Estado del Arte de la Participacion Ciudadana en Chile." Santiago de Chile. www.innosocialafta.cl/documentos/ EstadodelartedelaparticipacionciudadanaenChile.pdf.

Garretón, Manuel Antonio. 1989. *The Chilean Political Process*. Edited by Sharon Kellum and Gilbert W. Merkx. Thematic Studies in Latin America. Boston: Unwin Hyman.

2003. *Incomplete Democracy: Political Democratization in Chile and Latin America*. London: University of North Carolina Press.

Goffman, Erving. 1986. *Frame Analysis: An Essay on the Organization of Experience*. London: Northeastern University Press.

González, Felipe. 2018. "Crédito, Deuda y Gubernamentalidad Financiera en Chile." *Revista Mexicana de Sociología* 80 (4): 881–908. https://doi.org/10.22201/iis.01882503p.2018.4.57798.

Gonzalez, Ricardo, and Carmen Le Foulon. 2020. "The 2019–2020 Chilean Protests: A First Look at Their Causes and Participants." *International Journal of Sociology* 50 (3): 227–35. https://doi.org/10.1080/00207659.2020.1752499.

Gonzalez-Vaillant, Gabriela, and Gianmarco Savio. 2017. "Contentious Sites: Cultural Memory, Collective Organizing, and Symbolic Struggles Over the Park 51 Islamic Center." *The Sociological Review* 65 (2): 318–35. https://doi.org/10.1177/0038026116674885.

Goodwin, Jeff, James M. Jasper, and Francesca Polletta. 2001. *Passionate Politics: Emotions and Social Movements*. Chicago: University of Chicago Press.

Greaves, Edward. 2002. "Reorganizing Civil Society: Popular Movements, the State, and Municipalities in Post-Authoritarian Chile." University of Florida.

2004. "Municipality and Community in Chile: Building Imagined Civic Communities and Its Impact on the Political." *Politics & Society* 32 (2): 203–30. https://doi.org/10.1177/0032329204263070.

2005. "Panoptic Municipalities, the Spatial Dimensions of the Political, and Passive Revolution in Post-Dictatorship Chile." *City and Community* 4 (2): 189–215. https://doi.org/10.1111/j.1540-6040.2005.00111.x.

Gutman, Yifat. 2017. *Memory Activism: Reimagining the Past for the Future in Israel-Palestine*. Nashville: Vanderbilt University Press.

Guzmán, Romina, Henry Renna, Alejandra Sandoval, and Camila Silva. 2009. *Movimiento de Pobladores en Lucha: "A Tomarse Peñalolén para Conquistar la Ciudad."* Santiago de Chile: SUR.

Haines, Herbert H. 1984. "Black Radicalization and the Funding of Civil Rights: 1957–1970." *Social Problems* 32 (1): 31–43. https://doi.org/10.2307/800260.

Han, Clara. 2012. *Life in Debt: Times of Care and Violence in Neoliberal Chile*. Berkeley: University of California Press.

Hanisch, Carol. 2001. "Struggles Over Leadership in the Women's Liberation Movement." In *Leadership and Social Movements*, edited by Colin Barker, Alan Johnson, and Michael Lavalette, 77–95. Manchester: Manchester University Press.

Hardy, Clarisa. 1986a. "Estrategias Organizadas de Subsistencia: Los Sectores Populares Frente a sus Necesidades en Chile." In *Estilos de Desarrollo en América Latina y Desafíos del Futuro*. Santiago de Chile: CEPAL.

1986b. *Hambre + Dignidad = Ollas Comunes*. Santiago de Chile: Programa de Economía del Trabajo (PET).

Harris, Fredrick C. 2006. "It Takes a Tragedy to Arouse Them: Collective Memory and Collective Action during the Civil Rights Movement." *Social Movement Studies* 5 (1): 19–43. https://doi.org/10.1080/14742830600621159.

Hechos Urbanos. 1987. "Boletín de Información y Análisis." *SUR Documentación*, June 1987.

Hewitt, W. E. 1993. "Popular Movements, Resource Demobilization, and the Legacy of Vatican Restructuring in the Archidiocese of Sao Paulo." *Canadian Journal of Latin American and Caribbean Studies* 18 (36): 1–24. https://doi .org/10.1080/08263663.1993.10816696.

Hidalgo, Robinson Silva. 2008. "El Espacio Público Dictatorial: Edificios y Lugares Significados por el Poder Político." *Revista de Urbanismo* 30: 15–29.

Hidalgo, Rodrigo. 2004a. "De los Pequeños Condominios a la Ciudad Vallada: Las Urbanizaciones Cerradas y la Nueva Geografía Social en Santiago de Chile (1990–2000)." *Eure* 30 (91): 29–52. https://doi.org/10.4067/S0250–71612004009100003.

2004b. "La Vivienda Social en Santiago de Chile en la Segunda Mitad del Siglo XX: Actores Relevantes y Tendencias Espaciales." In *Santiago en la Globalizacion: ¿Una Nueva Ciudad?*, edited by Carlos De Mattos, María Elena Ducci, Alfredo Rodríguez, and Gloria Yáñez, 219–42. Santiago de Chile: SUR.

2005. *La Vivienda Social en Chile y la Construcción del Espacio Urbano en el Santiago del Siglo XX*. Santiago de Chile: Instituto de Geografía, Pontificia Universidad Católica de Chile, Centro de Investigaciones Diego Barros Arana.

Hildebrandt, Paula, Kerstin Evert, Sibylle Peters, Mirjam Schaub, Kathrin Wildner, and Gesa Ziemer. 2019. *Performing Citizenship: Bodies, Agencies, Limitations*. Cham: Palgrave Macmillan.

Hilgers, Tina. 2012. *Clientelism in Everyday Latin American Politics*. Edited by Tina Hilgers. New York: Palgrave Macmillan.

Hill, Lance. 2006. *The Deacons for Defense: Armed Resistance and the Civil Rights Movement*. Chapel Hill: The University of North Carolina Press.

Hiner, Hillary. 2010. "Voces Soterradas, Violencias Ignoradas: Discurso, Violencia Política y Género en los Informes Rettig y Valech." *Latin American Research Review* 44 (3): 50–74. https://doi.org/10.1353/lar.0 .0082.

Hipsher, Patricia. 1996. "Democratization and the Decline of Urban Social Movements in Chile and Spain." *Comparative Politics* 28 (3): 273–97. https://doi.org/10.1177/S0038038599000218.

1998. "Democratic Transitions as Protest Cycles: Social Movement Dynamics in Democratizing Latin America." In *The Social Movement Society*, edited by David S. Meyer and Sidney Tarrow, 153–72. Oxford: Rowman & Littlefield Publishers.

Holston, James. 1991. "Autoconstruction in Working-Class Brazil." *Cultural Anthropology* 6 (4): 447–65. https://doi.org/10.1525/can.1991.6.4.02a00020.

1999. *Cities and Citizenship*. Durham: Duke University Press.

2008. *Insurgent Citizenship: Disjunctions of Democracy and Modernity in Brazil*. Princeton: Princeton University Press.

2011. "Contesting Privilege with Right: The Transformation of Differentiated Citizenship in Brazil." *Citizenship Studies* 15 (3–4): 335–52. https://doi.org/10.1080/13621025.2011.565157.

Holston, James, and Arjun Appadurai. 1996. "Cities and Citizenship." *Public Culture* 8 (2): 187–204. https://doi.org/10.1215/08992363-8-2-187.

Hölzl, Corinna. 2018. "The Spatial-Political Outcome of Urban Development Conflicts: Emancipatory Dynamics of Protests against Gentrification in Peñalolén, Santiago de Chile." *International Journal of Urban and Regional Research* 42 (6): 1008–29. https://doi.org/10.1111/1468-2427.12674.

Hong, Pamela M., and Clayton D. Peoples. 2020. "The Ties that Mobilize Us: Networks, Intergroup Contact, and Participation in the Black Lives Matter Movement." *Analyses of Social Issues and Public Policy*, May: 1–16. https://doi.org/10.1111/asap.12230.

Hordijk, Michaela. 2005. "Participatory Governance in Peru: Exercising Citizenship." *Environment and Urbanization* 17 (1): 219–36. https://doi.org/10.1630/0956247053633728.

Huneeus, Carlos. 2014. *La Democracia Semisoberana: Chile Después de Pinochet*. Santiago de Chile: Taurus.

Inostroza, Marta. 2013. "Chile a 40 Años del Golpe: Silvia Leiva, Dirigente del Campamento Nueva Habana." *Estocolmo Noticias*, February 10, 2013. www.estocolmo.se/noticias/?id=2737.

Isin, Engin. 2000. *Democracy, Citizenship and the Global City*. New York: Routledge.

2002. *Being Political: Genealogies of Citizenship*. London: University of Minnesota Press.

2008. "Theorizing Acts of Citizenship." In *Acts of Citizenship*, edited by Engin Fahri Isin and Greg Nielsen, 15–43. London: Zed Books.

2009. "Citizenship in Flux: The Figure of the Activist Citizen." *Subjectivity* 29 (1): 367–88. https://doi.org/10.1057/sub.2009.25.

Isin, Engin, and Bryan S. Turner. 2002. *Handbook of Citizenship Studies*. London: SAGE.

Isin, Engin, and Patricia K. Wood. 1999. *Citizenship and Identity*. London: SAGE.

Jackson, Sarah J. 2021. "Black Lives Matter and the Revitalization of Collective Visionary Leadership." *Leadership* 17 (1): 8–17. https://doi.org/10.1177/1742715020975920.

Jara Ibarra, Camila. 2016. "The Demobilization of Civil Society: Posttraumatic Memory in the Reconstruction of Chilean Democracy." *Latin American Perspectives* 43 (6): 88–102. https://doi.org/10.1177/0094582X16669140.

Jargowsky, Paul A. 1997. *Poverty and Place: Ghettos, Barrios, and the American City*. New York: Russell Sage Foundation.

Jenkins, Craig, and Charles Perrow. 1977. "Insurgency of the Powerless: Farm Worker Movements (1946–1972)." *American Sociological Review* 42 (2): 249–68.

Jenkins, Richard. 1996. *Social Identity*. London: Routledge.

Johnson, Holly. 1985. *La Juventud Popular en Chile y el Movimiento Social*. Santiago de Chile: FLACSO. https://doi.org/10.1017/CBO9781107415324.004.

Joignant, Alfredo. 2019. *Acting Politics: A Critical Sociology of the Political Field*. New York: Routledge.

King, Gary, Robert Keohane, and Didney Verba. 1994. *Designing Social Inquiry: Scientific Inference in Qualitative Research*. Princeton: Princeton University Press.

Klandermans, Bert, and Dirk Oegema. 1987. "Potentials, Networks, Motivations, and Barriers in Social Movements." *American Sociological Review* 52 (4): 519–31. www.jstor.org/stable/2095297.

Knoke, David, and James R. Wood. 1981. *Organized for Action: Commitment in Voluntary Associations*. New Brunswick: Rutgers University Press.

Koppelman, Carter. 2016. "Deepening Demobilization: The State's Transformation of Civil Society in the Poblaciones of Santiago, Chile." *Latin American Perspectives* 44 (3): 46–63. https://doi.org/10.1177/0094582X16668316.

Kurtz, Marcus J. 2004. "The Dilemmas of Democracy in the Open Economy: Lessons from Latin America." *World Politics* 56 (02): 262–302. https://doi.org/10.1353/wp.2004.0013.

La Tercera. 2019. "Cuando las Declaraciones Juegan una Mala Pasada: El Listado de Frases Polémicas de los Ministros y Subsecretarios de Piñera." 2019. www.latercera.com/politica/noticia/gobierno-pinera-frases-polemicas/852188/.

Labbé, Francisco J., and Marcelo Llévenes. 1986. "Efectos Distributivos Derivados del Proceso de Erradicación de Poblaciones en el Gran Santiago." *Estudios Públicos* 24: 197–242.

Lamont, Michele, and Virag Molnar. 2002. "The Study of Boundaries in the Social Sciences." *Annual Review of Sociology* 28: 167–95.

Lapegna, Pablo. 2013. "Social Movements and Patronage Politics: Processes of Demobilization and Dual Pressure." *Sociological Forum* 28 (4): 842–63. https://doi.org/10.1111/socf.12059.

2016. *Soybeans and Power: Genetically Modified Crops, Environmental Politics, and Social Movements in Argentina*. Oxford: Oxford University Press. https://doi.org/10.1093/acprof:oso/9780190215132.001.0001.

Laraña, Enrique, Hank Johnston, and Joseph R. Gusfield. 1994. "New Social Movements: From Ideology to Identity." In *New Social Movements: From Ideology to Identity*, edited by Enrique Laraña, Hank Johnston, and Joseph R. Gusfield, 185–208. Philadelphia: Temple University Press.

Lazar, Sian. 2008. *El Alto, Rebel City: Self and Citizenship in Andean Bolivia*. London: Duke University Press.

2013. *The Anthropology of Citizenship: A Reader*. Oxford: Wiley-Blackwell.

Lenin, Vladimir. 1974. "The Dual Power." In *Collected Works (April–June 1917)*, 24, 38–42. Moscow: Progress Publishers.

Lewicka, Maria. 2010. "What Makes Neighborhood Different from Home and City? Effects of Place Scale on Place Attachment." *Journal of Environmental Psychology* 30 (1): 35–51. https://doi.org/10.1016/j.jenvp.2009.05.004.

Lichterman, Paul. 1995. "Piecing Together Multicultural Community: Cultural Differences in Community Building among Grass-Roots Environmentalists." *Social Problems* 42 (4): 513–34. https://doi.org/10.2307/3097044.

Lim, Chaeyoon. 2010. "Mobilizing on the Margin: How Does Interpersonal Recruitment Affect Citizen Participation in Politics?" *Social Science Research* 39 (2): 341–55. https://doi.org/10.1016/j.ssresearch.2009.05.005.

Lima, Nisia Veronica Trindade. 1989. *O Movimento de Favelados do Rio de Janeiro*. Rio de Janeiro: IUPERJ. www.arca.fiocruz.br/handle/icict/12454.

Lister, Ruth. 2003. *Citizenship: Feminist Perpsectives*. 2nd ed. New York: Palgrave Macmillan.

Lock, Wigbert. 2005. "Pobreza y Autoorganización en Santiago de Chile. Un Estudio Etnográfico en el Barrio José María Caro." *Revista Mexicana de Sociología* 67 (1): 1–30.

López-Morales, Ernesto. 2013. "Insurgency and Institutionalized Social Participation in Local-Level Urban Planning: The Case of PAC Comuna, Santiago de Chile, 2003–2005." In *Locating Right to the City in the Global South*, edited by Tony Roshan Samara, Shenjing He, and Guo Chen, 221–46. London: Routledge.

Lotem, Itay. 2016. "Anti-Racist Activism and the Memory of Colonialism: Race as Republican Critique after 2005." *Modern and Contemporary France* 24 (3): 283–98. https://doi.org/10.1080/09639489.2016.1159188.

Lovera, Domingo. 2018. "Derecho de Reunión." In *Manual de Derechos Fundamentales. Parte Especial: Derechos Civiles y Políticos*, edited by Pablo Contreras and Constanza Salgado, 397–424. Santiago de Chile: LOM Ediciones.

Luna, Juan Pablo, Elizabeth J. Zechmeister, and Mitchell Seligson. 2010. "Cultura Política de la Democracia en Chile, 2010: Consolidación Democrática en las Américas en Tiempos Difíciles." In *American Public Opinion Project*. Nashville: Vanderbilt University. www.vanderbilt.edu/lapop/chile/Chile-2010-cultura-politica.pdf.

Marshall, Thomas Humphrey. 1950. *Citizenship and Social Class: And Other Essays*. Cambridge: Cambridge University Press.

Martin, Deborah G. 2003. "'Place-Framing' as Place-Making: Constituting a Neighborhood for Organizing and Activism." *Annals of the Association of American Geographers* 93 (3): 730–50. https://doi.org/10.1111/1467-8306.9303011.

McAdam, Doug. 1986. "Recruitment to High-Risk Activism: The Case of Freedom Summer." *American Journal of Sociology* 92 (1): 64–90. https://doi.org/10.1086/228463.

McAdams, Dan P., Ruthellen Josselson, and Amia Lieblich. 2006. *Identity and Story: Creating Self in Narrative*. Washington: American Psychological Association. https://doi.org/10.1037/11414-000.

McIntosh, Hugh, and James Youniss. 2010. "Toward a Political Theory of Political Socialization of Youth." In *Handbook of Research on Civic Engagement in Youth*, edited by Lonnie R. Sherrod, Judith Torney-Purta, and Constance A. Flanagan, 23–41. New Jersey: Wiley.

McLaughlin, Janice, Peter Phillimore, and Diane Richardson. 2011. *Contesting Recognition: Culture, Identity and Citizenship*. Basingstoke: Palgrave.

McLean, Kate C., Monisha Pasupathi, and Jennifer L. Pals. 2007. "Selves Creating Stories Creating Selves: A Process Model of Self-Development." *Personality and Social Psychology Review* 11 (3): 262–78. https://doi.org/10.1177/1088868307301034.

McNevin, Anne. 2011. *Contesting Citizenship: Irregular Migrants and New Frontiers of the Political*. New York: Columbia University Press.

Medio a Medio. 2013. "Comunicado de Organizaciones Sociales y Vecinos de Lo Hermida." *Medio a Medio*, September 11, 2013. www.agenciadenoticias.org/comunicado-de-organizaciones-sociales-y-vecinos-de-lo-hermida/.

Melucci, Alberto. 1980. "The New Social Movements: A Theoretical Approach." *Social Science Information* 19 (2): 199–226. https://doi.org/10.1177/053901848001900201.

    1996. *Challenging Codes: Collective Action in the Information Age*. Cambridge Cultural Social Studies. Cambridge: Cambridge University Press.

    2000. "Social Movements in Complex Societies: A European Perspective." *ARENA Journal* 15: 81–100.

Merkle, Caspar. 2003. "Youth Participation in El Alto, Bolivia." *Environment and Urbanization* 15 (1): 205–12. https://doi.org/10.1630/095624703101286466.

Milkman, Ruth. 2017. "A New Political Generation: Millennials and the Post-2008 Wave of Protest." *American Sociological Review* 82 (1): 1–31. https://doi.org/10.1177/0003122416681031.

Ministerio de Desarrollo Social. 2014. "Reporte Anual de Estadísticas Comunales." Santiago de Chile: Ministry of Social Development, Government of Chile. http://observatorio.ministeriodesarrollosocial.gob.cl/indicadores/index.php.

MIR. 1972. *Lo Hermida: La Cara Más Fea del Reformismo*. Santiago de Chile: Ediciones El Rebelde.

    2000. "Mensaje de los Pobladores de Lo Hermida a los Pobres de Todo Chile (8 de Agosto de 1972)." In *La Izquierda Chilena (1969–1973): Documentos para el Estudio de su Línea Estratégica*, edited by Víctor Farías, 2944–52. Santiago de Chile: Centro de Estudios Públicos (CEP).

Molina, Jorge, and Nicolás Molina. 2015. "Construcción del Imaginario Revolucionario de Jóvenes Pincoyanos y la Lucha Armada en el Chile de los Años Ochenta." *Revista de Historia y Geografía* 31: 95-115. https://doi.org/10.29344/07194145.31.379.

Morales, Eduardo, Susana Levy, Adolfo Aldunate, and Sergio Rojas. 1990. *"Erradicados en el Régimen Militar. Una Evaluación de Los Beneficiarios."* 448. Santiago de Chile: FLACSO.

Morris, Aldon, and Suzanne Staggenborg. 2004. "Leadership in Social Movements." In *The Blackwell Companion to Social Movements*, edited by David A Snow, Sarah Anne Soule, and Hanspeter Kriesi, 171–96. Blackwell Companions to Sociology. Malden: Blackwell.

Moulian, Tomás. 1997. *Chile Actual: Anatomía de un Mito*. Santiago de Chile: LOM Ediciones.

Moya, Laura, Claudia Videla, and Ricardo Balladores. 2005. *Tortura en Poblaciones del Gran Santiago (1973–1990)*. Santiago de Chile: Corporación José Domingo Cañas.

Moyano, Cristina. 2010. *El MAPU durante la Dictadura: Saberes y Prácticas para una Microhistoria de la Renovación Socialista en Chile 1973–1989.* Santiago de Chile: Ediciones Universidad Alberto Hurtado.

Muñoz Tamayo, Victor. 2017. "Militancia, Facciones y Juventud en el Partido Socialista Almeyda (1979–1990)." *Izquierdas* 37: 226–260. https://doi.org/10.4067/S0718-50492017000600226.

Oberschall, Anthony. 1973. *Social Conflict and Social Movements.* Englewood Cliffs: Prentice-Hall.

———. 2000. "Social Movements and the Transition to Democracy." *Democratization* 7 (3): 25–45. https://doi.org/10.1080/13510340008403670.

O'Byrne, Darren J. 2003. *The Dimensions of Global Citizenship: Political Identity Beyond the Nation-State.* London: Frank Cass.

O'Donnell, Guillermo A., and Philippe C. Schmitter. 1986. *Transitions from Authoritarian Rule: Tentative Conclusions About Uncertain Democracies.* Baltimore: Johns Hopkins University Press.

Ortiz, Jorge, and Severino Escolano. 2013. "Movilidad Residencial del Sector de Renta Alta del Gran Santiago (Chile): Los Patrones Socioespaciales de Segregación." *EURE* 39 (118): 77–96.

Otano, Rafael. 1995. *Crónica de la Transición.* Santiago de Chile: Planeta.

Oxhorn, Philip. 1995. *Organizing Civil Society: The Popular Sectors and the Struggle for Democracy in Chile.* Pennsylvania: Pennsylvania State University Press.

Parraguez, Leslie. 2012. "La Reconstrucción del Movimiento Social en Barrios Críticos: El Caso de la 'Coordinadora de Pobladores José María Caro' de Santiago de Chile." *Revista INVI* 27 (74): 217–46. https://doi.org/10.4067/invi.v27i74.630.

Paulsen-Espinoza, Alex. 2020. "La Política de Vivienda de la Despolitización: Gobernanza Neoliberal, Tecnocracia y Luchas Urbanas. El Caso del Movimiento de Pobladores Ukamau, Estación Central." *Investigaciones Geográficas* 59 (June): 41. https://doi.org/10.5354/0719-5370.2020.57141.

Peña, Cristóbal. 2007. *Los Fusileros: Crónica Secreta de una Guerrilla en Chile.* Santiago de Chile: Debate.

Peñalolén Municipality. 2011. "Summary Lo Hermida Neighborhood Units (17, 18, and 19)." Santiago de Chile: Peñalolén Municipality. http://observatorio.penalolen.cl/unidades/lista.

Pérez, Cristián. 2013. *Vidas Revolucionarias.* Santiago de Chile: Editorial Universitaria.

Pérez, Miguel. 2018. "Toward a Life with Dignity: Housing Struggles and New Political Horizons in Urban Chile." *American Ethnologist* 45 (4): 508–20. https://doi.org/10.1111/amet.12705.

———. 2019. "'Uno Tiene que Tener Casa Donde Nació'. Ciudadanía y Derecho a la Ciudad en Santiago." *Eure* 45 (135): 71–90. https://doi.org/10.4067/S0250-71612019000200071.

———. 2022. *The Right to Dignity: Housing Struggles, City Making, and Citizenship in Urban Chile.* Stanford: Stanford University Press.

Pinto, Diego. 2012. "Estado y Pobladores en la Configuración del Territorio: Del Campamento Nueva Habana a Población Nuevo Amanecer." Universidad de Chile. https://repositorio.uchile.cl/handle/2250/100484.

Pinto, Julio. 2005. "Hacer la Revolución en Chile." In *Cuando Hicimos Historia: La Experiencia de la Unidad Popular*, edited by Julio Pinto Vallejos, 9–33. Santiago de Chile: LOM.

Piven, Frances Fox, and Richard A. Cloward. 1977. *Poor People's Movements: Why They Succeed, How They Fail*. New York: Vintage Books.

Polletta, Francesca. 1998. "'It Was Like a Fever...' Narrative and Identity in Social Protest." *Social Problems* 45 (2): 137–59. https://doi.org/10.2307/3097241.

——— 1999. "'Free Spaces' in Collective Action." *Theory and Society* 28 (1): 1–38. https://doi.org/10.1023/A:1006941408302.

Portes, Alejandro. 1976. "Occupation and Lower-Class Political Orientation in Chile." In *Chile: Politics and Society*, edited by Arturo Valenzuela and Samuel Valenzuela, 201–37. New Brunswick: Transaction Publishers.

Posner, Paul W. 2004. "Local Democracy and the Transformation of Popular Participation in Chile." *Latin American Politics and Society* 46 (3): 55–81.

——— 2008. *State, Market, and Democracy in Chile: The Constraint to Popular Participation*. New York: Palgrave Macmillan.

Punto Final. 1972. "Expediente Negro de Lo Hermida." *Supplement Edition 165*, August 29, 1972. www.pf-memoriahistorica.org/PDFs/1972/PF_165_doc.pdf.

Purcell, Mark. 2003. "Citizenship and the Right to the Global City: Reimagining the Capitalist World Order." *International Journal of Urban and Regional Research* 27 (September): 564–90.

Putnam, Robert. 2000. *Bowling Alone: The Collapse and Revival of American Community*. New York: Simon and Schuster. https://doi.org/10.1017/CBO9781107415324.004.

Rasse, Alejandra. 2019. "Lo Hermida: Botar el Muro y Abrir el Imaginario." In *Hilos Tensados: Para Leer el Octubre Chileno*, edited by Kathya Araujo, 339–52. Santiago de Chile: Editorial USACH.

Razeto, Luís, Arno Klenner, Apolonia Ramirez, and Roberto Urmeneta. 1990. *Las Organizaciones Económicas Populares, 1973–1990*. 3rd ed. Santiago de Chile: Ediciones PET. www.luisrazeto.net/content/las-organizaciones-económicas-populares-1973-1990.

Renna, Henry. 2011. *Siete y Cuatro. El Retorno de los Pobladores: Lucha por la Vivienda, Autogestión Habitacional y Poder Popular en Santiago de Chile*. Santiago de Chile: Quimantú.

Reyes, Jaime. 2016. "La Autodefensa de Masas y las Milicias Rodriguistas: Aprendizajes, Experiencias y Consolidación del Trabajo Militar de Masas del Partido Comunista de Chile, 1982–1987." *Izquierdas* 26 (January): 67–98. https://doi.org/10.4067/S0718-50492016000100004.

Reyes, Luis. 2011. "Capital Social e Identidad. Dialéctica de una Transformación: Aproximación Histórica al Movimiento de Pobladores en Lo Hermida (1970–2010)." Universidad de Chile. http://tesis.uchile.cl/handle/2250/110010.

Rodríguez, Alfredo, Marisol Saborido, and Olga Segovia. 2012. *Violencias en una Ciudad Neoliberal: Santiago de Chile*. Santiago de Chile: SUR.

Rodríguez, Juan Pablo. 2020. *Resisting Neoliberal Capitalism in Chile: The Possibility of Social Critique*. Marx, Engels, and Marxisms. Cham: Palgrave Macmillan. https://doi.org/10.1007/978-3-030-32108-6.

Rojas-Corral, Hugo, and Miriam Shaftoe. 2021. *Human Rights and Transitional Justice in Chile*. London: Palgrave Macmillan.

Roth, Benita. 2010. "'Organizing One's Own' as Good Politics: Second Wave Feminists and the Meaning of Coalition." In *Strategic Alliances: Coalition Building and Social Movements*, edited by Nella Van Dyke and Holly J. McCammon, 99–118. Minneapolis: University of Minnesota Press.

Rubio, Rodrigo. 2006. "Lecciones de la Política de Vivienda en Chile." *Bitácora Urbano Territorial* 10 (1): 197–206. https://revistas.unal.edu.co/index.php/bitacora/article/view/18722.

Ruiz-Tagle, Javier. 2017. "Territorial Stigmatization in Socially-Mixed Neighborhoods in Chicago and Santiago: A Comparison of Global-North and Global-South Urban Renewal Problems." In *Social Housing and Urban Renewal*, edited by Paul Watt and Peer Smets, 311–49. Bingley: Emerald Publishing Limited. https://doi.org/10.1108/978-1-78714-124-720171009.

Salazar, Gabriel. 2012. *Movimientos Sociales en Chile: Trayectoria Histórica y Proyección Política*. Santiago de Chile: Uqbar Editores.

Sandoval, Carlos. 2014. *Movimiento de Izquierda Revolucionaria: Coyunturas, Documentos y Vivencias*. Santiago de Chile: Quimantú.

Santa María, Ignacio. 1973. "El Desarrollo Urbano mediante los 'Asentamientos Espontáneos': El Caso de los 'Campamentos' Chilenos." *EURE* 3 (7): 103–12.

Sassen, Saskia. 2005. "The Repositioning of Citizenship: Emergent Subjects and Spaces for Politics." *Globalizations* 2 (1): 79–94. https://doi.org/10.1080/14747730500085114.

2008. *Territory, Authority, Rights: From Medieval to Global Assemblages*. Princeton: Princeton University Press.

Schlotterbeck, Marian E. 2018. *Beyond the Vanguard: Everyday Revolutionaries in Allende's Chile*. Oakland: University of California Press.

Schneider, Cathy Lisa. 1991. "Mobilization at the Grassroots: Shantytowns and Resistance in Authoritarian Chile." *Latin American Perspectives* 18 (1): 92–112.

1995. *Shantytown Protests in Pinochet's Chile*. Philadelphia: Temple University Press.

Schuck, Peter. 2002. "Liberal Citizenship." In *Handbook of Citizenship Studies*, edited by Engin Isin and Bryan S. Turner, 131–44. London: SAGE.

Schwartzman, Luisa Farah. 2007. "Does Money Whiten? Intergenerational Changes in Racial Classification in Brazil." *American Sociological Review* 72 (6): 940–63. https://doi.org/10.1177/000312240707200605.

Sepúlveda, Daniela. 2014. "Memoria y Reparación: El Tratamiento Institucional a las Víctimas de Violación de Derechos Humanos en Chile." *Revista de Ciencia Política* 52 (1): 211–27. https://doi.org/10.5354/0719-5338.2014.33105.

Shotter, John. 1993. "Psychology and Citizenship: Identity and Belonging." In *Citizenship and Social Theory*, edited by Bryan S. Turner, 115–38. London: SAGE.

Silva, Eduardo, and Federico M. Rossi. 2018. *Reshaping the Political Arena in Latin America: From Resisting Neoliberalism to the Second Incorporation*. Pittsburgh: University of Pittsburgh Press.

Skewes, Juan Carlos. 2005. "De Invasor a Deudor: El Éxodo desde los Campamentos a las Viviendas Sociales en Chile." In *Los con Techo: Un Desafío para la Política de Vivienda Social*, edited by Ana Sugranyes and Alfredo Rodríguez, 101–22. Santiago de Chile: SUR.

Skocpol, Theda, and Margaret Somers. 1980. "The Uses of Comparative History in Macrosocial Inquiry." *Comparative Studies in Society and History* 22 (02): 174–97. https://doi.org/10.1017/S0010417500009282.

Snow, David A. 2001. "Collective Identity and Expressive Forms." In *International Encyclopedia of the Social & Behavioral Sciences*, edited by Neil Smelser and Paul Baltes, 2212–9. London: Elsevier Science. https://doi.org/10.1016/B0–08-043076-7/04094-8.

Snow, David A., E. Burke Rochford, Steven K. Worden, and Robert D. Benford,. 1986. "Frame Alignment Processes, Micromobilization, and Movement Participation." *American Sociological Review* 51 (4): 464–81. https://doi.org/10.2307/2095581.

Somers, Margaret R. 1994. "The Narrative Constitution of Identity: A Relational and Network Approach." *Theory and Society* 23 (5): 605–49. https://doi.org/10.1007/BF00992905.

Somma, Nicolás M., and Matías A. Bargsted. 2015. "La Autonomización de la Protesta en Chile." In *Socialización Política y Experiencia Escolar: Aportes para la Formación Ciudadana en Chile*, edited by Cristián Cox and Juan Carlos Castillo, 207–40. Santiago de Chile: Ediciones UC.

Somma, Nicolás M., Matías Bargsted, Rodolfo Disi, and Rodrigo M. Medel. 2020. "No Water in the Oasis: The Chilean Spring of 2019–2020." *Social Movement Studies* 20 (4) 1–8. https://doi.org/10.1080/14742837.2020.1727737.

Somma, Nicolás, and Rodrigo Medel. 2017. "Shifting Relationships Between Social Movements and Institutional Politics." In *Social Movements in Chile: Organization, Trajectories, and Political Consequences*, edited by Marisa Von Büllow and Sofía Donoso, 29–61. New York: Palgrave Macmillan. https://doi.org/10.1057/978-1-137-60013-4.

Staeheli, Lynn. 2003. "Cities and Citizenship." *Urban Geography* 24 (2): 97–102. https://doi.org/10.2747/0272-3638.24.2.97.

Staggenborg, Suzanne. 1998. "Social Movement Communities and Cycles of Protest: The Emergence and Maintenance of a Local Women's Movement." *Social Problems* 45 (2): 180–204. https://doi.org/10.2307/3097243.

Staggenborg, Suzanne, and Josée Lecomte. 2009. "Social Movement Campaigns: Mobilization and Outcomes in the Montreal Women's Movement Community." *Mobilization* 14 (2): 163–80. https://doi.org/10.17813/maiq.14.2.04l4240734477801.

Stahl, Kenneth A. 2020. *Local Citizenship in a Global Age*. Cambridge: Cambridge University Press.

Stokes, Susan C., Thad Dunning, Marcelo Nazareno, and Valeria Brusco. 2013. *Brokers, Voters, and Clientelism: The Puzzle of Distributive Politics*. Cambridge: Cambridge University Press.

Straubhaar, Rolf. 2015. "Public Representations of the Collective Memory of Brazil's Movimento Dos Trabalhadores Rurais Sem Terra." *Latin American Perspectives* 42 (3): 107–19. https://doi.org/10.1177/0094582X15570891.

Sugranyes, Ana. 2005. "La Política Habitacional en Chile, 1980–2000: Un Éxito Liberal para Dar Techo a los Pobres." In *Los con Techo: Un Desafío para la Política de Vivienda Social*, edited by Ana Sugranyes and Alfredo Rodríguez, 23–58. Santiago de Chile: SUR.

Sugranyes, Ana, and Alfredo Rodríguez. 2005. *Los con Techo: Un Desafío para la Política de Vivienda Social*. Santiago de Chile: SUR.

Swartz, David. 2013. *Symbolic Power, Politics, and Intellectuals: The Political Sociology of Pierre Bourdieu*. London: Chicago University Press.

Swerts, Thomas. 2017. "Creating Space for Citizenship: The Liminal Politics of Undocumented Activism." *International Journal of Urban and Regional Research* 41 (3): 379–95. https://doi.org/10.1111/1468-2427.12480.

Tarlau, Rebecca. 2013. "Coproducing Rural Public Schools in Brazil: Contestation, Clientelism, and the Landless Workers' Movement." *Politics & Society* 41 (3): 395–424. https://doi.org/10.1177/0032329213493753.

Tarrow, Sidney. 2011. *Power in Movement: Social Movements and Contentious Politics*. 3rd ed. New York: Cambridge University Press.

Tavie Díaz, Cristian. 2018. "Lonco: Rol y Representación de la Autoridad Ancestral Mapuche en la Ciudad." Universidad Academia de Humanismo Cristiano. http://bibliotecadigital.academia.cl/xmlui/handle/123456789/4535.

Taylor, Verta, and Nancy E. Whittier. 1992. "Collective Identity and Social Movement Communities." In *Frontiers in Social Movement Theory*, edited by Aldon D. Morris and Carol McClurg Mueller, 104–29. London: Yale University Press.

1998. "Collective Identity in Social Movement Communities: Lesbian Feminist Mobilization." In *Social Perspectives in Lesbian and Gay Studies: A Reader*, edited by Peter M. Nardi and Beth E. Schneider, 104–29. London: Routledge.

Thompson, Lisa, and Chris Tapscott. 2010. *Citizenship and Social Movements: Perspectives from the Global South*. New York: Zed Books. https://doi.org/10.1017/CBO9781107415324.004.

Till, Karen E. 2005. *The New Berlin: Memory, Politics, Place*. Minneapolis: University of Minnesota Press.

Tironi, Eugenio. 1990. *Autoritarismo, Modernización y Marginalidad: El Caso de Chile 1973–1989*. Santiago de Chile: SUR.

Tulchin, Joseph S., and Meg Ruthenburg. 2007. "Citizens: Made Not Born." In *Citizenship in Latin America*, edited by Joseph Tulchin and Meg Ruthenburg, 281–4. London: Lynne Rienner Publishers.

Turner, Bryan S. 1986. *Citizenship and Capitalism: The Debate Over Reformism*. London: Allen & Unwin.

TVN. 2012. "Informe Especial: Infiltrado en los Guetos Capitalinos." Chile: TVN. May 14. http://no-ads-youtube.com/video/lugimore/tvn-informe-especial-infiltrado-en-los-guetos-capitalinos?v=lwijvg4wH88.

UNDP. 2017. *Chile en 20 Años: Un Recorrido a Través de los Informes sobre Desarrollo Humano*. Santiago de Chile: United Nations.

References 241

Universidad de Chile. 2015. "Becas y Beneficios, Quintiles de Ingreso." Bienestar Estudiantil. 2015. www.uchile.cl/portal/pregrado/bienestar-estudiantil/becas-y-beneficios/109037/quintiles-2015.

Valdés, Teresa. 1986. "El Movimiento Poblacional: La Recomposición de las Solidaridades." Santiago de Chile: FLACSO-Chile. http://cronopio.flacso.cl/fondo/pub/publicos/1986/DT/000859.pdf.

Valdivieso, Gabriel. 1989. "Comunidades Cristianas de Base. Su Inserción en la Iglesia y la Comunidad." Santiago de Chile: Centro Bellarmino - CISOC. www.memoriachilena.cl/602/w3-article-9586.html.

Valenzuela, Arturo. 1989. *El Quiebre de la Democracia en Chile*. Santiago de Chile: Ediciones FLACSO. www.salvador-allende.cl/Biblioteca/Valenzuela.pdf.

Valenzuela, Samuel. 1997. "La Constitución de 1980 y el Inicio de la Redemocratización en Chile." 242. https://kellogg.nd.edu/publications/workingpapers/WPS/242.pdf.

Venegas, Juan Ignacio. 2016. *¿Por qué los Jóvenes Chilenos Rechazan la Política?* Santiago de Chile: RIL Editores.

Wacquant, Loïc. 2008. *Urban Outcasts: A Comparative Sociology of Advanced Marginality*. Cambridge: Polity Press.

2009. *Punishing the Poor: The Neoliberal Government of Social Insecurity*. London: Duke University Press.

2010. "Urban Desolation and Symbolic Denigration in the Hyperghetto." *Social Psychology Quarterly* 73 (3): 215–19. https://doi.org/10.1177/0190272510377880.

Wacquant, Loïc, Tom Slater, and Virgílio Borges Pereira. 2014. "Territorial Stigmatization in Action." *Environment and Planning A: Economy and Space* 46 (6): 1270–80. https://doi.org/10.1068/a4606ge.

Weber, Max. 1978. *Economy and Society: An Outline of Interpretative Sociology*. Los Angeles: California University Press.

White, Aaronette. 1999. "Talking Feminist, Talking Black: Micromobilization Processes in a Collective Protest against Rape." *Gender & Society* 13 (1): 77–100. https://doi.org/10.1177/089124399013001005.

Wilson, William J. 1990. *The Truly Disadvantaged: The Inner City, the Underclass, and Public Policy*. Chicago: University of Chicago Press.

Wolff, Jonas. 2007. "(De-)Mobilising the Marginalised: A Comparison of the Argentine Piqueteros and Ecuador's Indigenous Movement." *Journal of Latin American Studies* 39 (1): 1–29. https://doi.org/10.1017/S0022216X0600201X.

Yiftachel, Oren. 2009. "Critical Theory and 'Gray Space': Mobilization of the Colonized." *City* 13 (2–3): 246–63. https://doi.org/10.1080/13604810902982227.

Young, Iris Marion. 1990. *Justice and the Politics of Difference. Journalism and Communication Monographs*. Vol. 18. Princeton: Princeton University Press.

Zerilli, Linda. 2016. "Politics." In *The Oxford Handbook of Feminist Theory*, edited by Lisa Disch and Mary Hawkesworth, 632–50. Oxford: Oxford University Press.

Zerubavel, Eviatar. 1999. *Social Mindscapes: An Invitation to Cognitive Sociology*. London: Harvard University Press.

Zivi, Karen. 2012. *Making Rights Claims: A Practice of Democratic Citizenship*. Oxford: Oxford University Press.

Zulver, Julia. 2017. "Building the City of Women: Creating a Site of Feminist Resistance in a Northern Colombian Conflict Zone." *Gender, Place and Culture* 24 (10): 1498–1516. https://doi.org/10.1080/0966369X.2017.1387105.

# Index

For EU product safety concerns, contact us at Calle de José Abascal, 56–1°,
28003 Madrid, Spain or eugpsr@cambridge.org.